Idiosyncratic
Person-Centred
Therapy

From the personal
to the universal

Edited by
Suzanne Keys

PCCS BOOKS
Ross-on-Wye

First published in 2003

PCCS BOOKS LTD
Llangarron
Ross-on-Wye
Herefordshire
HR9 6PT
UK
Tel +44 (0)1989 77 07 07
www.pccs-books.co.uk

**Idiosyncratic Person-Centred Therapy:
From the personal to the universal**

British Library Cataloguing in Publication Data.
A catalogue record for this book is available from the British Library.

ISBN 1 898059 56 X

Cover design by Old Dog Graphics
Printed by Bath Press Ltd., Bath, UK

Contents

Acknowledgements

Many thanks from the editor and contributors to the following people for their invaluable insight, help, support and encouragement: Conal Percy, Dorothea Kast, Tony Merry, Brian Thorne, Pete Sanders, Maggie Taylor-Sanders, Henry Keys, Freda Keys, John Keys, Anthony Stone, Genevieve Smyth, Jokhim Meikle, Debbie Butler, Carolyn Dougill, Margaret Laws, Sandra Pedevilla, Mary Roche, the workshop participants at Egmond aan Zee, Peter Schmid, Helen Cunliffe, Jeffrey John, Emma Sawyer, Carolyn under the trees and the supervison group, Michael Farrell, Ros Watling, Charlie Moritz, Mike Worrall, Marie Adams, Anne Daley, Keemar Keemar, Mart and the kids, Chris, John Fraser, Peggy Natiello, Ian, Tom and Nell.

Thanks also go to Windy Dryden for his original idea for the 'Idiosyncratic Therapy' series.

Foreword

Counselling and psychotherapy in Britain have reached a critical stage in their evolution. The increasingly litigious climate of contemporary society, the move towards the statutory registration of therapists and the attempt to shoehorn therapeutic processes into the framework of national vocational qualifications are all, in their different ways, indications of a desire to control and render risk-free an essentially unpredictable activity. Abject capitulation to such pervasive forces threatens to reduce therapy to a series of 'empirically validated' procedures and therapists themselves to little more than psychological technicians fearful of stepping out of line and, as a consequence, of incurring professional censure or even public ignominy.

This book provides a passionate counterblast to the prevailing Zeitgeist. Its contributors are all person-centred practitioners who are deeply committed to the fundamental belief in the trustworthiness of the human organism and in the primacy of the relationship in the therapeutic enterprise. They are faithful to the legacy of Carl Rogers, the quiet revolutionary, but their courage takes them into terrain which even the intrepid Rogers might only dimly have envisaged. These are therapists whose levels of self-acceptance and empathic commitment are such that they dare to be fully themselves in their therapeutic relationships and, as a result, they trust the promptings of the intuitive core of their own beings in the service of their clients. What is more, they have taken the risk of putting the outcome of such dedicated commitment into the public domain and, in so doing, they reveal poignant moments of life-enhancing or even life-saving intimacy and self-offering. In some cases the clients themselves tell their own stories and provide further compelling testimony to the efficacy of their therapists' courageous willingness to develop their unique and idiosyncratic ways of being person-centred. Carl Rogers loathed the adjective 'Rogerian' and he would rejoice that there are no Rogerians in the pages of this book. Instead we find person-centred practitioners who bring to their work the fullness of their own beings and refuse to sell their clients short with pale imitations of Rogers or any other luminary in the person-centred firmament. Both seasoned veterans of the approach and comparative newcomers are represented among the contributors but all demonstrate the same determination to eschew inauthenticity and resist the temptation to seek refuge behind a pseudo-professionalism. These are vibrant human-beings who know that being truly alive is a risky business and that to avoid risk-taking is to court sterility and paralysis.

I have little doubt that the book will incite controversy and, in some quarters, hostility or even contempt. If it does not do so it will probably have failed to communicate its essentially seditious challenge. It is this same challenge, however, which will be a source of inspiration for those therapists who long to bring to their therapeutic work the richness of their own creativity and the power of their unique empathic responsiveness. Suzanne Keys is to be congratulated on bringing together so varied a team of contributors and on enabling them to provide such compelling glimpses into the disciplined freedom of an approach to therapy which is only now revealing the full implications of its radical nature.

Brian Thorne
Harlech, Holy Week 2003.

Editorial comments

Contributors were deliberately chosen who work in the UK, including England, Scotland and Northern Ireland. Unfortunately there is no contributor from Wales. All but one of the contributors are also working in private practice. The reason for this was to limit the variables impacting on the idiosyncrasies of each contributor. Working in different settings and different countries inevitably affects the idiosyncrasies of a therapist. The focus of this book is to explore the range of practice and the commonalities within a limited set of variables.

The term *therapy* is used in this book to cover both counselling and psychotherapy. There is ongoing debate as to what, if any, distinction there is between these two terms. The Person-Centred Approach to a client is the same whether it is called counselling or psychotherapy.

Some contributors refer to person-centred theoretical terms such as core conditions, congruence, empathy, unconditional positive regard, external/internal locus of evaluation, conditions of worth, actualising tendency and self-concept which are explained briefly in the *Introduction*. Every effort has been made to stop jargon inhibiting the accessibility of the text.

In order to have gender-inclusive language the plural is often used throughout this book when the gender of the subject could be either masculine or feminine.

Suzanne Keys

1

Suzanne Keys

Introduction

I want this book to be for anyone interested in the intricacies of human relating. It is for both clients and for therapists. I particularly have in mind all those who may be struggling in vain to become the 'ideal therapist'. This book is about trusting and valuing the person you are and what you have to offer. It is about therapeutic practice which is person-centred, unique and ethical. It is about the idiosyncrasy of the therapist and the idiosyncrasy of each relationship between therapist and client.

The Greek roots of the word idiosyncrasy translate as 'private mixture' (*idios*, private, *sun*, with, *krasis*, mixture) and this book concerns the 'private mixture' each person brings to the therapy relationship and how each relationship itself is a 'private mixture'. 'Private' here means both unique and personal as well as the fact that neither one's own mixture nor the relationship between therapist and client can ever be completely known by another. 'Mixture' encompasses the range of things that go into making an individual unique and this includes the complexity of both external and internal factors. Thus the 'mixture' is influenced and made up of social and environmental factors as well as what some theoreticians refer to as configurations (Mearns and Thorne, 2000) or plurality of selves (Cooper and Rowan, 1999). Thus the mixture is both within each individual and between the therapist and client.

Through ten chapters from different person-centred therapists in private practice in the UK, the reader enters into the therapy room and into the intimate moment-by-moment encounter between two people. These chapters explore how the 'private mixture' of the unique and unpredictable so often produces wonderful and unexpected moments of personal and professional discovery.

Idiosyncrasy
The aim of this book is to reclaim the concept of idiosyncrasy. In modern-day English language, idiosyncratic has come to mean anything from peculiar, eccentric or quirky to the more pejorative weird, odd, strange, irregular or abnormal. This book embraces idiosyncrasy as an essential part of a therapist's practice and goes so far as to state that person-centred therapists and relationships are by definition idiosyncratic. The key concepts of person-centred practice have idiosyncrasy at their heart. That does not mean that a person-centred therapist is weird, abnormal or irresponsible. To be idiosyncratic is not to be sloppy or lacking in discipline or a sense of professional responsibility. On the contrary, as the contributors in this book demonstrate, to be a person-centred therapist and to value idiosyncrasy demand a high degree of integrity, rigorous self-discipline and an ongoing dedication to being as fully human as possible in the service of the client and the relationship. To be fully human is to be able to acknowledge both strengths and weaknesses and to be unafraid of being vulnerable in the meeting with another person.

The voices of idiosyncratic therapists come through this book not only in terms of their personal journeys, the way that they work and how they understand their therapeutic relationships but also in the way they write. This has led to a fascinating editorial task and has highlighted the crux of the problem around the concept of idiosyncrasy: every writer/therapist has their own style but this has to be seen in relation to the other — the reader/the client. The right to be idiosyncratic comes with responsibility. As human beings we do not exist in isolation; we live and thrive in relationship. Idiosyncrasy is about our own 'private mixture' but this is of no value if we cannot communicate it to others in a way that does not alienate them. As an editor, I have discovered that writing conventions, like therapeutic boundaries, have their place. They are often there to promote clearer relating. Conventions cannot be disregarded simply because an individual's right to be idiosyncratic must be valued above all else. Nevertheless conventions can be challenged and idiosyncratic writing/therapy may well involve taking risks, questioning assumptions and challenging parameters. Paradoxically, as some contributors explore in this volume, it is often the convention itself which permits freedom of expression, the passionate belief in a theory which allows for real encounter, and discipline which lets idiosyncrasy flourish.

Person-Centred Therapy
Person-Centred Therapy developed out of the work of Carl Rogers[1] (1902–1987), without doubt one of the twentieth century's most influential thinkers and practitioners in the field of human relating. He developed a theory of relating which he applied not only to counselling and psychotherapy but also to education, group work and conflict resolution. The focus of this book is on the details of Person-Centred Therapy in practice. It explores the unique practices of different therapists, all of whom, nonetheless, share a person-centred philosophy and all but one of whom work as counsellors in private practice.

The exception is Omar Sattaur, who writes as a counsellor in training. He takes us to the heart of his personal journey of becoming a person-centred therapist as he explores his own 'private mixture' and how it relates to his training. Whilst different Person-Centred Therapy training courses may share much theory and philosophy, each person in training interprets and brings meaning to those theories and that philosophy in personal ways. This subjectivity is encouraged and welcomed as an essential prerequisite of anyone in person-centred training. The trainee's task is to embody the theory, to make it their own.

Person-Centred Therapy, along with other humanistic approaches to therapy, is grounded in a phenomenological approach to the person. An approach described by Tony Merry as meaning

> ... that we behave in the world in response to our personally experienced reality. The way we experience the world, and therefore the way we respond to it, results from the sense and meaning we each derive from our unique mixture of needs, history and expectations. (Merry, 2002, p. 18)

It is, therefore, the duty of a person-centred therapist not only to be aware of their own 'unique mixture of needs, history and expectations' and how it affects them but also to develop their own idiosyncratic understanding of theory. Rogers warned of therapists becoming 'insecure disciples' for whom theory becomes 'iron chains

---

[1.] For those readers not familiar with Rogers' work nor the theory of person-centred therapy there are no better starting points than Rogers' *On Becoming a Person* (1961), Howard Kirschenbaum and Valerie Henderson's edited collection of his writings *The Carl Rogers Reader* (1989), Dave Mearns' and Brian Thorne's *Person-Centred Counselling in Action* (1999), Tony Merry's *Learning and Being in Person-Centred Counselling* (2002) and Paul Wilkins' *Person-Centred Therapy in Focus* (2003). There is, of course, also a range of information on Person-Centred Therapy on the internet. A good starting point is <www.bapca.org.uk> the website for the British Association for the Person-Centred Approach.

of dogma' rather than 'a fallible, changing attempt to construct a network of gossamer threads . . . a stimulus to further creative thinking' (Rogers, 1959, p. 191). Embodied theory is an evolving process and a lifelong task. If the trainee person-centred therapist is to make the theory their own they must assume the profound and ongoing task of discovering who they really are. In *What it Means to Become a Person,* Rogers was astonished at the nineteenth century philosopher Kierkegaard's accuracy in picturing the dilemma of the individual:

> . . . the deepest form of despair is to choose 'to be another than himself.' On the other hand 'to will to be that self which one truly is, is indeed the opposite of despair,' and this choice is the deepest responsibility of man [sic]. (Rogers, 1961, p. 110)

It is the therapist's responsibility to 'will to be that self which one truly is', not only for themselves, but in order that their encounter with clients can be as authentic and therefore as fully human and healing as possible. The therapist cannot ask of their client what they do not aspire to themselves:

> So often, professionalism results from the possession of specialized knowledge and skills which others need for the conduct of their lives. For the person-centred therapist, however, the knowledge and the skills reside in the courage and the capacity to become more fully human so that others in turn may discover confidence in their own human resourcefulness. A strange profession indeed which requires of its practitioners that they simply become more fully themselves. (Thorne, 2002, pp. 21–2)

The process of becoming more fully oneself, more fully in touch with one's selves, more fully human and thereby more fully competent and professional as a counsellor is explored by all the contributors to this volume but particularly by Sholto Thompson, who explores the *process* of becoming not only in terms of his personal journey but also in relation to the process of a particular therapy relationship with a client.

As Thorne states above, part of being 'fully human' is to have 'confidence in [your] own resourcefulness'. This is another philosophical underpinning of the Person-Centred Approach to therapy: trust in the *actualising tendency*[2] of the organism. What this means is that all person-centred therapists believe that human beings can be trusted to have within them the capacity and resources to grow towards fulfilment. Rogers famously described this process as being like potatoes left in a bag in the cellar, whose shoots grow up towards the light despite the darkness and cramped conditions (Rogers, 1980, p. 118).

Psychologically, the conditions which contort human development come in the form of *conditions of worth*. These may develop when a person's desire for love from significant others means they have to adapt their behaviour and the way they think about themselves in order to get some *positive regard*: warmth and acceptance.

---

[2] *Actualising tendency* and other theoretical terms are used by some contributors without explanation, so the following paragraphs are a brief and simplified explanation of some of the most common person-centred terms used in the book.

These conditions of worth depend on an *external locus of evaluation.* In other words they depend on opinions, judgements and evaluations from others, external to the person. Thus the person develops a *self-concept,* or self-concepts, based partly on others' judgements. This can be at odds with the parts of a person which want to actualise and become more *fully functioning.* One of the identifying signs of a more fully functioning person is that they have an *internalised locus of evaluation*: they can trust themselves to make their own decisions, taking into account others' opinions without being unduly influenced by their conditionality. In short, they can trust their idiosyncrasies; they can trust that their own 'private mixture' is not harmful to themselves or to others.

The Person-Centred Approach to therapy then is based on trust rather than suspicion. It is based on having confidence in oneself as the therapist, but also in the client and their capacity to grow. This confidence is based on a trust that to be idiosyncratic, to be fully oneself, to be fully human is life-enhancing — not only for an individual but also for relationships. To achieve this confidence is an ongoing, lifelong process involving much struggling, risk-taking and questioning.

The client's voice
The degree of trust possible between therapist and client is emphasised in this book by the high degree of authority accorded to client experiences. References to these experiences come not only in the form of transcripts of recorded sessions but also in the form of collaborative writing, indeed we often hear directly from clients. In a recent article, Sue Genest explores the lack of 'client perspective' in the counselling literature: 'What is strikingly evident in seeking out this literature and reading it, is that the client perspective is an important yet all too scarce source of information for understanding the experience and outcomes of counselling' (Genest, 2003, p. 18). Gillian Proctor, however, adds a note of caution, when deconstructing discourses of client empowerment. She quotes from Lowe (1999, p. 82).

> How collaborative can collaboration be, and how transparent can transparency be, if they are institutionalised within a particular mode of practice? It is one thing to offer clients a voice within a professional therapeutic discourse, but it might be quite another thing to allow them a discourse of their own. (Proctor, 2002, p. 60)

It is up to the reader to decide in the following chapters whether they really can hear authentic, empowered client and therapist voices in this book.

Terry Daly has transcripts of sessions with three clients exploring different aspects of therapy. Jan Hawkins has included written feedback from a client about the process of reading her therapy notes. Person-centred therapist Dick McDonald and 'art as therapy' group facilitator Caryl Sibbet have collaborated on a chapter with his client Anna who also attends Caryl's group. Anna's art work is included as a 'fourth voice' in their journey together. Tracey Walshaw includes the transcript of a session where she and her client discuss idiosyncrasy and their relationship specifically for this book. Irene Fairhurst has written her chapter around her client's journal extracts and restrospective commentary. Rose Battye includes written feedback from clients about how they see the therapy relationship and the particular idiosyncrasies of their counsellor.

The therapist's voice

The therapists in this book write about themselves and their work. Some focus more on themselves in relation to their work and others more on therapeutic relationships. All display a great level of trust and honesty in revealing their own 'private mixtures'. They have researched their own practice for this work, much as a practitioner researcher would do: valuing their experience and their subjectivity; reflecting on it; learning from it; and sharing it ethically with others to see if there is common ground (McLeod, 1999). Any therapy at its best involves reflexive research, with the emphasis on the self-awareness of the therapist and the importance of ongoing supervision or collaborative inquiry (Merry, 2002, p. 173). This collection of unique stories of individual person-centred therapists' work therefore involves elements of theory, practice and research. It resembles supervision in public, with the reader invited to collaborate in the inquiry. It is an ongoing process.

Among the tools contributors have used to examine their work are transcripts of tape recorded sessions. Transcripts are an immediate way for the reader to be involved in the details of a therapist's work. Rogers, in an interview in the final year of his life, emphasised the importance of the use of recorded therapy material:

> the importance of recording interviews cannot be overestimated . . . to have the opportunity to listen to what went on . . . to try and understand the process of what went on, should be a tremendous learning experience . . . I think that the careful review of recorded interviews is essential. (Baldwin, 2000, p. 51)

In this book we have the opportunity to share in that learning experience with therapists and clients through transcripts, notes and reflections. Therapists share with us their 'mistakes' and their imperfections, particularly Terry Daly and Tracey Walshaw. Rogers considered the therapist's awareness of his or her imperfection as crucial to their helping role:

> The therapist needs to recognise very clearly the fact that he or she is an imperfect person with flaws which make him vulnerable. I think it is only as the therapist views himself as imperfect and flawed that he can see himself as helping another person. (Baldwin, 2000, pp. 50–1)

In the BACP[3] Ethical Framework for Good Practice in Counselling and Psychotherapy (2002) there is a list of personal moral qualities 'considered of the utmost importance to clients . . . personal qualities to which counsellors and psychotherapists are strongly encouraged to aspire.' These include:

> humility: the ability to assess accurately and acknowledge one's own strengths and weaknesses
> courage: the capacity to act in spite of known fears, risks and uncertainty. (BACP, 2002, p. 4)

All the contributors in this book display ample amounts of humility and courage, both in the work they do and in their preparedness to share it publicly.

---

3. British Association for Counselling and Psychotherapy. Website <www.bacp.co.uk>.

From the personal to the universal
It is in this public sharing that the personal may become the universal. This book takes as its premise Rogers' 'learnings':

> I can trust my experience ... experience is, for me, the highest authority ... what is most personal is most general. (Rogers, 1961, pp. 22–6)

In other words, the therapist and client experiences in this book are trustworthy and have authority and validity precisely because they are personal. It is their personal nature that touches our common humanity. In what we read we may recognise our own struggles, fears, joys and passions, our own desire to be in authentic relationship.

Each therapist describes a different style of working, a different interpretation of person-centred theory. They are a diverse group. They have trained in different places, live all over the UK, are different ages, genders, have different ethnic backgrounds and sexual orientations. All these variables of course make a difference in how they embody the theory. Nevertheless, common threads emerge: the therapist's respect for the client as the expert in their own lives, the therapist's trust in their own and the client's resources, the courage to share intimate experiences, the importance of the core conditions, including idiosyncratic empathy, the centrality of the spiritual and philosophical underpinnings of the therapist's practice, the quality of presence and the ongoing questioning of what it really means to be a person-centred therapist.

Core conditions
Repeated reference is made throughout this book to Rogers' 'core conditions' as the bedrock of therapists' practice. Jenny Biancardi most specifically explores her idiosyncrasies through looking at each of the core conditions in turn. In the recent WAPCEPC[4] journal Germain Lietaer writes about the 'cruciality' of the core conditions when discussing the common ground shared by all person-centred therapists (2002, p. 10). Rogers describes these three conditions for successful therapy as follows:

> On the basis of research findings, three attitudes or conditions appear to be most important for the success of therapy: (1) the therapist's genuineness or congruence, (2) the therapist's complete acceptance of or unconditional positive regard for the client, and (3) the therapist's sensitive and accurately empathic understanding of the client's feelings and personal meanings. In successful therapy, these attitudes are effectively communicated to the client. It is believed, although not definitely confirmed by empirical evidence, that the conditions for therapy are probably stated above in the order of their importance. Although there may be some difference of opinion, genuineness appears to be the most basic: the other two are important but probably less so. Therapy appears to be maximally effective when all three attitudes are present in high degree. (Rogers and Sanford, 1980, p. 1487)

[4.] World Association for Person-Centered and Experiential Psychotherapy and Counseling. Website <www.pce-world.org>.

The three core conditions are inextricably linked but Rogers here stresses the importance of congruence. Idiosyncrasy within the Person-Centred Approach to therapy is meaningless without understanding congruence. Congruence has many meanings. A recent book on congruence begins:

> Congruence, genuineness, transparency, authenticity, realness — these are all words that are used to convey Rogers' condition of congruence. The concept has been described as an attitude, a state of being, a way of living. (Wyatt, 2001, p. vii)

In geometry when two shapes are congruent they are identical when matched up, they fit perfectly. So too the therapist who is congruent can match up their feelings and be clearly aware of what is going on internally and express that authentically. Congruence then is to be aware of one's own 'private mixture', to value it and to be able to communicate it honestly when appropriate. Idiosyncratic practice is useless if it is not congruent and congruence is nothing if it is not idiosyncratic. Thus the idiosyncrasy of a person-centred therapist is highly prized and seen as essential to the therapeutic endeavour.

Idiosyncratic empathy
Bozarth's concept of idiosyncratic empathy links congruence and empathy:

> Idiosyncratic empathy emphasizes: (1) the transparency of the therapist in relationship to the other person; (2) the person-to-person encounter in the relationship; and (3) the intuition of the therapist. (Bozarth, 1984/2001, p. 139)

Empathy is not merely about the therapist being in the client's world, nor is it merely about the therapist reflecting the client's feelings or repeating the last thing that the client has said. What idiosyncratic empathy emphasises is the congruence of the therapist and of the relationship. First, the therapist, in being congruent, is aware that they also bring their subjectivity into the client's world. Second, the meaning that emerges from this unique meeting of two people depends on how much the therapist and client match up, whether there can be an authentic encounter. The meaning-making which emerges in this meeting is unique to the two people involved. In this way even a transcript of a taped therapy session gives only a glimpse at what is occurring between therapist and client at any one moment. Terry Daly highlights the relative poverty of transcripts in this respect; the words often do not give us an idea of the fullness of the therapist's empathic understanding. It can, in fact, sometimes seem as if the therapist's words are totally unrelated to what the client has just said — and yet this may be a deeply empathic idiosyncratic response, reflecting an accurate understanding of the client's world at that particular moment. This is Bozarth's third point about 'the intuition of the therapist'. Most of a therapist's understanding of the client's world is not picked up through words, but rather through the therapist's overall sensing, both rational and intuitive, of a client. Idiosyncratic empathy therefore requires the therapist to be in tune or congruent with themselves, the client and the relationship between them.

Spiritual discipline
In order to be in tune, the person-centred therapist must embody the core conditions

of empathy, congruence and acceptance. The conditions work together in what some person-centred therapists refer to as a 'dance'. Research has shown that these conditions are a prerequisite for any functioning therapeutic relationship (Beutler, Machado and Neufeldt, 1994, p. 243). However, one of the challenges for a person-centred therapist lies in being able to experience these attitudes towards themselves: to be accepting, understanding and honest with themselves. This would be the 'living out of the core conditions', which Thorne writes of as a 'spiritual discipline':

> the person-centred therapist who commits himself or herself to the living out of the core conditions is exercising the spiritual discipline which is the expression of a practical mysticism. (Thorne, 2002, p. 84)

Several authors in this book explore this 'practical mysticism' in different ways, among them Jan Hawkins, Omar Sattaur, Annette Ansell, Sholto Thompson, Dick McDonald and Rose Battye. Annette Ansell writes in detail about her practical, emotional and spiritual preparation to meet clients in a way that recent research has named 'preparing the ground for presence' (Geller and Greenberg, 2002). For many person-centred practitioners it would seem that a spiritual underpinning to their practice is a most important part of their 'private mixture'. It not only sustains and grounds them as they face the demands of their work but ultimately enables a deeper, more healing connection with their clients, perhaps because they are more deeply connected to themselves.

Presence
In the final year of his life Rogers emphasised the importance of the self of the therapist being present in the therapeutic relationship. He even suggested that he had over-emphasised the importance of the core conditions whilst underestimating the importance of the self of the therapist being clearly present:

> I am inclined to think in my writing perhaps I have stressed too much the three basic conditions (congruence, unconditional positive regard and empathic understanding). Perhaps it is something around the edges of those conditions that is really the most important element of therapy — when my self is very clearly, obviously present. (Baldwin, 2000, p. 45)

He considers the self, or 'private mixture', of the therapist as of great therapeutic value. Some therapists talk about the 'use of self' in this context. I am very grateful, however, to Marge Witty[5], who introduced me to the 'instrumentality' of this term. What I think she means by 'instrumentality' is that if I talk about my 'use of self' it implies that it is for a purpose. I become an instrument to make something happen: a means to an end. I, the therapist, am defining that end. This takes the emphasis away from the client and my trust in their resources. Moreover, the therapist as a person is erased and somehow becomes an object to be manipulated or used by the client. This is different from me as a therapist valuing my self in the therapeutic encounter and aiming to be as in touch with my self as possible with

---

[5.] At the 2002 British Association for the Person-Centred Approach (BAPCA) 'Dialogues' Conference in Durham.

the intent of remaining open to the client and following their lead. Therefore my aim is to be present to my self rather than to use my self. This 'being present to my self' may then become *presence* in the relationship. Rogers wrote:

> I find when I am closest to my inner, intuitive self, when I am somehow in touch with the unknown in me, when perhaps I am in a slightly altered state of consciousness, then whatever I do seems to be full of healing. Then simply my *presence* is releasing and helpful to the other. There is nothing I can do to force this experience, but when I can relax and be close to the transcendental core of me, then I may behave in strange and impulsive ways in the relationship, ways which I cannot justify rationally, which have nothing to do with my thought processes. But these strange behaviors turn out to be *right,* in some odd way: it seems that my inner spirit has reached out and touched the inner spirit of the other. Our relationship transcends itself and becomes a part of something larger. Profound growth and healing and energy are present. (Rogers, 1980, p. 129)

This relaxing and getting close to the 'transcendental core of me' which may lead to 'strange and impulsive' behaviours which cannot be justified rationally but are nevertheless 'right', brings us back again to a definition of idiosyncratic person-centred practice. Contributors to this book may describe behaviours which, in another context, would seem 'strange' but which in the context of a particular relationship are absolutely 'right'. This can only be possible if they are as accepting and as close as they can be to their own 'private mixture' as well as to that of their client.

Person-centred identity crisis?
The paradox of Person-Centred Therapy is that because its identity is idiosyncratic, it cannot be easily pinned down or firmly grasped; it has to be experienced to be understood; it only comes into being as it comes into play. Some would claim that any therapist could call themselves 'person-centred'. I hope by now to have given some idea that this is not the case. The dilemma for Person-Centred Therapy is that it is highly individual and yet to be professionally identifiable it needs to be fixed to some degree.

Rumbling behind the pages of this book are the echoes of an ongoing debate within the person-centred and experiential therapy field, a debate on professional identity. This debate is reflected in the contributions of the inaugural WAPCEPC journal, *Person-Centered and Experiential Psychotherapies* (2002). The desire for identity and definition has been exacerbated by the seemingly global drive to regulate, codify and professionalise therapy. In this it can be understood as a response to an externalised locus of evaluation — ironic given that one of the signs of a healthy organism in terms of person-centred theory is an internalised locus of evaluation. However it is true that Person-Centred Therapy may need to assert a more coherent identity in order for it to be identifiable in relation to other therapies, especially if it is to continue to be recognised and valued in the therapy field and beyond.

The contributions to this book reflect this debate not only through the range of practice presented under the one person-centred umbrella but also in the common threads explored in this introduction. These common threads reflect some of the distinguishing characteristics of Person-Centred Therapy posited by two current person-centred theoreticians. Peter Schmid identifies three characteristics: the client and therapist spring from a fundamental 'we', the client is the expert and the therapist is present (Schmid, 2002). For Pete Sanders, the primary principles are the primacy of the actualising tendency, the assertion of the necessity of therapeutic conditions and the primacy of the non-directive attitude *at least* at the level of content but not necessarily at the level of process (Sanders, 2000, p. 67).

For many practitioners the debate about whether they are being person-centred or not centres around the idea of 'nondirectivity'. When Rogers first wrote about counselling in the 1940s he termed it nondirective counselling in response to the more analytic therapeutic approaches which saw the therapist as the expert whose job it was to 'direct' the client round to their way of thinking. In the 1950s he started using the term 'Client-Centred Therapy' and then later 'Person-Centred Approach' as the theory and philosophy of therapy was increasingly transferred to other settings. The concept of nondirectivity, however, has remained key to the understanding of Person-Centred Therapy. For some, nondirective therapy is misinterpreted as meaning that the therapist is 'passive'. In this understanding an 'active' therapist would be a 'directive' therapist. This has caused confusion as to what is or is not person-centred and in some cases 'rules' seem to have emerged indicating, for example, that any active involvement by the therapist is wrong. Barry Grant is extremely helpful in his exploration of what he terms 'principled nondirectiveness', which he defines as a moral stance, an 'expression of respect'. So, instead of prescribing what should or should not happen in a therapeutic relationship he brings the concept back to the attitude and intention of the therapist. He describes what principled nondirectiveness might look like in practice and it is not at all 'passive'.

> The paradox of principled nondirectiveness is that a therapist who wholeheartedly lives the attitude may at times appear to be extremely directive. A client may request direction, advice, interpretations, or instructions, and the therapist may offer these. The decision to do so does not depend on a determination of the client's needs, best interests, diagnosis, or learning style. It rests, rather, on whether the therapist wants to honor the request, judges himself or herself competent to honor it, and believes it moral to do so. The therapist has no stake in having things come out one way rather than another. (Grant, 1990, pp. 374–5)

This 'principled nondirectiveness' comes from a respect for the client and a lack of therapist investment in a prescribed outcome. From it flows the active engagement of the therapist in whatever way emerges from the idiosyncratic encounter. Bozarth goes so far as to say that:

> Any ethical activity or action that emerges from the attention to the internal world of the client is a viable and congruent activity in Person-Centred Therapy. (Bozarth, 1998, p. 128)

Contributors in this book are definitely actively engaged with their clients. Rose Battye and Jenny Biancardi, in particular, explore this engagement in the light of their learning from other therapeutic approaches. How person-centred therapists ethically integrate their intellectual curiosity and expanding knowledge into their everyday practice and whether this somehow takes them away from person-centred practice is an ongoing debate amongst person-centred therapists. Some contributors are aware that they may be judged 'non-person-centred' because of what they describe in this book. Tracey Walshaw and her client deal specifically with this fear of being judged. They explore how the questioning, so important to person-centred therapists, can become doubting, and can be internalised as 'thought police'. Many person-centred therapists live with an internal voice which tells them there is a right and a wrong way to 'do' the Person-Centred Approach to therapy, as if there were a list of rules that they must keep to in order to 'be a good person-centred therapist'. This doubting relies on an externalised locus of evaluation and hinders idiosyncrasy. It can have a stunting and debilitating effect on budding and struggling therapists. Nowadays therapists are more than ever susceptible to this kind of doubting as the society around them increasingly disparages idiosyncrasy, preferring instead measurable outcomes and regulatory codes.

Idiosyncrasy in a wider context

With the possibility of the statutory regulation of therapy in the UK[6], this book about idiosyncratic Person-Centred Therapy and the idiosyncrasy of Person-Centred Therapy is particularly pertinent. The risk is that regulation will demand that therapists fit more rigid criteria, conform to predetermined norms and endeavour to be alike rather than their own 'private mixture'. This system is based on fear rather than trust. If the therapist cannot be trusted to be both idiosyncratic and ethical it is not only the therapists who will suffer but ultimately their clients too. If the 'private mixture' of therapists is not trusted, how can they begin to trust their clients and their 'private mixture'? The very essence of the Person-Centred Approach in terms of its valuing of the 'private mixture' of the therapist, the client and their relationship would be under threat if conformity were somehow confused with ethical, accountable practice.

> One danger inherent in the increased clamour for accountability and professionalisation is that the therapist who takes an individualistic and unorthodox stance will have their voice ignored, or, worse still, find themselves scapegoated and driven underground. . . . many therapists may decide it is safest to eliminate improvisations and idiosyncrasies from their practice on the assumption that these will be construed by others as poor practice, or worse. (Wosket, 1999, p. 12–14)

In her chapter Jenny Biancardi remarks on how her practice has become less idiosyncratic in the light of the current climate. This saddens me but it is nevertheless important to acknowledge the context that we are working in.

Most therapists in the UK in 2003 are aware of the possibility, and some would say likelihood, of formalised complaints from clients and public procedures being part of their professional experience. This inevitably has an impact on how we practice. So the dilemma for therapists may be, 'How do I live with a continual internal questioning of my practice as well as being present and ready to meet the

---

[6.] For a full and frank exploration of registration and professionalisation, see Mowbray (1995), House and Totton (1997) and Bates and House (2003).

client as a human being?' At what point do the 'what if' questions, or the 'I've got to cover my back' thoughts, inhibit our ability to be authentic in relationship? Each person needs to find that balance for themselves and it will surely change in each relationship.

Ethical dilemmas are an everyday part of a therapist's working life as they are part of all our lives in many different situations and relationships. Therapists need to be aware of what their personal codes of ethics are and how they relate to the wider community and its codes. These external codes are useless if they are 'abided by' or 'adhered to' begrudgingly and in a manualistic way, rather they need to be experienced, enlivened and discussed. The new BACP *Ethical Framework for Good Practice in Counselling and Psychotherapy* allows much more scope for idiosyncratic practice focusing as it does on values, principles and personal moral qualities. It also emphasises the complexity of ethical decision-making:

> A decision or course of action does not necessarily become unethical merely because it is contentious or other practitioners would have reached different conclusions in similar circumstances. A practitioner's obligation is to consider all the relevant circumstances with as much care as is reasonably possible and to be appropriately accountable for decisions made. (BACP, 2002, p. 3)

The contributors to this book have put themselves on the line by revealing their practice to the reader, my hope is that they will be treated with respect and care. Inevitably as readers we will position ourselves, we will critique and we will judge. In fact this book is intended to be responded to — there is such a range of practice here that it would be strange if the reader could identify or agree with all of it. This is the richness of debate and dialogue. As the editor I want to make clear that what is presented here are personal accounts of lived experience — reflections on moments in a particular relationship at a particular time. They are not examples of how a therapist should or should not behave. I, as the editor, am not saying 'this is right' or 'that is wrong'. We each need to make up our own minds where we stand and what 'ethical' and 'professional' mean for us. This book has been put together in the hope that the difficult and complex issues therapists and clients face can be honestly and openly acknowledged and discussed.

The current danger is that idiosyncratic practice will become synonymous with irresponsible, reckless or unethical behaviour and that therapists will endeavour to conform to norms rather than explore authentic person-to-person relating. David Mearns and Brian Thorne provide a hard-hitting critique of our culture and the risks it poses for person-centred therapists:

> The greatest danger for an approach which aims to be 'person-centred' is to function within an environment which does not allow latitude for persons. The environment of professional counselling has not reached this point, but we should recognise that the processes of institutionalisation tend to accompany professionalisation and be aware of the drift in that direction. In monitoring that movement (Mearns, 1999) we might pay attention to: the slide from potentiality model to deficiency model, the drift from functionalism to structuralism, pressures towards manualisation, the politics of appearance, and the loss of humanity. (Mearns and Thorne, 2000, p. 32–3)

If they are right and we do live in an environment which 'does not allow latitude for persons', where there is a consequent 'loss of humanity' then idiosyncrasy is indeed under threat. It is also needed more than ever. To that end, perhaps Tracey Walshaw is right to wonder in her chapter whether idiosyncrasy will be 'the new buzzword for the twenty-first century'. This would be a hopeful sign for humanity: a powerful antidote to fear, rigidity and conformity. Person-Centred Therapy, by placing idiosyncrasy at the heart of its theory and practice, plays a significant role in providing this antidote. This book celebrates idiosyncrasy by giving it voice.

References

Baldwin, M. (ed.) (2000) *The Use of Self in Therapy*, 2nd edition. New York: The Haworth Press.

Bates, Y. and House, R. (eds.) (2003) *Ethically Challenged Professions: Enabling innovation and diversity in psychotherapy and counselling.* Ross-on-Wye: PCCS Books.

Beutler, L.E., Machado, P.P.P., and Neufeldt, S.A. (1994) Therapist Variables. In A. Bergin and S. Garfield (eds.) *Handbook of Psychotherapy and Behaviour Change*, 4th Edition, New York: Wiley.

Bozarth, J.D. (1984/2001) Beyond reflection: Emergent modes of empathy. In R.F Levant and J.M. Shlien (eds.) (1984) *Client-Centered Therapy and the Person-Centered Approach.* New York: Praeger, pp. 59–75. Reprinted in S. Haugh and T. Merry (eds.) (2001) *Rogers' Therapeutic Conditions: Evolution, Theory and Practice. Vol 2. Empathy.* Ross-on-Wye: PCCS Books, pp. 131–43.

Bozarth, J.D. (1998) *Person-Centred Therapy: A Revolutionary Paradigm.* Ross-on-Wye: PCCS Books.

British Association for Counselling and Psychotherapy (2002) *Ethical Framework for Good Practice in Counselling and Psychotherapy.* Rugby: BACP.

Cooper, M. and Rowan, J. (eds.) (1999) *The Plural Self: Multiplicity in Everyday Life.* London: Sage.

Geller, S.M. and Greenberg, L.S. (2002) Therapeutic presence: Therapists' experience of presence in the psychotherapy encounter. In *Person-Centered & Experiential Psychotherapies, WAPCEPC Inaugural Special Double Issue*, 1(1&2): 71–86.

Genest, S. (2003) The necessity of client perspectives on counselling for clients, counsellors and researchers (part two), In *Ipnosis: an independent journal for practitioners*, 11 Autumn: 18–20.

Grant, B. (1990) Principled and instrumental nondirectiveness in Person-Centered and Client-Centered Therapy. *Person-Centered Review,* 5 (1): 77–88. Reprinted in Cain, D.J. (ed.) (2002) *Classics in the Person-Centered Approach.* Ross-on-Wye: PCCS Books, pp. 371–7.

House, R. and Totton, N. (eds.) (1997) *Implausible Professions: Arguments for Pluralism and Autonomy in Psychotherapy and Counselling,* Ross-on-Wye: PCCS Books.

Kirschenbaum, H. and Henderson, V.L. (1989) *The Carl Rogers Reader.* Boston: Houghton Mifflin.

Lietaer, G (2002) The united colors of person-centered and experiential psychotherapies. In *Person-Centered & Experiential Psychotherapies, WAPCEPC Inaugural Special Double Issue*, 1(1&2): 4–13.

Lowe, R. (1999) Between the 'no longer' and the 'not yet': postmodernism as a context for critical therapeutic work. In I. Parker (ed.) *Deconstructing Psychotherapy,* pp. 71–85. London: Sage.

McLeod, J. (1999) *Practitioner Research in Counselling*. London: Sage.

Mearns, D. (1999) Professionalisation and institutionalisation. In *Counselling*, 28 (5): 344–5.

Mearns, D. and Thorne, B. (1999) *Person-Centred Counselling in Action,* 2nd edition. London: Sage.

Mearns, D. and Thorne, B. (2000) *Person-Centred Therapy Today: New Frontiers in Theory and Practice*. London: Sage.

Merry, T. (2002) *Learning and Being in Person-Centred Counselling,* 2nd edition. Ross-on-Wye: PCCS Books.

Mowbray, R. (1995) *The Case Against Psychotherapy Registration: A Conservation Issue for the Human Potential Movement*, London: Trans Marginal Press.

Proctor, G. (2002) *The Dynamics of Power in Psychotherapy: Ethics, politics and practice*. Ross-on-Wye: PCCS Books.

Rogers, C.R. (1959) A theory of therapy, personality, and interpersonal relationships, as developed in the client-centered framework. In Koch, S. (ed.) (1959) *Psychology: A Study of a Science, Vol.3. Formulations of the Person and the Social Context*. New York: McGraw-Hill, pp. 184–256.

Rogers, C.R. (1961) *On Becoming a Person*. Boston: Houghton Mifflin.

Rogers, C.R. (1980) *A Way of Being*. Boston: Houghton Mifflin.

Rogers, C.R. and Sanford, R.C. (1980) Client-centered psychotherapy. In Kaplan, G., Sadock, B., and Freeman, A. (eds.) *Comprehensive Textbook of Psychiatry, Vol. 3*. Baltimore: Williams and Wilkins.

Sanders, P. (2000) Mapping person-centred approaches to counselling and psychotherapy. *Person-Centred Practice*, 8 (2): 62–74.

Schmid, P. (2002) Paper presented at the Carl R. Rogers 100th Birthday Symposium 2002, La Jolla, California.

Thorne, B. (2002) *The Mystical Power of Person-Centred Therapy. Hope beyond Despair*. London: Whurr.

Thorne, B. (2003) *Carl Rogers,* 2nd edition. London: Sage.

Wilkins, P. (2003) *Person-Centred Therapy in Focus*. London: Sage.

Wosket, V. (1999) *The Therapeutic Use of Self: Counselling Practice, Research and Supervision*. London: Routledge.

Wyatt, G. (ed.) (2001) *Rogers' Therapeutic Conditions: Evolution, Theory and Practice. Volume 1: Congruence*. Ross-on-Wye: PCCS Books.

2

Terry Daly

Acceptance, Power
and the Velveteen
Rabbit

'What is REAL? asked the rabbit one day, when they were lying side-by-side near the nursery vendor, before Nana came to tidy the room. 'Does it mean having things that buzz inside you and a stick out handle?'

'Real isn't how you are made,' said the Skin Horse. 'It's a thing that happens to you. When a child loves you for a long, long time, not just to play with, but REALLY loves you, then you become Real.'

'Does it hurt?' asked the rabbit.

'Sometimes,' said the Skin Horse, for he was always truthful. 'When you are real you don't mind being hurt.'

'Does it happen all at once, like being wound up,' he asked, 'or bit by bit?'

'It doesn't happen all at once,' said the Skin Horse. 'You become. It takes a long time. That's why it doesn't often happen to people who break easily, or have sharp edges, or who have to be carefully kept. Generally, by the time you are real, most of your hair has been loved off, and your eyes drop out and you get loose in the joints and very shabby. But these things don't matter at all, because once you are Real you can't be ugly, except to people who don't understand.'
(Williams, 1922, p. 5)

Introduction

When I was initially asked to write a chapter for this book I was delighted: I thought it was a wonderful idea. However, in the past year I have gone from delight to frustration in my attempt to articulate my process as a counsellor, in a way that would make sense to others. I now realise as a severely dyslexic person that the written word is not a welcome place for me. Indeed I would describe it as quite a demanding and hostile environment.

I had completely underestimated the effort that it would take to translate my understanding, my way of working, into a format that would make sense to others. As a person-centred therapist I strive to offer unconditional acceptance to my individual clients and value their journey without expectations of formats or traditional structures.

Writing this chapter has highlighted that I am not offering this acceptance to myself. With great irony I am trying to force myself into those traditional formats of writing which for me are full of barriers rather than allowing myself to find my own creative way. This learning alone has been most valuable to me and well worth the struggle. So, like the velveteen rabbit, I feel worn and rubbed, but with it a sense of growing self-love and acceptance.

In disability equality awareness training the social model of disability offers an alternative to the medical model approach where my dyslexia would be seen as the problem. The social model suggests that barriers prevent me from fully participating not my dyslexia. So, for instance, the lack of a wheelchair ramp is a barrier, not the fact the person uses a wheelchair (Oliver, 1990).

One of my challenges has been to accept that my own individual barriers cannot be fully removed if I want to communicate through the written word. My own preferred way of communication is spoken and interactive. Like my dyslexia, writing this chapter has been like a jigsaw puzzle for me, although it's like one jigsaw puzzle in four or five different boxes, without actually knowing what the picture is. Gradually what emerges, in a very haphazard way, are my thoughts that might make sense to others.

My work with students certainly has highlighted that I am not alone in this process of frustration in putting words to paper. However, I have learnt a huge amount regarding my self and what my needs are in the process. One of my idiosyncratic ways of working is based on this experience: I have deep belief in the right of the individual to express themselves in their own way. Each individual should find their words, their expression. There is validity in that process. This is one of the main reasons why I was so attracted to the Person-Centred Approach from such an early age.

My own experience of not being 'acceptable' has been a direct and powerful influence on my work and is subsequently a major idiosyncratic part of me.

In this chapter I approached three clients and asked their permission to use recorded transcript material and work on it to look at how I am as a therapist. What I would like to highlight in each of the three pieces of work is the issue of power: how understanding power in the therapeutic relationship is a crucial part of offering acceptance.

• The first transcript reflects my misuse of power, which, although unintentional, could still be considered damaging to the client.
• In the second transcript I highlight the importance of how the counsellor's understanding of the social issues that affect a client can itself be very powerful and communicate acceptance.
• The third piece of work focuses on feedback from a client who describes herself as a deeply private person with an abhorrence of counsellors. This particular relationship is characterised by a depth of mutuality and an equality of power.

My background in relation to power and the Person-Centred Approach
Before I continue with the transcripts I would like to say something more about why I embrace the Person-Centred Approach. At 14 years old, I remember a magical moment in my life when I was offered unconditional acceptance. This shone like a beacon amongst what was otherwise a dark and hostile world. I realise as I am describing it in words it does not seem remarkable; however, for me the experience was profound and, without exaggeration, life-changing. The fact that it might not seem remarkable now is in itself very significant.

I was going through a very troubled time at school and home. One day I decided not to attend school and spent time walking with friends on the streets of my home town. We passed our parish church and were invited in to meet a group of student priests. As was typical of me and my friends at that time, we met this invitation with aggressive curiosity. A short time later we found ourselves sitting in a large circle in something they called an encounter group.

At this point in my life the only experience of groups that I had was family and the school environment with me confronting teachers, arguing and generally challenging systems that I found oppressive and unfair. This is how I began my first encounter group, with the expectation of being shouted down.

I remember one student priest in particular noticing how angry I had become in the group and he asked me why I was angry, in fact he encouraged me to express what I was feeling which left me strangely inarticulate. Within moments I found him sitting beside me and he simply placed a hand on my shoulder. We sat like this for many moments with complete silence in the group. I increasingly felt turmoil and my anger turned to sadness. I was unable to say or articulate this sadness but what was miraculous for me was that this student stayed by my side with his hand on my shoulder and made no demands on me to speak. More importantly, he did not move away — he just simply sat silently by me for the rest of the group.

At that time I had not the language or the experience to understand it, but it left me with the belief that things could be different in my world. The moment grabbed me fully and left me startled and hungry for more.

Now, many years on, I know what was offered to me was what we call 'psychological contact'. I do not know the name of this young student priest as he left on the same day, but what he communicated was warm interest and respect.

Because of this experience at 14, I joined an encounter group aged 15, and I became resolute that I wanted to receive and offer what was for me a fantastically different way of being, and so I began a long journey with many wrong turns.

Over a period of 15 years I worked in a variety of social work settings looking to offer some of the acceptance and challenge I discovered in my early years of group work. Unfortunately, I was to discover a very different culture in many of the large and often institutionalised organisations that I worked for. I know that I could be described as naïve: I was certainly constantly surprised at the difference in attitudes of my colleagues and, in particular, my managers to issues of power and equality in the workplace. The idea that the client should always be at the centre was not something that was readily shared or understood.

Most of the wrong turns were related to power and its misuse. I naïvely believed then, and now, that those of us wanting to 'help' do so with a desire not to disempower the person seeking help. However, I believe that individuals wanting to help are intrinsically linked to the structures they work within.

Gillian Proctor, the author of the recent book, *The Dynamics of Power in Counselling and Psychotherapy*, captures well what can go wrong when trying to support oppressed people:

> **Structural positions of power and psychological distress**
> I would argue that the higher prevalence of members of oppressed groups in psychiatry reflects the positions of power of the groups involved. There is much evidence to associate the likelihood of suffering from psychological distress with the individual's position in society with respect to structural power. The higher rates of diagnosis for women compared with men of many disorders, such as depression, anxiety and eating disorders, reflects women's position in society with respect to power . . . Yet the response by psychiatry to women is characterised by 'tending to *remove* power and control from women, to *deny* her feelings, and to *ignore* the meaning behind her actions' (Johnstone, 1989, p. 120). (Proctor, 2002, p. 3)

So I now look back with regret at my own attempts at helping as a residential worker, social worker and active listener. In my attempts to offer support, often the reverse would take place. Now I would suggest it was my, and my colleagues', lack of personal development and failure to enter into the client's frame of reference which contributed to our incongruent way of working with clients. Carl Rogers clarifies this for me:

> This has raised in my mind the strong suspicion that the optimal helping relationship is the kind of relationship created by a person who is psychologically mature. Or to put it in another way, the degree to which I can create relationships which facilitate the growth of others as separate persons is a measure of the growth I have achieved in myself. In some respects this is a disturbing thought, but it is also a promising or challenging one. It would indicate that if I am interested in creating helping relationships I have a fascinating lifetime job ahead of me, stretching and developing my potentialities in the direction of growth. (Rogers, 1961, p. 56)

Who I am as a therapist?

Many of these early difficult experiences I now find help me to hold firm boundaries, which paradoxically allow me to work on the edge. The British Association for Counselling and Psychotherapy (BACP) *Ethical Framework for Good Practice in Counselling and Psychotherapy* frees me to risk intimacy in relationships as opposed to restricting me. This subject is a chapter in itself, which I will reluctantly refrain from exploring now. I make no apologies in stating that I get immense satisfaction from my work and that it meets a need in me to have some effect on the aggression and emotional turmoil that seems so prevalent in the world today.

What allows me to stay so energised in my work is the firm belief that my clients do not have to be a certain way to meet my needs. I believe it is crucial that I find my own mechanisms to look after myself, which include supervision, therapy, and my relationship with my partner, friends and colleagues.

In ensuring that I am fulfilled in my own personal and professional world, I can then embark on my therapeutic relationships with a hopeful intention of leaving my own needs aside.

It would be naïve and dishonest of me if I claimed that my own process does not have needs popping up in therapeutic relationships: curiosity, judgements, attractions and gossip. They often show themselves during a session but thankfully, when I am in touch with my ethical self those 'demons', as I call them, can be kept at bay.

It has been my experience and constant delight that within the Person-Centred Approach attempts at dealing with issues of power have been up front and this offers a frame of reference which allows me to constantly monitor myself in the therapeutic relationship.

This, then, partly answers for me why I have chosen a person-centred approach to working. I have now come to the belief that I am a powerful individual with many social constructs, values and fears, which can easily be passed on to, or triggered by, the counselling process and so the Person-Centred Approach demands that I am constantly vigilant in how 'I am' with the client.

When I am centred and in good contact with the client the relationship is characterised by a lack of misuse of power by myself and a willingness to work with power struggles within the relationship.

In this context the magic of the core conditions can emerge. In this chapter I hope, with the support of my three clients, to look briefly at how this magic manifests itself for the clients and myself during therapy and also how it can easily go wrong.

My experience of therapeutic work is often similar to finding my way in unfamiliar territory: the start is usually with me not knowing where I am with the client process. In my early years this not knowing was accompanied by panic, which in turn became a need to organise, help the client (or rather, me) to focus and find a direction.

Now at the beginning of new relationships I find I am excited by the anticipation of not knowing and the challenge of building a relationship where I can communicate confidence and willingness to stay with the client, which is not seen as passive or ineffective.

I believe that a relationship should be very active and full and that my just 'being' should be experienced by the client as fully present: I am in unfamiliar territory, walking beside the client noticing many small details, allowing the client's reality to gradually fill my senses and the client senses my warmth and interest as active and not lacking in transparency.

As the relationship builds I am welcomed into the world of the client. I am increasingly convinced that it is only when the client offers me acceptance, in other words welcomes me into their reality, that the process of therapy really begins.

I believe that I must know who I am and constantly monitor my own levels of self-acceptance so that my own lack of acceptance does not contaminate client relationships. I am aware that contaminate is a strong word, but I believe it to be very appropriate. When my clients have sensed in me a lack of acceptance it is usually of myself, but experienced by the client as directed at them.

A dear friend of mine, who works as a person-centred therapist in San Diego, uses a wonderful phrase, which suggests the need for the therapist to take responsibility for balance within a session and remain integrated whilst working.

Tears can be shared with the client, but remember, somebody must mind the store. (Elsie Zala)

Acceptance

For me the very essence of the Person-Centred Approach is about individuality, which leads to a community of acceptance characterised by difference. In a world where brute strength often is valued, I am hopeful that the strength of the Person-Centred Approach can be offered as an alternative but effective way of being.

As individuals become more self-accepting, they in turn offer more acceptance with empathy as a result. My neighbour becomes a friend not foe, the unfamiliar becomes exciting not a threat, difference offers the possibility of growth not loss.

So, for me, my work with the individual is as important as the collective social action that I have undertaken in the past. Again I find the words of Carl Rogers inspirational in relation to the possibilities of change in society:

I conclude that if nations follow their past ways, then, because of the speed of world communication of separate views, each society will have to exert more and more coercion to bring about a forced agreement as to what constitutes the real world and its values. Those coerced agreements will differ from nation to nation, from culture to culture. The coercion will destroy individual freedom. We will bring about our own destruction through the clashes caused by differing world views.

But I have suggested an alternative. If we accept as a basic fact of all human life that we live in separate realities; if we can see those differing realities as the most promising resource for learning in all the history of the world; if we can live together in order to learn from one another without fear; if we can do all this, then a new age could be dawning. And perhaps — just perhaps — humankind's deep organic sensings are paving the way for just such a change. (Rogers, 1980, pp. 107–8)

Transcript 1: Anne

The first transcript took place several years ago and I have chosen it because it highlights how easy it is for me to get lost as a therapist. The particular session extract demonstrates what happens when I lose confidence in being centred on the client and use my power to defend myself unnecessarily as opposed to being open to the client's experience of me. My hope in showing this particular piece of client tape is that it might generate some discussion that supports exploration of mistakes as a valuable learning tool.

To briefly introduce the background to this transcript: I had been working with Anne for several years on a weekly basis. I believe we had a strong therapeutic relationship where there was a high level of mutuality. In the session I have chosen to transcribe, we had met the day before for one hour and agreed to a follow-up session the next day because of practical problems of holidays.

After the close of the session the previous day, I made a statement, in passing, about my feelings towards the part of Anne that was still unaccepting of her successes. I recall feeling warm and affirming towards her when I made this statement. However, I used the phrase, 'I would like to thrash that part of you that is so unaccepting of you.' As the following transcript shows this left Anne with a profound sense of unacceptance.

Anne 1: The last thing you said, do you remember? Not on the tape.
Terry 1: Oh, the incongruence? Of being congruent.
Anne 2: Of being congruent?

(At this point I simply could have asked the client to remind me rather than guessing incorrectly.)

Terry 2: Yeah I think I remember. I can't remember the very last thing and I can remember some of the things.
Anne 3: (*Laughing in background*) Yeah it's come up before, you know that you just like to thrash that part.
Terry 3: Oh yeah that's right! (*Sounding defensive*)
Anne 4: It's come up before.
Terry 5: Is that the last thing I said?
Anne 6: Well it's the last thing I remember.
Terry 6: Mmm.
Anne 7: I just want to talk about that a bit.
Terry 7: Mmm.
Anne 8: What did you mean?

Terry 8:   (*Pause for twenty seconds*) irritated, by (*pause for five seconds*) yeah, by all the feelings that I would have. You know it's fascinating that you remember just that bit and not the other things.

Anne 9:   Yeah.

Terry 9:   Why is that? Can I throw it back to you? (*I use this as an example of misusing my own power — struggling with my lack of congruence at this point. It would have been more appropriate for me to share how I felt about having hurt Anne rather than trying to convince her that my intentions were good.*)

Anne 10:   Yeah, because I started to get angry about it. I do remember the other things actually.

Terry 10:   You do?

Anne 11:   I sort of felt . . . em, (*pause for ten seconds*) I think it's your stuff.

Terry 11:   (*Nodding*) Let me say it to you again then, and see if it's what you heard. Is that all right if I do that?

(Now I find myself cringing when listening to the tape. I am amazed at how clumsy, arrogant and dismissive I was, simply because I was quite rightly challenged by the client.)

Anne 12:   (*Nodding head*)

Terry 12:   There is a part of me that's irritated with that part of you that undermines or can't let you accept your successes. And of course that's my stuff. So that irritation is, is almost a lack of acceptance.

Anne 13:   Yeah, well I don't think I quite understood that you meant it was a part in me that undermines.

Terry 13:   Oh what did you think?

Anne 14:   I think I thought it was that hurt, frightened part.

Terry 14:   That I'm angry with your hurt, frightened part?

Anne 15:   Yeah, that I would allow it to take over.

Terry 15:   Yeah, I'm smiling, because, no that's not it at all.

Anne 16:   Right, so it's the bit that . . .

Terry 16:   (*Interrupting*) It doesn't really matter what bit it is.

(Again this is an example of me trying to make it better, but is quite rightly misunderstood by the client.)

Anne 17:   It does to me, it does to me.

Terry 17:   But it's like I'm not accepting, you know, I'm trying to make you into this, I can't compartmentalise you.

Anne 18:   Yeah.

Terry 18:   There is a part of me that does find a part of you irritating.

Anne 19:   But what does it evoke in you?

Terry 19:   My stuff?

Anne 20:   Like what?

Terry 20:   So what's happening now is that I'm angry with the message you've got that you're not good enough, I'm angry with (*pause*) I'm angry that you got the message, and am irritated that it still has such a powerful effect on you. It irritates me, yeah.

Anne 21: It irritates you?

Terry 21: I could never in a million years be angry with the hurt part or the frightened part. But it's the, it is that condition of worth so I'm not accepting it, I'm lacking acceptance for it. And it comes from, well, that's my stuff that's where it comes from. (*Silence for one and a half minutes*) and what I should be offering is acceptance to all of who you are.

Anne 22: If you don't, how could I?

Terry 22: (*Nodding in agreement.*)

(Silence for two minutes.)

Terry 23: Yeah, that's my stuff, I'm angry with me as well I suppose. And irritated with me. That covers the irritation, about my own lack of acceptance, my message that I'm not good enough. (*Pause*) So I'm not really irritated with you at all, no, it's not you at all, no, I don't feel any irritation or anger at all now that it is in focus, I just feel sad.

Anne 23. Something you also said, what was that? You know that, if I went ahead and took the risk what about the cost? And that left me thinking last night I think I'm too scared not to take the risk, it's like, almost there are some things I do, that I try and escape from but a lot of things I don't have any choice about. And I don't know whether that's a good or a bad thing.

Terry 24: So it's got nothing to do with bravery, you don't have the choice.

Anne 24: I do have a choice, but it's not much of a choice and it would be harder to live with myself if I didn't do it.

Terry 25: It doesn't sound like much of a choice, but you're right you do have a choice. (*Pause*)

Anne 25: I suppose it's the word thrash, because that's the word that daddy used as well so it's like, and I feel that that part of me was thrashed. That's what happened. Every sensitive feeling I showed was trampled over, it's like new grass growing, it comes up, and then it gets trampled over. And it comes up again but never gets very far; he used to say — never (*this part of the tape unintelligible*).

Terry 26: And now?

Anne 26: And now the voice is in my head, and it got, gentler when I was an adult, before it was angry, when I was an adult it was more like, (*this part of the tape is unintelligible*) so backing off wasn't an option.

(Silence for two minutes.)

Anne 27: What are you thinking?

Terry 27: I'm wondering why you're smiling?

Anne 28: I do that I suppose.

Terry 28: Mmm, but even with that shrug it feels like you're still left with a huge burden.

Anne 29: Yeah when I tap into it, it's what I was thinking about last night too, with ... with the guilt thing, she gets so irritated. And I was thinking, fuck her.

Terry 29: And so were you saying fuck Terry too?

Anne 30: (*Laughing*) No I wasn't actually, because I knew that I had to address it with you and I knew where it was coming from. But it's like it was good that I could address the guilt thing.

This transcript highlights how a casually made statement at the end of the session can do a great deal of damage, especially when it is followed up by defensiveness on the part of the counsellor. Fortunately Anne and I had had a strong relationship, which enabled us to work through my clumsiness and, more importantly, my lack of acceptance.

I think configurations theory illustrates well the mistakes that I made during the session; my valuing of one part of the client more than the other. Dave Mearns in *Person-Centred Counselling Today* talks about the importance of valuing 'the not for growth part of the client'.

> Arguably the most common mistake made by person-centred therapists is not to be as aware of those configurations which carry an opposite imperative — those which caution against change because of the disruption and loss which might result. It is important that the person-centred therapist offer an equally full therapeutic relationship to *not for growth* configurations, like: 'the 'me' that just wants to curl up and do absolutely nothing'; 'the part that wants to go back', and 'the bit of me that wants to destroy this therapist'. Person-centred therapists often have a mistaken understanding that therapy should always be pointing in a 'growthful' direction. (Mearns and Thorne, 2000, p. 115)

I hope if the same situation arose now, I would be less verbose, more apologetic and more empathic from the start of Anne's challenge of me. Although it is easy for me to highlight my mistakes, on a positive note I found great reassurance in the fact that once I had actually got in touch with what was really going on for me in relation to the client and was able to be congruent, the focus shifted away from my clumsiness thereby allowing the client to explore what my lack of acceptance meant in her reality.

This piece of work shows how powerful and effective the use of recording can be. Carl Rogers was often quoted as saying that tape recording was one of the most powerful mediums for learning within counselling training. I personally believe it is essential that recording from time to time is kept up throughout the life of a counsellor's work.

It has highlighted two particular parts of my idiosyncratic way of being:

• Mistakes are common to me and if I can work on those mistakes with the client in an open way, they in themselves can become a very valuable part of the process.
• The need for feedback from others in order to explore mistakes or struggles with my therapy work, which usually takes the form of a supervision group.

As part of the preparation for this chapter I shared the transcript with Anne and it raised some very interesting additional points:

- She experienced me as being transparent during the session, which encouraged her to explore her own anger and express it in a congruent way.
- Despite the many mistakes I made, my openness and level of self-disclosure was experienced by her as modelling relationship.
- Finally, much is lost in the text in relation to the tone of the voices and the humour. There is a much bigger context of the long-term relationship, which supported us. This particular session allowed for some risks to be taken on both sides.

Transcript 2: Bill
The second transcript is very important to me in that it brings together two important parts of myself. Firstly, my belief that counsellors should have a level of social awareness, so that when the client comes to counselling with a background of oppression, be it lesbian, gay, black, religious or gender related, they do not have to take on the role of educating the therapist. Secondly, my conviction in the importance of the quality of presence offered by the therapist.

In introducing the next transcript I'd like to call on my notes that relate to the particular session.

Today's session was, as with previous sessions, very powerful for me personally and very moving. Bill has, once again, caught beautifully the process of therapy in allowing me to simply enter into his world fully. Bill often comes without an agenda, with no idea of where he wants to start, but quickly moves into connecting with some very deep feelings.

Today was no exception with him encountering his experience of HIV and the implications of being HIV positive, in relation to medicine. Bill allows me to really get behind his fears and anxieties, to stay with what he calls a 'murkiness' so that we can together explore the implications and the changes to his health.

Towards the end of the session, Bill described really well this whole idea, he jokingly apologised today for saying that he didn't feel he was bringing what would be appropriate for the chapter in the book, and then in our laughter I realised that this is exactly what he was doing in simply bringing himself with a deep desire to understand and accept who he is. That deep desire to accept who he is was demanding and harrowing because it requires him to look rigorously at all aspects of his life, to allow himself to scrutinise the parts which he now has to accept as no longer fitting.

This section is roughly twenty minutes before the end of the session. The focus has been on the client's sense of judgement of himself and a lack of self-acceptance.

Bill 1: It's funny I get spun off in different directions by what people say and what I read so I get to the point that I think I'm OK about things generally then I read something that says (*pause*) I stopped reading a lot because I feel a lot of the reading . . . Knowledge is power but it can also . . .

Terry 1: If it knocks you off your axis.

Bill 2: Yeah, so I've been reading lots about HIV, I still do, it's good to know the latest but I feel it will be more pertinent when I'm on medication because there's so much about the best cocktail and new drugs and I try not to . . . I don't read about all the new drugs coming out because I think you get yourself fixating what is going to cure you, what is going to fix you, I try not to do that but some of the stuff you read is very honest and that's good but it can be frightening. There was an article recently in . . . Fact Sheet and it was about . . . we think of things as being a lot better, people are living a lot longer and people dying of AIDS all that stuff gone, but is it? The side-effects of medication totally controlled by drug regimes just going through all the different things and I added it all up I thought fucking hell, you know it is really still tough and it makes you feel a bit low and then fine again. And then Paul talks about his partner, the medication didn't work for him so they knew he was going to die after so many years, all the time. So I am always worrying a little bit about what it will be like when I start being on medication. Will it work, won't it work? Part of me just wants to get it over with, to find out if it will work, on the other hand I want to keep it away as long as possible. So it's all these little things . . . all the time.

Terry 2: And they're not little things! They're colossal things! (*Humour and exasperation in my tone.*) That is that rawness, about you, what you consider to be little things now is a sign of your metamorphosis because other people would be overwhelmed with even the possibility of thinking like that whereas you have had to learn to accommodate all of those thoughts so . . . It's incredible what you're doing. So how can you stay on your axis? And be aware of all these things, so that's what you're asking me earlier on about what direction you should go in and now I'm thinking how can you make sure you are compassionate and loving of yourself.

Bill 3: (*Nodding.*) Yes.

Terry 3: (*Noticing a different expression on the client's face.*) What are you feeling?

Bill 4: No, I agree with that, but I'm almost thinking am I compassionate towards myself? I don't feel, I feel hazy about how I would measure that, be aware of that because I know I'm tough on myself and sometimes I do feel I'm too tough on myself, catching myself all the time and it almost like I have other moments when I'm consciously thinking . . . 'God you're being hard on yourself, because of the way you are but the good thing is you are aware of how you are, most people aren't aware of these things.' So I deserve a pat on the back for, you know, knowing that I'm doing these things. And yet I'm still giving myself a hard time, well not always sometimes I do think 'good for you'. But you are right, all these little things as I call them you are right they are . . . Like now when I get, I always thought when I got diagnosed, if I start getting little things wrong with me . . .would I be like . . . 'my God my God!' I didn't, so when I did get a cold I just think, 'well I got a cold'. But that's been creeping in as well, and I notice when I'm run down, probably since I got that low blood cell count and I just had a really heavy weekend and it was great fun and I felt OK after it but see yesterday and today I just feel exhausted absolutely exhausted and it's a different . . . Funny kind of exhaustion not an 'I want to go to bed and sleep' exhaustion it's just a 'have no energy' exhaustion. And a few years ago I would have thought 'bloody hell I better take it easy this weekend' whereas now I'm thinking of 'my God I've killed off cells what have I done?' You know, I should go to bed and get lots and lots of sleep. To try and build that back up. And it's just that little subtle paranoia about my health.

Terry 4: You use the word paranoia. I feel that is so unfair.

Bill 5: Right.

Terry 5: That just does not feel right, it's like, it's a reality, it's a possibility it's not paranoia. How on earth can you know the difference between . . . (*humorous tones*) And now I feel like slapping your ankles young man! For having one of your crazy weekends, you should be looking after yourself, of course you're tired, you've burned the candles. But the reality is, is it that or . . . or is it the illness? Not knowing feels like an incredible burden.

Bill 6: So now I think I'm resistant to, it's like I recognise the cover of me which is I'm HIV-positive and I have accepted that. And so to say I have HIV is nothing it's just a word. So I recognise that I'm HIV-positive and I know that I have a virus. I know all the things in my head, but, I think, I don't want to accept what the implications of that are in the long-term so it's like I don't want to worry about not being well, or about what will drugs do to me. I just want to be terribly well, terribly balanced optimistic HIV-positive person where nothing ever goes wrong, that's what I want to be. It's like I probably could be that person, realistically that's who I am but . . . What am I trying to say? It's like I don't really want to deal with that, I am dealing with it but in a bad way because it's making me feel old and ill.

Terry 6: Yeah and if you could welcome these negative feelings into your terribly healthy, positive, young, self-concept it would enhance it. Rather than work against it, welcome it.

(A major theme in previous sessions had been to work on accepting and making space for uncomfortable negative feelings which the client identified as his shadow self. He didn't feel these feelings had a right to surface.)

Bill 7: OK, I understand that, but again it's like how do I do that? Occasionally when you say something it makes such sense but then I become hazy about . . . Is it just more talking that will help me do that or how do I?

Terry 7: No, no, I haven't got a clue how we do it . . . to be honest except that when you catch yourself with that feeling of that shadow it's like 'I'm not surprised' rather than 'What the fuck am I doing?' (*Phrase used earlier by client*) When I think of my own shadow, over childhood and I now say to myself: 'What do you expect? Of course you feel this or that.' And at the same time I might say to myself, 'That's not all of who I am.'

Bill 8: I like that . . . I feel comforted all of a sudden. (*Pause for five minutes when the client goes into some deep feelings*) That feels good, because I probably have been, been hard on myself. Probably too hard on myself. (*Pause, heavy sigh*) I don't think I've actually allowed myself to be scared. Just never let that. (*Long pause*) I can't get that sentence out of my head. It's buzzing in me like an electric power station.

Terry 8: I'm not surprised.

Bill 9: (*Long pause*) It almost annoys me that I don't get more, all that stuff is there but I don't really get frightened, a bit sad sometimes. I talk about it but, and sometimes I wish I did feel. (*Long pause*) Sorry am I overtime?

Terry 9: No, we started ten minutes late, so we haven't gone over time.

Bill 10: Nearly there . . . it's because I think I am so, I am so terrified at the start of being scared and not coping and am so relieved when I got through the first year without everything falling apart that I probably never allowed myself to just stop and let . . . just even a little bit.

Terry 10: Yeah, that's it.

Bill 11: I feel a bit sad now and I also feel good because I liked what you said.

Terry 11: Yes, I feel sad as well and it feels good.

Bill 12: I will try not to be so hard, not hard I mean tough.

Terry 12: Yes, like one of those lieutenants in the Navy we were talking about; there's no room for sadness or being scared you have to be vigilant, on guard all the time.

Bill 13: Yes, that's what I do but I admire myself as well. I see all the good things about how I have been.

Looking over these lines now once again fills me with a mixture of feelings: taking the individual lines separately I could quickly become judging of myself. In Terry 5, I am clearly expressing my view as opposed to offering empathy. Again in Terry 6, I am offering advice in a directive way. In Terry 7, a wonderful opportunity for the client to find their own way and I can't resist a suggestion.

In reality this client has a strong internalized locus of evaluation and in over-analysing each sentence I would lose the integrity of the whole session. My willingness to explore the client's reality compensates for my clumsy and sometimes directive statements. My deep sense of acceptance for the client is communicated despite my apparent non-acceptance in the words.

Genuineness and transparency are critical in this particular relationship: a high degree of self-disclosure is characteristic. If I can be real with this client he will trust my experiencing of him. What appears to be inappropriate humour in Terry 5, actually communicates a great deal of understanding. Humour is without doubt one of my idiosyncratic ways of being.

My humour and sexual identity play an important role in my work. Transparency requires that I am fully open. As a gay man this can often create anxieties for me. In this particular relationship my sexual orientation is valued, as the client himself is gay. However, transcribing this tape has reminded me how vulnerable lesbian and gay counsellors can be to the attitudes of their clients. My experience has been that this has not been well documented in a counselling text.

I believe it is very important that the counsellor is familiar with cultural difference. In this instance my understanding of HIV and AIDS plays an important part during the session. I believe we communicate a huge amount of acceptance to clients in our willingness to familiarise ourselves with social issues, so that the client themselves does not have to take on the role of educator.

Nevertheless understanding in the context of relational depth is not everything, as Dave Mearns so aptly puts it:

> I believe that the counsellor's understanding of the client is much overemphasized in counselling. Most of the time it is not important that the counsellor understands what the client is relating. Indeed, a trap for the person-centred counsellor is to be deflected away from being close to the experiencing of the client and drawn into trying to understand what the client is saying. Usually this has the result of pulling the client out of his experience in an effort to explain it to the counsellor! Much more facilitative to the client's movement into his experiencing is to be as close to that experiencing as possible. (Mearns, 2003, pp. 6–7)

This highlights another of my idiosyncratic traits: a balance between social awareness, understanding of cultural difference and the ability to hold this awareness so that it does not affect the *quality of presence* that Mearns refers to, but rather enhances it.

Transcript 3: Cathy

In contrast to the two previous examples I examine my work with Cathy by exploring my client notes and reflecting on these notes with her in the hope that we might capture something of the essence of our relationship which might highlight my idiosyncratic ways of working.

I have been working with Cathy for several years with a focus on supporting her through the reality of multiple sclerosis.

We already knew each other from an introduction to counselling course where Cathy was a participant and I was the trainer.

In the initial discussion with Cathy regarding the possibilities of exploring some of our work, she responded with a great deal of humour — a characteristic of our relationship.

Often we would find the work we were doing, which was intense and deeply moving, to also be amusing, full of joy and laughter. In the early days my client would often remind me of some of my more outrageous statements, usually made when I was struggling to stay within the client's frame of reference. It got to the point where my client would be able to tell me quite quickly that she knew when I wasn't with her, because I had switched into what she called my 'counsellor mode'.

Below is an extract from my client notes, which Cathy agreed to respond to.

Today's session was approximately one hour and it was characterised by celebration. Cathy has for some time been struggling with a loss of mobility that over the past five or six years has been seriously restricting her freedom. After struggling for many years, Cathy finally accepted the need to use a wheelchair in the latter half of 2001. Cathy described that period as a very dark time in her life where the world was shrinking more and more. Movement and flowing is incredibly important to this client. Not only was she being restricted from this flow of movement, but also the idea of having to rely on others was quite abhorrent to her.

In stark contrast today was recognition that for the past five or six months, the wheelchair has been unnecessary and that mobility has returned and with it a joyful movement and freedom.

During this session with Cathy I had noticed several times an absence of particular feelings and now when I reflect I realise that the absence was of this sense of being trapped and it is being replaced with a tremendous, joyful and spiritual freedom.

Today I had the pleasure and the joy of simply accompanying Cathy with this sense of joyfulness. Several times the client used metaphors and if I can call on one, it was the image of two butterflies on a spring/summer's day spinning around each other with no particular balance or movement, but with tremendous grace and freedom. This was my experience of working with Cathy today and, after accompanying her into some very dark places, I was also able to accompany her in this place of absolute freedom and joy.

In the following transcript Cathy comments on the above notes and our relationship.

Cathy 1:   I am very hostile to the counselling/therapy kind of way of looking at people. The way people can trick round things, like if I was to say something, like a proper counsellor or therapist would respond, 'I think you are in denial there'. And all those tricks I get really annoyed about.

It is so easy, 'Ah — denial!' You know all those tricks, I have come across so many counsellors like that I wouldn't let any of them into my head.

But I remember coming straight to see you from seeing this neurologist and you were really upset and I wasn't. He had diagnosed multiple sclerosis, partly it wasn't a surprise and partly I go into totally rational, 'we can deal with this'. Let's forget about feelings, that is a good thing. I found that moving and surprising more because it made me aware of how I am not in touch with emotional effects and things and how I can't be in touch and it helped me deal with reactions to people like my family as well.

Terry 1:   They would have similar . . .

Cathy 2:   Yes, they all had similar reactions. I like it when you say things like, 'I don't think that people have got their money's worth unless they have a good cry once a session.' I like being able to lighten things.

I can't bear it when things get very heavy and I can't bear it when things get very serious and I think the dynamic between us is the ability to lighten things without it seeming trivial or making things superficial, it is nothing like that.

I have at times been told that I don't take things seriously enough by people when I make some flip comment. I can't, that is just not the way I work. I much prefer you as an improper counsellor.

Because I couldn't work with someone who can't see things from the sideways point of view.

Terry 2: The way I see it, it is allowing you to be who you are?

Cathy 3: Oh yes, I tend to reflect back, I have always done this and partly because it gives me a lot of personal privacy. I don't reflect back with you . . . think, 'what is Terry wanting today?' I feel quite free. Like that time particularly when you were doing the Egan Solar position, you suddenly went into counselling mode. I thought, 'oh God! I have lost him'. I actually said, 'am I boring you because you have gone into counselling mode?' You had gone into this kind of posture, leaning forward trying to look alert, your eyes slightly wider apart than normal, with a slight glazed look as you are trying very hard to concentrate and eye contact. (Laughter) But that was early days.

Terry 3: Oh dear. It was, actually, wasn't it? Maybe it was when I was bit panicky with what you were talking about. Maybe that is what it was. Like, I realise now, when I become like a counsellor when I panic.

Cathy 4: I have got a deep, deep privacy, a deep need for it, that it takes a lot for me to trust somebody and it does have to be somebody real. I have to feel that someone is real, rather than doing this or doing that job.

It is the real connection rather than the textbook connection, rather than the model that really matters to me. Remember on that course you were very, very flippant at times and that is why I thought maybe I could talk to you. I have not come across anybody working in the counselling field that I thought I could actually let into my head.

Terry 4: That is a compliment.

Cathy 5: It is striking actually looking back. How unique you were and are with me in terms of in my life. I just have met so many people who are counsellors. They are head cases. Mostly I think counsellors have their own issues to deal with and it encourages them to come into the counselling field. But some counsellors are definitely projecting; they are not dealing with their stuff but putting it onto other people. You can't open your mouth. I remember one woman, she is a fully qualified counsellor, done a degree in psychology and the rest of it and I cannot say anything. Her response is always 'has something upset you?'

It's the lightness that comes in, even if you don't say anything, the gleam in your eyes, amusement, just something, that twitch of your facial muscles.

Terry 5: The one thing that I find curious is that you say you like things light and yet I experience you as very deep.

Cathy 6: This is the difference between light and shallow. I hesitate about using the word light, because people tend to think it means superficial or shallow and it is not. It is light, it is illumination, and it's bringing a sparkle into things. Which could get heavy and dark and bogged down and choked up.

Terry 6: Crushing.

Cathy 7: Yes, and really, really crushing. About bringing a little bit of sparkle in at times. Makes it feel that it is sometimes possible to bear with and that is what really matters to me. Not somebody saying it is awful. On some sort of lighter comment but not shallow.

Terry 7: That is really helpful the difference between lightness and shallow.

Cathy 8: Yes, I mean, it is really important to me because I've stuck with you over the time. My need for light and bubble and sparkle and this superficiality stuff. I know it isn't that but at times what I am trying to find out what I like about people and the rest of it. The idea of putting in a flippant comment. Again I don't think, for example, I ever do it incongruently and you never ever do it. Its just like you throwing a handful of sparkly dust over me, it is lovely and it really helps and I don't feel in the slightest bit denied or em . . .

Terry 8: Disrespected.

Cathy 9: When somebody would make light of what you are doing. That is never a positive thing but giving a light to it, lightening it. So I don't feel it is ever made light of or dismissed.

People do make light of it a lot, you know and say the usual 'it is not as bad as that'. There are too many people that feel that they know how you can deal with things or what you should be doing.

This relationship reminds me of my belief in the absolute sharing of power in all of my therapeutic relationships. The level of sharing will depend on the client's locus of evaluation and the level of mutuality in the relationship. Paradoxically, I believe most challenge takes place when the client experiences a high level of equality and acceptance in the relationship and empathy can be received openly.

My own lack of 'respect' for systems and structures is reflected in how I am with this client, striving to avoid any semblance of technique or approach and just trying to be real within the core conditions.

I find it interesting that Cathy described my approach as offering 'lightness' as opposed to 'heaviness'. This is despite the fact that the work is profound and deep.

Conclusions

I am increasingly excited about my client work based on the fact that the sharing of power in relationships has a dramatic effect on therapeutic outcome despite class, creed or cultural differences. This has far-reaching implications for working with diversity.

My idiosyncratic way of being is clearly based on my own experiences in relation to power and inequality. This awareness is balanced by an intrinsic belief in the power of the core conditions. In looking over these transcripts I am aware of my failures to hold the core conditions. In my opinion, however, the levels of mutuality in each relationship balance this. Nevertheless, I must ask myself the question: why impose my thoughts or ideas onto the client in the first place? Although my experience provides me with a high degree of self-awareness this does not give me license to be less vigilant in relation to how I use my power and less consistent in how I offer the core conditions.

I have discovered, like the velveteen rabbit, that, although the costs of being real are high, the outcome is immensely rewarding both in therapeutic relationships and life.

References

BACP (2002) *Ethical Framework for Good Practice in Counselling and Psychotherapy.*

Johnstone, L. (1989) *Users and Abusers of Psychiatry.* London: Routledge.

Mearns, D. (2003) *Developing Person-Centred Counselling.* Second Edition. London: Sage.

Mearns, D. and Thorne, B. (2000) *Person-Centred Therapy Today: New Frontiers in Theory and Practice.* London: Sage.

Oliver, M. (1990) *The Politics of Disablement.* London: Macmillan Press Ltd.

Proctor, G. (2002) *The Dynamics of Power in Counselling and Psychotherapy. Ethics, Politics and Practice.* Ross-on-Wye: PCCS Books.

Rogers, C.R. (1961) *On Becoming a Person. A Therapist's View of Psychotherapy.* Boston: Houghton Mifflin.

Rogers, C.R. (1980) *A Way of Being.* Boston: Houghton Mifflin.

Williams, M. (1922) *The Velveteen Rabbit.* New York: Bantam.

3

Jan Hawkins

'Softly, I can do it Softly'

I felt I had come home when I first read Carl Rogers' *On Personal Power* (1978). I was no longer an alien, born at the wrong time, on the wrong planet, equipped only with the wrong phrase book. My preceding psychodynamic training had interested me intellectually, but working with clients made me question the assumptions made about their motivations. Reading Rogers I found affirmation of my view of the world. I didn't need to work to understand the ideas and theory. It all made complete sense to me. Rogers spoke what I felt; he too saw positive change and healing not only as a possibility, but as crucial issues for the future of humanity. What a wonderful revelation: I might hope to find like-minded people and learning opportunities. I might be able to develop as a therapist by living out my values about social interactions, rather than applying a set of techniques and a range of interpretations to my clients. My way of being in the world at last found some link.

The holistic nature of the Person-Centred Approach allows me both to be fully myself, as well as to meet others in relationship. But exactly because this approach obliges me to be fully open to myself and what I am experiencing, as well as to my clients, it was, and continues to be, far more of a challenge for me than my previous training had been. Part of the process of letting go of my earlier counselling training involved liberating myself from the impulse to find the 'right way' with a client. Rogers' emphasis on creativity as one of the characteristics of 'persons of tomorrow' (1978) encouraged me to be open to creative exploration within therapeutic relationships. It is this creativity, along with the recognition of the unique nature of each individual and each therapeutic relationship, that appealed to me as a theme when I was invited to contribute to this book. My title comes from Richard, a client I will talk about. His phrase 'Softly, I can do it softly', spoke deeply to me from himself, yet it also touched my own sense of how I feel in being with my clients, and how I am in the world. I *can,* like Richard, do it softly: being with my clients I want to access the whole of myself, of who I am, and bring myself into relationship with my client. I tread softly alongside them, so that they can feel my presence, yet maintain contact with their own feelings, concerns, struggles and tensions. I want to tread softly, yet remain purposeful and firmly grounded, as I attempt to understand my client's world from his or her own perspective.

I have, as I write, just returned from teaching a group of therapists on an intensive training weekend focusing on working with adult issues resulting from childhood abuse. I recognised throughout that weekend how often I caught myself reminding the group of students that interventions I mentioned should not be taken as prescriptive. Many of the most intense moments of connections I have experienced within sessions are when a different, perhaps rather unusual, mode of relating has evolved and often these have never been repeated. This is because the individuality or uniqueness of the communication, whatever the creative idea or mode of interaction, evolved with that particular individual in that specific session.

The Person-Centred Approach allows me, with my client, to 'explore the full range of what happens when two people find intimacy' (Kreinheder, 1980, p. 17). I want to listen to my client with all of who I am, and enter into their world, open to exploring that world in that person's own particular way. It is in being open to the other, and being open to myself, that I experience a variety of languages with my clients. It may be that I am called upon to engage through spoken language, music and song, image, fantasy, action, silence. The possibilities seem limitless.

I offer here a few of the experiences I have shared with clients which have required me to go beyond face-to-face spoken interaction in order to meet at depth. Each example illustrates a different mode of interacting which evolved in particular and unique relationships. I begin with Richard, who has severe learning disabilities.[1]

Richard

We began the session with my usual reminder of what I was there for, and where would he like to begin. The room I use for counselling when I visit Richard is, in fact, an office. It has hard-backed office chairs, desks all round the room, computers, boxes and files in every available space. I always clear a space on a desk for the brightly coloured pencils, pens and other objects I bring to facilitate communication, but the distractions are numerous, and it is far from ideal. Despite this, Richard did begin this session facing me in the chairs I had placed alongside the desk where my array of objects sat invitingly. He glanced sideways at me and began:

Richard: The Hoover. The fridge. The radio. The electric razor.
Me: (*Waiting for something to respond to, and aware of a familiar sense of intense concentration as I try to figure out if I am missing something from these utterances, which pepper our every contact.*)
Richard: The electric toaster, the vacuum cleaner. The razor.
Me: These things seem important to you Richard . . .
Richard: Yi.

He turns now, his body away from me, and looks at the objects, glancing quickly again at me. Richard decides to draw, as he often does.

Richard: The drawing?
Me: (*Nodding.*)

He takes up a grey pencil and begins drawing. I am waiting and recognising in myself a desire for connection, yet respecting too his need to maintain connections only briefly. After some focused effort on his drawing I say:

Me: Your drawing seems interesting.
Richard: Earphones.
Me: Earphones, aah, I see, grey earphones.

He shows me the holes in the ear-pieces where the sound comes from and the lead to plug into the record player, for music.

---

[1] Severe learning disabilities have been defined since the 1920s as an IQ of less than 50. A discussion of euphemisms used to describe people with learning disabilities is in Sinason (1992). In real terms those described as having severe learning disabilities need lifelong support in many areas of their lives, being unable to function independently. A full exploration of the issues involved in person-centred counselling with people with learning disabilities can be found in Hawkins (2002).

Me: Music, through the earphones to your ears. (*Stating the obvious, but attempting to reach out to him.*)
Richard: (*Pleased*) Yi.
Me: Music is important to you?
Richard: Yi.
Me: I'm wondering about that music
Richard: Mummy and Daddy. (*Glances towards me, then very quietly.*) One, two, three o'clock, four o'clock rock.

He begins to sing under his breath. I join him. Now he turns his chair and body towards me again, and we sing quietly together the whole song. This song from the 1950s is luckily familiar to me.

Immediately after we finish, he very quietly begins the Scottish song 'You take the high road and I'll take the low road', so quietly, almost inaudible, yet clear. I join him almost as inaudibly, and he gains in confidence so that we are singing clearly, still quietly, but now we are definitely singing.

During this song, he clasps his hands together and draws up and into his body, smiling broadly and with a look of absolute exquisite joy. At the very same time, his eyes well up with tears as his face flushes — and still we sing. We begin again, and he is enraptured. I too am feeling an intense connection, my eyes too fill with tears, and I feel the intensity of a moment of agony and ecstasy where he and I, through this simple song, are able to transcend our differences and he can know that I am really in touch with him. As we draw to ending the song, I become aware that we have been holding hands — very gently.

We finish the song, and immediately his volume drops again as he tentatively begins 'Ten green bottles'. Again I join him, and with my company, he sings a little louder, more clearly, and now, as we slowly sing from ten to one green bottle, his mood shifts. Gradually the joy diminishes, and he seems heavily burdened, and sad. He barely pauses for breath:

Richard: Simone screaming. Screaming and shouting.
Me: Simone screams and shouts, and I'm wondering how you are feeling, Richard.
Richard: Sad. Screaming in the kitchen. Throws plate.

He looks anxious and very sad.

Me: I see you are sad, and I'm sensing something else too about Simone throwing the plate and shouting.
Richard: Sad and frightened.
Me: You're sad and frightened when Simone throws the plate and screams and shouts.

I sense that he is more in that scene than with me now.

Me   And what happens next?
Richard: No breakfast for Simone. (*Looking anxious.*)
Me: When she screams and shouts and throws the plate Simone gets no

breakfast and you feel sad and frightened.

Richard: (*Back to the room, though not to connecting with me.*) The electric razor. The vacuum cleaner. The toaster.

Me: Maybe sometimes it's easier to talk about things than people and feelings?

He glances, still looking anxious and burdened, before turning to the paper and pencils again, and carefully draws. It is a microphone.

Richard and I have only recently made any kind of physical contact — it is not his way. But recently that has changed, and he greets me when I arrive with a wonderful smile and an outstretched hand. It is important to allow Richard to lead in all ways. Making psychological contact with anyone seems very difficult for him, and I must be able to respect this. It has taught me that part of what I get for myself as a therapist is connection at the deepest levels. Usually, in therapy, I am meeting with people at depth, and I know that is something that feeds me too. Relating at depth does not happen in everyday life with acquaintances. Even with those with whom one is most close, relating at that kind of depth is something relegated to 'quality time'. So, as a therapist, my own desire to relate at depth must not hinder me in working with someone like Richard, who suddenly dives to depths, and then, just as suddenly, stays in the shallows. I notice that I am very conscious of these shifts, and occasionally have felt irritated by the confabulations. Sometimes I have been angry too, at the people in Richard's history who have caused him such fear that the remoteness of objects is safer than being with another person. His story has come out in fragments like those transcribed above. When he begins the naming of objects, I must try to stay as open and aware of him as I can, lest I miss something important hidden among them. The effort involved in this is enormous at times as I struggle to remain aware of what is happening in myself, yet not let that overshadow even the objects named before me.

Some weeks later, I arrived for our session to find Richard, uncharacteristically, bouncing about clapping his hands. As soon as he saw me, he bounced over, towering over me, waving a coffee cup. Without pausing in his mostly incoherent verbalising, he took my hand.

Me: Hi Richard, it's good to see you.

He was ready to take me to the office we meet in, but I needed to check in with staff and get the key. I told him this and assured him I'd be ready very soon. During my preparations, I wondered what was happening for him. I had never seen him like this.

We begin the session, facing each other. He is talking continuously and bouncing slightly on his chair. I gently take his hands in mine and say nothing for what seems a very long while. He speaks at times and mumbles incoherently at others, but there is nothing I can grasp.

I am aware that Richard has a tendency to bite or hit out suddenly, though he has never done this to me. This awareness hits me as he suddenly leaps to his feet and says, 'Have coffee?' I ask if we can spend some time together first and he sits again. More rambling ensues, interjected with an occasional snatch of a song. I join him for 'You take the high road and I'll take the low road', and he calms a little.

Now his verbalisations are becoming clearer and he is describing numerous violent and disturbing images: bombs, fires, things being thrown at him. There is little affect but a sense of almost amused hysteria, so quietly contained that I could see why this could be misunderstood as him simply being 'high'. Later too, it occurs to me that Richard, who like so many of his peers spends long hours in front of television sets, must recently have been bombarded by images of the tragedy of September 11th. It must have been even more difficult for Richard to comprehend what these events meant, and could only serve to remind him of what a dangerous and violent world he lives in.

Our intermittent connection at depth with each other is painful for me, as if I am feeling the horror and fear he is not in touch with, but which spins in his head between object naming, mumbling, descriptions of incidents, and singing. I am unusually close and holding one or both of his hands very gently most of the time, and this contact seems calming and grounding. Eventually I say, 'All these things spinning round in your head, it's hard to be still. You are safe now, it's not happening now, and I am with you to hear what you are feeling and seeing.' He turns to the paper and pens on the desk.

He draws himself with a wound on his head and says, 'Richard's head cut open.' Occasionally he glances at me quickly between drawing a detailed picture of himself, and more clearly describing what he is seeing. Several times he says. 'Staff nurse threw . . . at me.' The dots signify a variety of objects in this repeated sentence, objects he was remembering were thrown at him, 'Hit me with hammer.' Between these descriptions I respond with, 'Your head feels like it's cut open' and 'It's a dangerous world' and 'People and objects hurt you'.

He seems sporadically dissociated[2], returning to me at times between reporting on what he is seeing, yet there is little or no affect, even when he is present rather than obviously dissociated.

Suddenly, in a very present moment, he gives an extremely threatening open-mouthed facial gesture. I know of the risk of his biting behaviour, but I do not feel frightened, I am caught up in his world. He says, 'shout, be loud' in a clear and audible (unusual for him) voice. I respond, 'You want to shout and be loud?' — he looks at me as if this is a revelation to him — 'Can you shout and be loud? It's OK here to shout and be loud', but the moment of clarity and connection has passed. He is drawing and rambling again. I have one hand resting on his arm and one on his back, and I'm praying as I listen, praying that Richard may find some peace within himself.

He turns to me and says, 'Softly, be nice. I can do it softly. Do it softly.' He is reminding himself of how he has to be. This brings tears into my eyes as I respond, 'Yes Richard, you can.' He returns to the staff nurse throwing things and hitting him because he is a *nuisance* and a *bad boy*. I feel his hurt deeply. The staff nurse, who might legitimately have been expected to bring comfort and care, instead

---

[2.] Dissociation can be thought of as a creative survival skill developed by people experiencing extremely traumatic events. It allows the person to distance themself psychologically and/or emotionally from the trauma, thereby allowing survival. Unfortunately, where chronic trauma necessitates repeated dissociation, it can result in a lifelong tendency to dissociate even when there is no current danger. For a fuller description see, for example, Herman (1992), Gartner (1997) and Warner (2000).

perpetrates violence. I find it extremely, almost physically, painful. Richard grew up in an institution because of his learning disabilities. How much more were his difficulties exacerbated by the treatment he received there? Now that he is free from that regime, the fear, anxiety and flashes persist. He is not free of the damage caused to him. Aware as I am of the intensity of physical and emotional pain, I am calm and feeling a connection with him that seems open and unwavering; his connection to me is disjointed. He says, 'I'm calm'. I stroke his arm. We have been together in this process for an hour and I must stop. He is reluctant to stop and I give him a few more minutes. He finishes colouring his drawing. On finishing he says, more to himself than to me, 'can keep away from staff'. He bounces out into life where, even with the best intentions in the world, he is continually disempowered.

I am again conscious of the one hour a week he gets with me and how much effort and energy I expend in that hour, simply to stay with his experience of the world. I am aware, from what he tells me about his life, that the fear and powerlessness continue, and there is not a thing in the world I can do to end his suffering. This knowledge is heavy in me.

Being with Richard really stretches me, as I allow myself to enter into his idiosyncratic mode of relating which is so very different from mine. It feels very different from my relationship with clients who do not have severe learning disabilities, as our modes of relating to the world and each other have more in common.

Jessie

Jessie has been working with me at home for about six months. She wants to overcome her bulimia, and other addictive issues in her life. Throughout her early life she endured experiences of neglect and sexual abuse, and has come to understand the connections between those experiences and the addictive patterns that now pervade her life. We have explored what triggers each of these different addictive behaviours, which include taking drugs and other behaviours distressing to her. She has made connections between the feelings that precede these events, and those that precede a binge/vomit episode.

It seems to me that addictions, as well as a whole range of behaviours which are accompanied by feelings of compulsion, communicate a common theme: these behaviours are not the problems, they are the solutions to the problems. It follows that if compulsive and addictive behaviours are solutions, we need to look deeper for the problem. Often the problem is actually some degree of distress, which to greater or lesser degrees compulsive and addictive behaviours temporarily relieve. With this recognition in mind, I have come to see compulsive and addictive behaviour as distress flares. Vessels that journey on water always carry distress flares for when there is trouble, and no other means of communicating is possible. Compulsive and addictive behaviours seem to me to be a way of communicating a problem. If we can attend to the distress flare, and recognise what the distress is about, there may be less, or even no need to engage in that behaviour.

I have shared my distress flare image with Jessie when she talks of her sense of compulsion around the various behaviours she wants to change. I have supported her in her attempts to recognise the triggers, and encouraged her to care for herself, rather than engage in the obligatory self-battering (physical and verbal) that follows each episode. She still actively engages in all the behaviours she wishes to stop, but she now has a sense of sleeves rolled up in the task of fully understanding herself, and is beginning to show some self-acceptance after each episode.

In this session we are sitting on the floor, where she has taken herself, and I have joined her. She is exploring a box of objects I keep in my therapy room. This box contains a variety of objects: stones, crystals, keys, shells, tiny multi-cultural dolls, balls, bells etc. Sometimes people use the objects to explore various parts of themselves, choosing different objects to represent different parts of themselves. Sometimes they use the objects to represent people in their lives, and their relationships to self and others. Very few people actually use the objects, but they are there for those who do find it useful to touch and hold different textures. They enable communication where sometimes words cannot be found.

So, Jessie was touching the objects in the box, and had chosen three different objects to represent parts of her self. These were chosen quickly, and with much pleasure. Then she chose a rusty little horseshoe. There was a pause, and then she placed her hand on her belly.

Jessie: (*with great surprise*) I'm feeling something in here.
Me: In your belly, you're feeling something in there.

Great pause as she is held rapt and I too feel a sense of wonder as such a change has come over her.

Jessie: (*even more surprised*) I think I'm hungry.
Me: (*after a long pause*) You sound surprised about that.
Jessie: I never feel hungry. I'm never hungry. Not hungry. Not in here.
Me: (*I am aware that we are on the edge of something very important, and I'm feeling a slight anxiety; she so easily loses contact with her feelings.*) Can you hold onto that feeling? What does it tell you?
Jessie: It says I need to eat something.
Me: And could you eat something?
Jessie: I don't know. I haven't got anything. Well, anyway . . .
Me: Would you like to try something, something different? . . . I have some things in the kitchen. (*At this point I'm wondering which school of thought would even begin to accept me.*)
Jessie: (*still holding the horseshoe with a look of wonder, and a hand on her belly*) Hmmm.

I make a quick dash to the kitchen, where I gather up some different tastes and textures: dried apricots, creamy yoghurt, cheese, nuts. She is looking younger by the minute as I lay out the different tastes before her. She shyly asks to be fed, and I do feed her. She closes her eyes, and tastes the different tastes, smelling each one before she takes it into her mouth, where she savours it for a long time. Time and space seem suddenly fluid. She is completely involved in tasting foods, saying yes and no, and playing with that power over what enters her mouth. She is overcome with the sense of smell and taste, enraptured. I am enraptured too, overcome by the sense that something so simple could be so huge for her.

After the session was over, and I saw her to the door, she fairly skipped up the road. Looking back and smiling, she looked young and refreshed, quite unlike the burdened waif-like person I was used to.

In the sessions that followed, Jessie reported that she had been playing with her desire to be fed, sometimes asking her partner to feed her. They had been playing with this and having fun. Most importantly, she felt she had discovered a sense of taste that she had not known before. Subsequently this was clarified as being due to her having been orally abused. She had literally switched off her sense of smell and taste as a way of having some power over what was happening to her. The switch had stayed off for all those years. This particular session, representing something outside her own experience in that she was able to take pleasure and have control over what she put in her mouth, had allowed her to reclaim something very important. She was then able to use this experience in her efforts to cope with her bulimia. One aspect of her bingeing had been to not taste, or even notice, what she had been cramming down. Now she could taste and feel what she was eating. She also, for the first time, recognised what hunger felt like.

This strange experience for me, of actually leaving the room, gathering up foods, and feeding my client, came purely from an intuitive response to where she was at the time. I felt very shy of discussing it with people and wondered how I might be judged for it. All sorts of possibilities ran through my head of the possible psychoanalytic interpretations of my behaviour, and my own concern about 'bringing in something from outside the client's frame of reference'. Yet, subsequent events allowed me to trust what had happened, and to recognise those times when my client and I have entered another realm, where a healing opportunity presents itself in the here and now. Moments like these are rare within the confines of the therapy hour.

Rachel

Rachel was a woman I had been seeing for about two years, when she began deeply exploring her feelings towards her father, who had sexually and emotionally abused her throughout her childhood. These complex feelings ranged from understanding and tender loving feelings, to ones of rage and a wish to kill him, or at least hurt him as he had hurt her. Rachel expressed her frustration at having these angry and violent feelings trapped inside her, knowing she would not act on them, because her father was now old and frail, and she loved him as the man he had become. Through our explorations, it became apparent to Rachel, and to me, that she needed a physical release for these feelings. Like many people who contain extreme levels of anger, Rachel feared that if she let it go, it would be uncontrollable and destructive, and that she might actually harm somebody. Talking simply was not going to do it for her; she felt some kind of physical release was the only way forward.

I happened to know somebody who owned a punch bag which was weighted at the bottom and could be punched from all angles without falling over. When I offered this to Rachel, she was both excited and nervous. Would she become a raving banshee who could never regain control? Would the release of her rage harm me, or harm my opinion of her? Was she really allowed to make noise and jump about in my therapy room? The attraction of the punch bag outweighed these concerns of hers, as we explored them. In myself I was aware that this was an unusual thing to be offering — once again coming from outside the realms of any of my training.

There was some planning for the session. How could we address Rachel's concerns about losing control, and about releasing as much as she needed to? We negotiated a two-hour session, to allow for sufficient processing. I had also borrowed a pair of sparring gloves, to ensure that Rachel did not harm herself during this process. We discussed too, by way of maintaining a sense of control, that she would announce how many punches would be enough, and I counted them. After reaching the arranged upon-number, I checked in whether that had been enough, and we began again each time with another set. Rachel reported afterwards that this had given her permission to 'lose it without losing it'. During some of the punching, which did become very violent at times, Rachel screamed at her father (the punch bag had now become him), and released feelings and words which she had suppressed for many years. When she felt she had finished, she sat back exhausted into a chair and sipped the water that was ready for her. It was a moving session for both of us. Not only had Rachel expressed this pushed-down rage and anger, but she had also exposed her most unacceptable self to me and found that I was not disgusted or horrified or frightened. This was an important milestone in our work together. It had been important that both her love and her anger for her father had been accepted and heard. Released from her rageful feelings, she subsequently was more able to spend time with him less afraid that the anger would creep to the surface.

The punch bag has been used only two or three times in my work as a therapist. Few of my clients have ever raised the desire to 'punch the lights out' of someone who had harmed or was harming them. Each individual, of course, has different ideas and fantasies about what would be helpful to them. My desire is to explore with my client how to safely make it possible for the release they so want to happen. This can lead me into uncharted territory. There is something important in the trust I have in my client, the process and my self, that allows unusual risks to be taken. I recognise too that if I did not feel sufficient trust in any of those aspects, I would be blocking rather than facilitating that connection, expression and potential release.

One of my interests in recent years has been in how angry feelings are expressed and transformed in therapy (Hawkins, 1997). In my own experience as a client many years ago, I tried the patience of more than one therapist who seemed to feel that I ought to be angry, or more angry than I appeared to be. This, at the time, confused me terribly, because I really did at that stage want to be a 'good client'. If these educated therapists thought I should be angry, then something was clearly wrong with me, because I wasn't; at least not for the things they thought I should be angry about. It has been important to me in my development and experience as a therapist to explore the issue of anger from a number of angles. This depth of understanding was missing for me in my early experiences as a client. In insisting I should be angry, my therapist missed my hurt and despair. This experience provided me with an important lesson in my own work: to honour my client's own understanding of their feelings, rather than impose what I think they should be feeling. I was also concerned that if I wasn't in touch with my anger perhaps I might not hear the client's anger when it was subtly present, or in some subtle way block my client's expression of their anger. It was for this reason that I engaged in a variety of anger workshops as a participant, and explored the available material, and then offered workshops myself focusing on anger. Healthy anger expression can be not only releasing, but deeply energising.

In the person-centred world there is sometimes a sense of sticking within the safety of positive and growthful feelings, perhaps focusing so much on the actualising tendency that the '*not for growth* configurations' are often avoided: 'Person-centred therapists often have a mistaken understanding that therapy should always be pointing in a 'growthful' direction' (Mearns and Thorne, 2000, p. 115). If anger is deemed to be a necessarily negative feeling, some therapists might, using selective empathy, steer clear of it, thereby denying the client the opportunity to experience and express their anger in an environment of acceptance and understanding.

> Rage needs to be *heard*. This does not mean that it simply needs to be listened to . . . the truth about rage is that it only dissolves when it is really heard and understood, without reservations. (Rogers, 1978, p. 133)

Ros

The final example of idiosyncratic practice comes from my work with Ros. We had been working together for about three years when, towards the end of a session, the subject of notes came up. At various times in my career I have kept session notes, especially during training and my early years as a therapist. During other periods I have not kept notes, partly because of concerns about the potential for summons of them in legal cases. A few of my clients over the years, who have been involved in legal cases, and at times of great vulnerability, signed consent forms to have their therapy session notes released to police and/or solicitors. I prefer, on the request of the client, to provide a report that the client has seen. This avoids the exposure of their most private thoughts.

I was able to have a long period without session notes due to having been blessed (sometimes this feels more like a curse) with a very good memory. However, when I was pregnant with my last baby, I was concerned I might not have the capacity to retain so much; pregnancy can send the mind into jelly. So I began to keep notes again. I have always felt that notes are as much my client's as my own, though this had always remained an idealistic and untested attitude. It had hit Ros as something of a shock when, for some reason, I mentioned notes. She was keen to see hers. There was a high level of trust in our relationship but I felt this was a moment of fragility. I agreed to check the notes to ascertain if I had included any personal reflections that I might prefer to keep private, and then let her see the notes next time. I asked her, if she read them, to record any feelings or responses for our next session.

Examination of my notes did not reveal anything of my own I felt was private, though there were reflections on my practice. Ros was, by now, a counselling student, and I felt these reflections could be entrusted to her. She took the notes home. I was very aware of the risk I was taking. I had never read, nor heard among colleagues, of the sharing with a client of session notes. I was aware too of the potential for accusations from other professionals of unprofessional conduct and lack of boundaries. Yet, I was being faced with a situation where I was being tested to 'walk my talk', to be honest and open and trusting. I trusted Ros and myself but wrestled with the question: was I simply being blind or arrogant? I was most concerned that the risk might hurt Ros, instead of enhancing things for her.

Before our next meeting Ros telephoned me, feeling very upset by what she had read. She had never telephoned me before between sessions. There is something very powerful about the written word. It can more starkly convey issues and feelings explored in sessions than the sessions themselves, as the sessions themselves include the whole range of non-verbal behaviour that enhances understanding, and demonstrates warmth and empathy. Seeing issues, concerns and fears she had raised in black and white frightened and overwhelmed Ros. Instead of the containment of one session, all her sessions were spread out in front of her at the same time, and it was quite a shock to see. Ros also felt frightened that some of her concerns, written down as they were, might, in fact, be my concerns about her life, not hers. Through our short conversation I was able to clarify that point and reassure her that if I did have particular concerns about issues she raised, I would certainly raise them with her. This reminded me of experiences when other clients would report to me things I had said in a previous session, for example, 'when you told me I was sad' when, in fact, I had only shared my understanding of what they had told me. I know from my own experience as a client that there have been times of confusion and distress when my own therapist's accurate empathic response has seemed stark and shocking and I have had to spend time processing what he has said, sometimes going back to check what I said which he seems to have more clearly articulated.

After our conversation I wondered if I had made a huge error of judgement. My desire to demonstrate my trust and remain transparent in our relationship should not add to my client's problems. My belief system should not impede my client's growth; she should not be held at the mercy of my idiosyncrasies.

In our next session Ros brought her more detailed written responses to both the session notes and our telephone conversation, and we explored these. It is now nine months since we completed our work together, and Ros has agreed to share, in her own words, what the process of sharing session notes was like for her:

> *When Jan made a passing reference one day to the notes which she had on my sessions with her, I felt taken aback. Notes? I had no idea that she had notes on me! I had shared my innermost thoughts, feelings and insecurities with Jan, shared things which I had never talked about to anyone else. Although I trusted Jan implicitly and common sense told me that it must be necessary to keep notes since I was just one of Jan's many clients, the thought of my most personal details being in note form felt slightly uncomfortable. It seemed to draw on childhood experiences of my being discussed in hushed tones behind closed doors, of sealed envelopes being sent to and from school, the contents of which were kept from me. Jan suggested that the notes were as much mine as they were hers and that she would let me see them. This was a revelation to me; to be treated with such openness and integrity felt empowering.*
>
> *I sensed that Jan felt ambivalent about allowing me to read the notes and that, for her, there was a degree of risk involved. My curiosity outweighed any misgivings, however, and with a slight feeling of apprehension, I took the notes home to read.*
>
> *My initial reaction was one of distress. In my sessions with Jan, the sharing of my feelings had been healing and comforting, but seeing them in writing*

seemed to have the reverse effect. Reading Jan's accurate portrayal of my pain and hurt somehow brought it all back with intensity. Unable to wait for another week until our next session, I called Jan on the phone. Whilst Jan was able to assuage my overwhelming feelings of sadness, at the same time I sensed that my phone call to her had compounded her doubts about letting me read the notes. The only way forward seemed to be to follow Jan's suggestion of making my own detailed 'notes on the notes' to take to our next session.

What followed in the next session was, I believe, a major breakthrough in my therapy. We were able to discuss my feelings (and Jan's) at a deeper level than before and to talk about our perceptions of one another with openness and sincerity. The sharing of Jan's notes and of my own notes in response brought a new depth to our sessions and seemed to open the way to a more profound level of communication.

The sharing of notes brought us closer together, and enabled Ros to explore our relationship more freely. She felt cared for, and this had previously, she feared, only been a fantasy. One extremely painful response was my occasionally, in my notes, quoting phrases she had used. This touched painful memories of having been bullied and ridiculed as a teenager. I was able to explain that, far from any disparagement, these quoted phrases were my own attempts to value her own particular words and thinking.

Some months later, we again swapped notes on our sessions, and spent the following sessions exploring the insights gained from this. On ending our work together some months later, we were able to reflect upon the shift in gear in our work, brought about by the risk she and I took. She dared to ask to see her notes. I dared to share them. It was not an easy process for either of us, but allowed our own relationship to be the more fully explored, and the issues she had raised throughout our work together to be reviewed from a different perspective.

The Person-Centred Approach can be both liberating and frightening, to both the client and the therapist. Being in a real relationship, where, often for the first time, a client can be fully open and receive acceptance, warmth and real responsiveness human-to-human can be terrifying, yet also deeply healing. As a therapist, there is no hiding place: I must maintain contact with myself in the deepest and most accepting way (an eternal struggle), in order to be able to offer contact with my clients in the deepest and most accepting way. None of the snapshots of the relationships described here should lead the reader to assume that all went smoothly thereafter. Each person's process is unique and ongoing whether in therapy or in other relationships and experiences. The illustrations I have offered demonstrate some of the ways I have found myself meeting with others in therapy; trying to do so softly.

References

Gartner, R.B. (1997) *Memories of Sexual Betrayal: Truth, Fantasy, Repression and Dissociation.* New Jersey: Jason Aronson.

Hawkins, J. (1997) A choice model for anger expression: encouraging responsibility. *Changes: An International Journal of Psychology and Psychotherapy,* 15 (3): 211–19.

Hawkins, J. (2002) *Voices of the Voiceless: Person-Centred Approaches and People with Learning Difficulties*. Ross-on-Wye: PCCS Books.

Herman, J.L. (1992) *Trauma and Recovery: From Domestic Abuse to Political Terror*. London: Harper Collins.

Kreinheder, A. (1980) The healing power of illness. *Psychological Perspectives*, 11 (1): 9–18.

Mearns, D. and Thorne, B. (2000) *Person-Centred Therapy Today: New Frontiers in Theory and Practice*. London: Sage.

Rogers, C.R. (1978) *On Personal Power: Inner Strength and its Revolutionary Impact*. London: Constable.

Sinason, V. (1992) *Mental Handicap and the Human Condition: New Approaches from the Tavistock*. London: Free Association Books.

Warner, M.S. (2000) Person-centred therapy at the difficult edge: a developmentally based model of fragile and dissociated process. In Mearns, D. and Thorne, B. *Person-Centred Therapy Today: New Frontiers in Theory and Practice*. London: Sage.

4

Omar Sattaur

Who am I?

Who am I?

I once thought the riddle of my life so convoluted that I had more reason than most to solve it. After all, I had crossed continents, strayed from the religious path set out for me by my parents, eschewed allegiance to any political party, relished being a professional misfit.

Most of us ask the question 'who am I?' at some time in our lives. And then, more often than not, the question seems to lose importance, becomes lost amid the practicalities of earning a living and 'making something' of one's life. As a child, I had noticed that I could 'surprise myself' and wondered how that could be. Who was surprised, and by whom? It seemed that I had many 'I's, all rising to prominence at different times. But what controls their rise and fall? Was it 'normal' to be all of these different 'I's, was it inevitable? Who I am seemed inextricably bound to who I was. A short poem by James Fenton, called *The ideal*, became very significant to me as my search progressed, and it remains so.

> This is where I came from.
> I passed this way.
> This should not be shameful
> Or hard to say.
>
> A self is a self.
> It is not a screen.
> A person should respect
> What he has been.
>
> This is my past
> Which I shall not discard.
> This is the ideal.
> This is hard.

The first question — 'who am I?' — raised many more questions. When, at a time of personal crisis, my 'external I' began to crumble, the urgency of answering the 'who am I?' question became inescapable, and I sought help from a therapist. This experience helped to keep that question alive in me and contributed, 15 years later, to my wanting to train as a counsellor. Beginning training as a person-centred counsellor in July 2000 was part of my process of trying to know myself more deeply.

I feel fortunate that I continue to ask that question, and I am confident that I will continue to ask it for the rest of my life. If I had any lingering doubts about the importance of addressing the question, studying for a counselling diploma took care of them. I had ample opportunity and good reason to look hard at myself, but with a compassionate eye. The most important consideration for me in training was to find a theoretical base that matched my own philosophy. I did not want to get half way through the training to discover that it was founded on ideas that were unacceptable to me or that contradicted my own experience of life. The fact that Person-Centred Therapy relies so much on the therapist's self-awareness appealed to me; that it also demanded commitment from therapists to bring all of themselves into therapeutic relationships also scared me a little. These were the most important factors in helping me to decide which type of therapy to study. Choosing the course was the next most important decision. I settled on a course which stressed experiential learning as this matched my own ideas about how I wished to learn. The following is an exploration of the riddle of my life, showing how person-centred theory and practice inform my understanding of who I am and therefore of what I hope to be able to offer as a person-centred counsellor.

My first is in meditation, but not in Islam

My understanding of certain personal spiritual experiences, both prior to training in the Person-Centred Approach and certainly during training, resonates with an important goal of Person-Centred Therapy; in Rogers' words, that clients will 'move toward more openly being a process, a fluidity, a changing' (Rogers, 1967, p. 171). Rogers quotes the Danish philosopher Kierkegaard in describing the person who truly has a sense of their existence: 'An existing individual is constantly in process of becoming . . . and translates all his thinking into terms of process' (ibid, p. 172). This idea of life as fluidity, as the individual being forever in the process of becoming rather than chipping away to find a predefined and fixed identity, appeals to the scientist in me. If every living organism on Earth follows the same natural law, of emergence and decay, of forming, reproducing and dying away, then why not our lives, our thoughts, emotions, and consciousness, too?

I was born a Muslim. The first words I heard would have been my father's as he whispered the Islamic creed in my ear: I bear witness that there is no god but God. As a youth I was much taken with Islamic ideas, the writings of Sufi poets, and I tried to live a Muslim life. As a university student away from home for the first time, I felt that I had no identity, no real way of describing myself to myself, even in everyday terms. I found, and still find, some of the ideas of Islam compelling. First, the simplicity and attraction of the idea of the oneness of God, and therefore of the unity of truth. And later, the ideas of Sufism. The 12th century Muslim mystic-philosopher and Sufi, Ibn al-'Arabi, taught the 'unity of being', the unity of all existence in which creation is ever new, in perpetual movement that unites the whole of creation in a process of constant renewal. There is a parallel with Rogers' view of the direction in which clients undergoing therapy are moving, towards being process and fluidity. At this time in my life, belonging was an urgent need, and finding acceptance was the most important drive for me. Now I can see that, at a deeper level, there was also a yearning for some way of experiencing more fully and understanding, to some extent, the body-mind, or material-spiritual connection. Given my Muslim background the experiential teaching of the Sufis seemed a good place to start. I treasure that background and, although I no longer practise the Islamic religious life, I'm sure I will find more to value in Islamic and Sufi teachings.

Nowadays, on waking, I sit in a corner of my work room for an hour, practising Vipassana meditation. Here, I focus my attention on sensations throughout my body. I seek to be an impartial observer of how sensations appear and vanish, how one sensation is replaced by another, how even the most persistent eventually, inevitably, die away. It seems such a simple task to perform and yet this lesson in the dynamism and impermanence of life is the hardest to learn. I find it only fleetingly possible to have no other but this single purpose occupying my mind. I learned this meditation technique on a 10-day course that I attended in 1996. It was a large course; perhaps 300 people attended. We were each assigned a two-feet-square cushion, one island in a vast archipelago. During the course of those 10 days, 'my' island became variously a haven, a fortress, a pinnacle, a cave, a cage, a hide, a prison and a bed, as I wrestled with the 'simple' task of being aware of what was going on internally, rather than what was going on around me. I can recall very un-compassionate thoughts arising in me, concerning the old Nepali peasant farmer on my right who frequently invaded 'my' territory. I remember that I was not particularly accepting of the more affluent-looking and, unfortunately, flatulent man on my left. I can recall how this barrage of 'difference' and 'otherness' that I had erected dissolved into amusement at my own weaknesses, negative attitudes, judgements and behaviours as I became more aware of what was arising and dying away in my own body with each passing moment. Dr Paul Fleischman, a Vipassana meditator and psychiatrist, puts it this way:

> No matter who we are, our inner lives are less like a box with separate compartments than like a flood-tide on a river. When we sit down to be still, a seemingly endless stream of memories, wishes, thoughts, conversations, scenes, desires, dreads, lusts, and emotionally driven pictures of every kind wells up in us, thousands upon thousands. The clearest, most immediate, and inescapable effect of meditation is to increase one's self-knowledge. This may be curious, exciting, and interesting but it could also be devastating. Taking this into account, therefore, the technique enables one's vision of one's true inner life to expand in the structured, protected, controlled, holding and nurturant environment essential to a safe launching on high seas . . . Nothing in the human condition will remain unknown or strange to one who has sat, hour after hour, thus safely stationed and continuously aware. (Fleischman, 1986, p. 2)

My Islamic roots and present spiritual practice are both important to me, and have influenced the way that I understand person-centred theory and how I relate to other people. My first experiences of the personal development (PD) group on my certificate course come to mind. When, I wondered, would the tutors give up this bizarre experiment and tell us the rules of the game? The answer, of course, was never. And so I sat musing on the other people in the group: what were they like? What did they 'do' outside of the course? How were they with 'normal' people? And then I began to resent the fact that some people hardly spoke up in the group. PD, or 'pond death' as I superciliously thought of it, became more and more of a trial. Then I began to observe how my mind, doggedly sticking to the external, slowly began to respond to an invitation to look within. The questions I had silently asked of others, I began to ask of myself: 'why don't I say anything? What would happen if I really said how I feel right now? Why, when I like so much to play the joker in other groups, am I so silent in this one?' And so on.

I valued even more the opportunity for reflection on my diploma course, during the ninety minutes that we set aside each week for community time. I began to notice other things about it; that I felt comfortable, secure, safe somehow, even when disturbing things were being discussed or when my own life was particularly turbulent. Some of my peers said they felt these 'general' feelings, too, sometimes at the same time that I did, sometimes not. Others had more profound experiences, of connectedness or of closeness with the group as an entity. I felt at once reassured and unsettled about being in the same boat as everyone else. Rogers' realisation that what is most personal is also universal (Rogers, 1967, p. 26) adds impetus to my desire to understand what I share with others through looking at what is unique to me.

I've wondered whether experiencing the simultaneous truths of being absolutely alone in the world and of oneness or being connected in some non-physical way to a room full of people, which I experience on meditation retreats, is similar to some people's rather more extraordinary experiences of being in community groups.

> Where the state of consciousness of a number of people within a workshop is involved, their individual self-systems seem to merge. A sense of underlying unity beneath their surface separation makes itself increasingly apparent. Both Bohm (1990) and O'Hara and Wood (1983) suggest that where a group displays a high degree of togetherness and coherence a form of group mind or collective consciousness is present. Bohm (p. 14) calls it participatory consciousness. O'Hara and Wood suggest that:
>> *Individuals achieve integration with other group members and with the collective mind. The collective mind is also integrated within itself and within the larger world of which it is a part. In these moments of isomorphic integration the individual and the group gain access to a vastness of possibilities which is of cosmic proportions* (O'Hara and Wood, 1983, p. 109).
>
> (Lago and MacMillan, 1999, p. 177).

Could the continuous mental and bodily awareness that I seek in meditation be a pre-requisite for the congruence I seek when I sit with my clients? Perhaps the 'structured, protected, controlled, holding and nurturant environment' that Fleischman talks about resembles the enabling environment that I wish to create for my clients, conducive to their 'safe launching on high seas'. There is the same delicate balance of awareness of the internal and external, the same understanding that I cannot make this happen at a particular moment on a particular day. There is no switch that I can simply turn on as I sit on my meditation cushion or as I greet my client. There's nothing I can do that will unfailingly ensure that I connect with other people in this larger sense. A certain kind of mental effort will, I know, facilitate the likelihood of this type of connection; concentrating on experiencing being, moment by moment: I am, this moment, this day. I wish that I could say that I was satisfied with this metaphysical truth but I am sometimes far from satisfied. There is a part of me that always seeks a more scientific understanding.

My second is in music, but not in science

As a schoolchild I discovered that science satisfies a hunger I have for analysing things and then piecing them together to give me a coherent view of the world. At the same time, I am aware of a different way I have of perceiving the world, which seems much less governed by laws and much more accepting of what arises naturally. This way is less clear, less solid, more fuzzy and fluid, but just as valid. These two ways of perceiving reality seem to divide people, let's say into scientists and artists. Scientists take things apart to see how they work. Artists want the holistic picture: how do all these different things co-relate, and how do they affect me?

I have a degree in biochemistry and therefore belong to the scientific category, but I have known about another way of seeing for a long time. It's only recently, though, that I have been able to allow it to co-exist with my 'scientific self'. It is as if I have two sets of spectacles: wearing one set I can perceive the world through my feelings, intuitively and through the way my body feels in the moment; wearing the other set enables me to see the components of my world and how they fit together. I no longer leave either set at home.

This was not always the case. For years I wore the scientific lenses permanently, without realising that I did so. Later I recognised this, and they became merely the preferred set. Permanent use of the scientific lenses blinded me to many interesting things, which, later on, became apparent as I changed and began to travel with both sets. For example, in the quotation above, Bohm, O'Hara and Wood allude to 'integration' with other people in a group, 'participatory consciousness' and the 'collective mind'. I have never experienced this deep connectedness in a person-centred community group but I have done so as a member of a group of meditators. This is something that is experienced with the senses rather than with the intellect — I needed to have the right pair of spectacles with me. Being without them on my first meditation courses led to some interesting internal conflicts. At the end of a course, participants are taught the meditation of loving-kindness. And I have felt these extraordinary vibrations taking my pain away and soothing me, emotionally and physically, even though, because of those other spectacles, a small part of my mind still sat in judgement. This part of me painted pictures in which I featured as a 1960s youth, high on 'good vibrations' with hopelessly woolly ideas of relationships. Actually, my generation was the 1970s, but such is the power of my scientist's introject about hippies that my artist can lose confidence in his way of seeing.

Yet the power of these sensations, this way of knowing, is ultimately undeniable. There is something extraordinary and positively powerful about a group of people in a collective endeavour to strive towards something. Towards what, though? Deeper understanding, greater connectedness? Another example that comes to mind can occur between the members of musical groups. I have felt how an uncertainty or a mistake can sometimes flow like an unpleasant wave through an entire orchestra. For a moment everything seems slightly out of kilter, like a few frames in a film, all slightly out of focus. The film may go on, the plot is intact, but there is an awareness that all could so easily have been lost. And, thankfully, there are times when the players are united; each equally important, none more prominent than the whole group or the one music that it makes.

Though I studied biochemistry, music was my first passion. Musical experiences have something in common with O'Hara's and Wood's idea of 'the collective mind'. Music seems to be much more often accessible both to participating music makers and between music makers and listeners. Perhaps this is because music can communicate what words cannot describe. People engaged in this type of focused, shared activity may be communicating in ways that are not discernible through scientific lenses. I wonder whether the same type of enhanced communication results from the enabling environment created by the core conditions of empathy, congruence and respect regardless of the particular therapeutic discipline followed by the counsellor. Jerold Bozarth's reading of Rogers' integrative statement

(1957) suggests that a therapist may employ a technique such as interpretation — which seems so completely at odds with empathic understanding — yet still manage to experience and communicate empathic understanding and unconditional positive regard.

> One explanation is that the experiencing of unconditional positive regard and empathic understanding with another is a highly personal experience that exists at some other level of communication. (Bozarth, 1998, p. 107)

It seems to me that there are other parallels, too. Music may be the perfect combination of mental and physical activity, a type of meditation in itself. In playing it is possible to be aware of both the moment and its significance to the whole piece, the whole expression. This demands a particular awareness, an out-of-the-ordinary presence that seems impossible to switch on at will. There are times when I have practised every day for months, am in good physical shape and have ample time, yet play clumsily; and expressing what it is that I feel about the music seems unattainable then. Playing at those times can be frustrating, hampered by anxiety, and can leave me feeling that I will never be able to play a particular passage properly because there are too many notes and not enough time. My body and mind seem out of sync. Yet there have also been times when I have not played for months, am flabby, overwhelmed with work and other commitments, and yet I am able to play effortlessly and feel alive in all of myself. When this happens, there seems to be all the time in the world, I can live in the moment, doing and observing my actions, yet not interfering with the process. For me, this fluency is unexpected, not an everyday occurrence. The feeling, when it comes, is similar to how I have heard experienced person-centred therapists describe particular sessions with clients. It is a kind of 'clicking in' with the other person. Like a gear on a bike; it can half work, but when it is fully engaged every push of the pedal seems so much more charged with energy, progress is so much more rapid. In reviewing sessions recorded with clients and peer counsellors on my course, we could hear when this synergy took place; sometimes client and counsellor would begin interacting in such a way that meaning and understanding seemed to be constructed so much more quickly, efficiently and effortlessly.

The place in consciousness where this becomes possible is special. It is a fertile, vital, secret garden, much coveted but often barred to entry. It is as if we all know about this garden but we have misplaced the key. My scientist has tried several strategies to enter this special place. He has tried to force entry, conducted systematic searches for the key, attempted to forge new keys, tried to steal skeleton keys, ignored the door and looked for other ways in, pretended there is no door and, in desperation, even pretended that there is no garden. All have proved futile; as, much to his amusement, my artist was able to see. My artist knows that if he is somehow aware of the garden and the door, he can be more an interested observer rather than a detective, and the door then opens, seemingly of its own accord.

These conflicts and arguments are old, and eternal. Herman Hesse personified the material-spiritual conflict within all of us in his novel *Narziss and Goldmund*. There is the Blake engraving in which Newton is depicted with a compass, attempting to reduce the wonder of the world to mere measurement. And my artist similarly judges my scientist: 'he cannot see the wood for the trees', 'he would explain everything away, including beauty and terror'. Science has become so dominant a paradigm for all of us that it is very difficult to admit to perceiving in any other way. There is no room for mystery in science. And even when science has no answer, it seems intolerant of older ways of understanding the world. But is this desirable, or even rational?

Suppose, for example, that it was proved that El Greco had a specific eye condition that made him see everything as significantly elongated. Would his paintings cease to be art? The 19th century German chemist Friedrich August Kekulé — puzzling over the chemical formula of benzene and in a state of tired, half-sleep — dreamed of the benzene molecule as a snake biting its own tail. This vision of a six-carbon benzene ring helped to make sense of the known facts of organic chemistry at that time, a branch of science that was then still in its infancy. Many experiences of this kind have been recorded; describing that state of consciousness with a sense of wonder and mystery. They have become part of cultural history. Time and again, great scientists pay homage to intuition for the vision that led to the great discovery, the missing piece in the puzzle. Does that invalidate science? Science will probably explain everything one day to its satisfaction; every 'mystery' will eventually succumb to its lenses. But will that necessarily render nature and life any less wonderful? It may be that, in a future world, a synthesis between scientific analysis and artistic experience will emerge to form a new and complete way of understanding the world and our part in it. Why then the conflict between the two?

My question has become how can I reconcile my scientist and my artist? I have said that I value them both, and I do. But that is only when I am in a reflective mood, writing this chapter, or enjoying one of those luxurious spells in which I am stripped from workaday responsibility because my train is stuck in the middle of nowhere, or the person I was supposed to meet has failed to arrive. It's much harder to be philosophical when my car won't start and I have forgotten to note the contact number of the client I am to see that morning. I suppose the fact that I acknowledge both scientist and artist is progress, although the 'integration' that Rogers' theory envisages seems bigger than that. Scientist and artist are only two among many other aspects of myself that I would like to integrate.

My third is in Guyana but also in India
I was born in Georgetown, the capital of what used to be called British Guiana and, since its independence from Britain, is called Guyana. Guyana was cleared of most of its original inhabitants, indigenous Amerindians, by American missionaries, Dutch colonists and later by British plantation owners. In the rainforests to the south of the country, there are still small Amerindian populations, but the moneyed population lives on the six-mile-deep coastal strip that is bounded by the Caribbean Sea and the Atlantic. This is a mixture comprising people of African descent, introduced there by the Dutch, people of Indian descent, brought over by plantation owners during the time of the Raj and a small proportion of Chinese, Portuguese and other ethnicities. My ancestors would have been illiterate peasants, poor and desperate enough to accept an offer of indentured labour on the other side of the world. Over the years the small population of Indians and their descendants lost their ties with 'mother India', and caste if not religion became largely irrelevant. Yet a fascination with India remains. The latest Bollywood blockbusters find an audience wherever

there is a sufficiently large population of the Indian Diaspora. Many Hindi and Urdu words describing familial relationships persist in the Caribbean English that almost every citizen claims as their first language and Hinduism and Islam still thrive, albeit in more relaxed, Caribbean forms.

To the east of Guyana lies Suriname, formerly Dutch Guiana, and further east, French Guiana, to this day an Overseas Département of France. The three are misfits in that continent. To the east and south they are bordered by Portuguese-speaking Brazil, to the west of Guyana lies Spanish-speaking Venezuela. Because of its originally African and Indian populations, the Guyanese consider themselves culturally part of the West Indies. People from the Caribbean islands inter-marry with Guyanese people; my aunt, for example, lived in Port of Spain, Trinidad. The three Guianas — largely Protestant, culturally Caribbean (but with South Asian/ West African ethnic roots) — are like an island in a Latin American, largely Roman Catholic sea.

Family lore has it that both sides of my family left India as Hindus. Deaths on board the ships that brought the Indians to Guyana left women and children without men, men without wives. Intermarriage between Hindu and Muslim emigrants resulted in one branch of my family converting to Islam. I had no idea about this until 1989, when I revisited my birthplace and discovered that some of my maternal family is Hindu. (The oldest female of that branch of the family, a lithe octogenarian, playfully insisted on calling me Kumar, rather than Omar.) My family emigrated to Britain in 1962, when I was four years old. Our first flat was in Dalston, in the East End of London. It soon became apparent to me that culture and, more immediately, language was different on either side of our front door. Outside, cockney was the lingua franca, inside it was West Indian. I remember a particular day when I felt that I had to choose how to sound — should I be like the cockneys outside or the West Indians inside? I did not feel comfortable with either and so tried to copy an accent from the radio. This must have amused if not confounded everyone around me for some time. I married someone who grew up near to Oxford and we have since decided to settle in the Peak District. Today, I think my accent is mostly southern, but it is beginning to take on Derbyshire traits. Nothing, however, can displace the West Indian in me when I talk to my mother.

My father used to tell me stories about India — the love story that laid the foundations of the Taj Mahal, the fight for Indian independence, the tragedy of partition. Yet he had never visited India. He declined to travel out to meet me in his sixty-ninth year and asked instead, in letters that found me at American Express travel centres all over Asia, if I would be his eyes and ears. I went with the desire to discover my cultural home and failed spectacularly. Conversations ground to an embarrassing halt as Indian questioners found that I knew neither the name of the village nor districts that my forebears inhabited nor, seemingly unforgivably, their caste. These experiences highlighted what had been a lifelong inquiry for me — who am I and where do I really belong, if anywhere?

I learn by observing patterns and making generalisations or 'laws' about the way the world works. But if I do not continually refine those 'laws' according to my experience of life then they can become a justification for pigeonholing people. For years before I first travelled to South Asia, the question 'where are you from?' would throw me into a state of confusion. What should I answer? I used to tailor

my response according to who asked the question. The questioner could be:
European, in which case, my answer could be: 'Guyana'
'Is that in West Africa?'
'No that's Ghana, Guyana is . . .' etc.

Or Indian:
'Where in India?'
'Well, I was born in Guyana but . . .' etc.

Or English:
'British.'
'But you look Indian.'
'Well, I am ethnically, but . . .' etc.

I am happy to be all of these labels, but I know that there is much more to me, too.
So nowadays I simply reply, Buxton. The remarkable thing about this answer is
that it is to do with the present and the question 'who am I?' is of course in the
present tense. However, in answering it, it is holding the tension between past and
present which can be so fruitful. The Fenton poem means much to me, reminds
me of everything that I am, of my roots and the good and the bad that have made
me who I am. But equally significant are T. S. Eliot's lines (1963, p. 222):

> We shall not cease from exploration
> And the end of all our exploring
> Will be to arrive where we started
> And know the place for the first time.

As a child it seemed to me that the sheer 'otherness' and 'difference' that there
was about me barred me from ever feeling entirely safe and secure in this country.
And this isolation kept my search for a cultural home alive. I now believe that the
search for identity is the important thing, and my home is with other seekers. I
have tried to put down the roots of the question 'who am I?', an idea of the factors
that gave rise to it. They are perhaps unusual, even exotic, but, listening to other
people's life stories, it is not the place names that matter: I might as well have
moved from Derby to Sheffield, the experience of alienation and the search for
belonging is what is important in asking the question. Some of my 'I's still contradict
one another and can still make me worried and anxious. I can still find myself
feeling vulnerable after biting off more work than I can chew, for example, and
then be mad at myself for doing so. I can still sometimes find myself doing things
I didn't really want to do and wonder, in frustration, why I took them on. I'm still
startled and horrified to hear, at a quarter to nine on a school day, the stern parental
voice that can leap out from somewhere at the back of my head, shouting at my
children for being children, for playing instead of hurrying to find their hats, lunch
packs, homework and the rest. But seeing these parts of myself emerge and be
accepted in therapy, in community time, in supervision has helped me to come to
terms with them. I note them here because their acceptance by others during the
course of study has made them clearer, more understandable to me. Allowing them
into my awareness, acknowledging their place in my make up is now my goal. The

more successful I am at doing this, the more facilitative I believe I can be as a therapist.

My last is in form, but not in content

I earn a living by writing and editing. I can find it fulfilling to share information or help someone to express what they feel strongly but find difficult to capture in words. I've been doing this kind of repackaging of information for more than 20 years, and inevitably, somewhere along the way I thought 'wouldn't it be wonderful to write fiction?' I still think that, but unfortunately that is as far as it goes. The overwhelming freedom of a blank piece of paper is enough to quench any creative fire I might have kindled. Walter Mitty-like, I fantasise about how I would feel when I hear my novel being read on Book at Bedtime, how I'd feel travelling to Haiti or Java or some equally romantic destination to research my second novel, or on seeing my children pointing out my hardbacks on the shelves of W. H Smith. And then I wake up. Novels need structure, a story line, but not too much; then something else must breathe life into the characters created.

Jazz and Indian classical musicians improvise, but their innovation is guided by clear rules. The heightened awareness that I have been able to perceive on a meditation retreat — and the sense of freedom and peace that that awareness can bring — is the result of gently coaxing the mind to attend to certain subjects, in this case the impermanence of sensations throughout the body, and not to others, such as the Mitty-like preoccupations I just mentioned, for example. The black dots on a page of manuscript are a necessary approximation of the music they hint at. Like the process of putting down the individual words, which will add up to a character in a novel, something else is at work in the writer; perhaps the same thing is at work in the musician, enabling him to breathe life into those dots to transform them into the truth of the music. Freedom makes sense only in relation to rules. At the same time, form and structure are enabling rather than determining.

I find more success in writing poetry because I am driven internally to do so, not by intellect, but by a desire to understand vague yet powerful feelings inside. My daily work of editing or writing articles is done via the computer keyboard, straight onto screen. My scientist has tried to tell me that there is therefore no reason why poetry cannot be written in the same way. I have even followed his advice, but there is absolutely no chance of poetic lines emerging from that process. Poetry for me comes with a bodily feeling, what Eugene Gendlin (1978) describes as a felt sense. I see, hear or read something that triggers an emotional memory. At that moment I enter the secret garden, my whole body is feeling something that seems urgent, true and important for me. This can happen anywhere and at any time and I feel always excited, alive and grateful when it does. If I am just waking — a creative time for me — I scribble down the phrase or the image. Sometimes reading the scribble later can be the key to the secret garden and I am able to re-enter. Then I write with a pen and paper (a friend recently pointed out to me how the physical holding of a pen seems to let the feeling flow out and onto the paper) and the poem usually writes itself. This experience is so very different from the other kind of writing that I do, which comes from thinking hard and analysing concepts and ideas, defining relationships between them, making logical sense of them. Here, my scientific lenses filter out ambiguity and uncertainty. But poetry needs the other pair of spectacles, as well as patience and trust in myself.

The same might be said of counselling. To cite Bozarth again:

> One of the greatest sources of misunderstanding of the Person-Centred Approach is that of focusing on how to do it. The focus then shifts to technical responding and leads to the emphases on such conceptualizations as reflecting, client-centred listening, client-centred communication and so on. The understanding of the client's meaning in a varied and deeply personal manner as conveyed by Rogers is distorted. (Bozarth, 1998, p. 99).

Bozarth (1998, p. 100) continues: 'When therapists are doing something that does not entail "being" their experiences with clients, then the "person-centredness" is contaminated.' Congruence, and how to be continuously congruent, seems to me to lie at the heart of this therapeutic approach.

My understanding so far of Person-Centred Therapy is that it is founded on therapists cultivating self-awareness and congruence — without this foundation it cannot be therapeutic. Increasingly, my practice reinforces this understanding. One of my clients, Fran, recalled a dream that she found significant. Fran had often told me of her liking for order and control. These qualities, she said, were characteristic of her father, whose approval she had spent much of her life trying to attain. In Fran's dream, she is driving a car, 'in control', as she pointed out. She knocks over a child, stops the car and attends to the child, making sure that the child is all right. The child's mother runs to the scene and, far from rebuking the driver, thanks her for attending to the child. Fran said that all three characters in her dream were aspects of herself. She talked about the driver, the parent, the vulnerable child and about integration of the three. She said, with some frustration, 'So the child part of me is upset because I never got recognition from my father — so what? What do I do with that?'

In the session that followed, Fran told me that she had slipped and fallen during the preceding week, and had hurt her back. She was in considerable pain during the session, and was clearly emotionally distressed by the incident. I noted how withdrawn and uncommunicative she was and commented on this. She also seemed to me to be rather child-like for some of the session, resting her head in the palm of her hand and keeping very still, but I failed to remark on this at the time. I was aware that there was much more than the physical incident of relevance here. Instead of reflecting my 'feeling' about the image of her as a child, I tried hard (probably too hard) to understand intellectually what was going on for her. I felt a pressure to understand but, at the same time, I knew that Fran was not responding in her usual way. Understanding came, but very slowly. In the next session I commented on this, and on my dismay that it had taken me so long to understand that the pain she had felt in the previous session had simply blocked everything else out for her. She reiterated how difficult she finds it to ask for help and how that, too, had probably contributed to the lower level of communication in that session.

The image of the vulnerable girl in her dream then suddenly flashed into my mind and I asked Fran if that image had any relevance to the way she had felt in the earlier session. She said that it had and then something unusual happened. I said that the vulnerable child that I carry within me was not only a vulnerable boy but many other things too — creative, for example — and that vulnerability was only one tiny part of him. I was aware of the energy with which I said this; I, too, was frustrated that other parts of myself could suppress 'my child's' creativity. Perhaps this is what imbued my statement with a relevancy that communicated on an emotional as well as an intellectual level? I went on to say that she seemed to have recognised that all three people in her dream were equally valid. The words creative and valid prompted a strong reaction in Fran, who said that she also saw the girl as a valid part of herself, as having a legitimate place in her life. She was clearly angry to have been told repeatedly that she was not creative.

Trusting in the image that sprang to my mind, and allowing the feelings that it evoked in me a voice, seemed to have benefited Fran (and me). It is difficult to analyse the mental and other processes that led to this exchange. This is another instance of my scientific lenses failing to deliver insight. What I can talk about is how I felt at the time. I was aware of some element of risk; I was not doggedly following the 'rules' but had discovered a freer space in which to act. In that space I was aware of my own feelings and intuitively matched them to my client's. There was some element of balance involved; being too much in my own feelings, I would risk losing the capacity to be helpful. Too little, and the spark would die without any chance of communicating what is shared and therefore possible to feel as synergistic energy. Finally, I knew myself enough to trust in myself. In this instance, being congruent followed with less conscious effort.

Through meditation, I allow myself regular opportunities for self-study and this helps me to know myself. It also offers me continuous practice of looking within; this is important when I spend so much of my life looking at the external, and renders my attempts at congruence less jerky. The way I felt with Fran is similar to how I feel when I am engaged in other creative processes. My own experiences of music making and writing, for example, share some of the risk and balance and feeling of freedom. Interestingly, all these examples rely on rules as a framework; they are there to support me, but they are the means to an end. They help me to live more creatively, to become much more of the person I really am.

References

Bohm, D. (1980) *Wholeness and the Implicate Order*. London: Routledge.

Bozarth, J. D. (1998) *Person-Centred Therapy: A Revolutionary Paradigm*. Ross-on-Wye: PCCS Books.

Eliot, T. S. (1963) From Little Gidding (1942). In *Collected Poems 1909–1962*. London: Faber, p. 222.

Fenton, J. (1993) The ideal. In the anthology *Out of Danger*. London: Penguin Books.

Fleischman, P. R. (1986) *The Therapeutic Action of Vipassana*. The Wheel Publication No 329. Kandy, Sri Lanka: Buddhist Publication Society.

Gendlin, E. (1978) *Focusing*. USA, Canada: Bantam Books.

Lago, C. and MacMillan, M. (Eds.) (1999) *Experiences in Relatedness: Groupwork and the Person-Centred Approach*. Ross-on-Wye: PCCS Books.

O'Hara, M. M. and Wood, J. K. (1983) Patterns of awareness: Consciousness and the group mind. *The Gestalt Journal*, 6 (2): 103–16.

Rogers, C. R. (1957) The necessary and sufficient conditions of therapeutic personality change. *Journal of Consulting Psychology*, 21 (2): 95–103.

Rogers, C. R. (1967) *On Becoming a Person*. London: Constable.

5

Annette Ansell

The Idiosyncratic Counsellor: Preparation, assessment, contracting and ending

In this chapter I focus on some of what I believe are my idiosyncracies as a person-centred counsellor. I outline my personal philosophy; how I acquired it and how it informs my person-centred theory. I then describe, in some detail, what I consider to be a most important, but often neglected, aspect of being a counsellor, the preparation for meeting clients. This preparation is about self-care and it is physical, social, emotional, intellectual and spiritual. It enables me to meet my clients in a helpful way. I then explore my approach to assessment, contracting and ending with clients. These aspects of my practice highlight some of my idiosyncratic ways of working. Some may find it paradoxical that my discipline and careful attention to boundaries enable me to be more fully present and to work more freely with my clients.

Personal philosophy
Since reading *The Celestine Prophecy* (Redfield, 1997) I have been deeply affected by the concept of synchronicity, defined by Joseph as 'a meaningful coincidence' or an event without any apparent cause (Joseph, 1999, p. xiv). He goes on to summarise Jung's definition of synchronicity:

> . . . any apparent coincidence that inspires a sense of wonder and personal meaning or particular significance in the observer. It is a perceived connection between two or more objects, events, or persons without any recognizable cause. (Joseph, 1999, p. xi)

I have experienced many synchronous events throughout my life and I now keep a synchronicity diary, which sharpens my awareness of acausal events — often only realising their significance retrospectively. This is not a complacent giving up of my life to Fate but rather an exciting and inspiring guide to the unfolding, formative and evolving self that is me. I often wonder how many therapists have had the experience of working on some aspect of their own psychopathology and then had enquiries from clients with almost (or exactly) the same problem. On innumerable occasions I have said, mostly to myself, that I need a couple more clients at home or in town and within a week they have come.

I can't account for any of this theoretically but I have heard other therapists say they have similar experiences. Sometimes going along with seemingly acausal or synchronous events feels like finding myself on a well-greased helter-skelter: terrifying on the way down but so great when I get to the bottom I want to try it again.

Another aspect of my approach to life is my love of natural history, biology, botany; anything to do with ecology, nature, or gardening. My learning about evolution was one of the few good school experiences I had. I remain an observer of the way nature will, without fail, make something out of (apparently) nothing: a pile of garden rubbish will, within a few days, start to develop its own ecosystem.

A further significant contributing factor in the development of my personal philosophy was the rise of various ideologies or styles of feminism. I experienced many feminist principles as affirmation of *my* ideas about sex roles and capabilities (notions that came from my inner locus of evaluation). They matched my experience of gross injustice and gave me permission to disregard the chauvinism and arrogance of the prevailing norms of my peers during my twenties and thirties. I could see how my actualising tendency (although I did not recognise it as such then) had been, and continued to be, stifled and ridiculed both by my family and by society in general. I became a fairly stereotypical man-hating feminist for several years as a way of defending myself and of gaining some inner strength and personal power (Proctor, 2002, Ch. 6). As pendulums go, the strategy became self-defeating because I had not resolved my difficulties with contacting and expressing my inner or core values; I had only exchanged them for another set of other people's values, yet another external locus of evaluation. However, what I did integrate into my self-concept was the principle of taking personal power and responsibility for my life.

I believe my current profession is where I fit into the Great Scheme of Things. When I am well grounded in my inner valuing I feel perfectly and inspirationally at home with myself, and with my life. When I am trying to live up to the externally imposed or introjected values of others (those that don't already accord with mine) I feel like a butterfly under water.

My history has resulted in a personal philosophy which I believe to be consistent with the philosophy and theory of the Person-Centred Approach. It can be summarised in this personal credo:

I believe that we have a formative or actualising tendency which is consistent with everything else in nature and that this tendency is universal.

I believe that the formative tendency in the universe is consistent with the notion of subtle energy (Cameron, 2002), which affects, is affected by and is the energy in all matter, including the atmosphere, stratosphere, and the outer reaches of the universe.

I believe that if I prepare myself for meeting my clients and supervisees in a way that has me remain mindful of the action of subtle energy, I will be most effective.

I believe, and experience, the six conditions for therapeutic change to be the pathway to mindfulness of both my power and limitations to being beneficial to my clients.

I believe that mindfully and willingly opening myself (by visualisation) to the power of subtle energy helps me to be clear and confident in the necessity and sufficiency of the six core conditions.

I believe that me, my philosophy, theory and practice continue to evolve.

My idiosyncrasies
The areas of my practice where my idiosyncrasies are most visible are: my preparation to meet clients and my assessment, contracting and ending with clients.

My preparation to meet clients

> . . . it is with self-love that the spiritual discipline of the person-centred therapist must begin, for without it the therapeutic enterprise is a charade where the therapist offers to the client an unconditionality of acceptance which he or she withholds from himself or herself . . . Self-love is a moral imperative for the person-centred therapist and no potential path towards it must be neglected. (Thorne, 2002, pp. 38–9)

In order to experience self-love I need to be in psychological contact with myself, which is essential if I am to be in psychological contact with my clients. I therefore place a great deal of emphasis on my preparation to meet my clients. It is, for me, another necessary condition, or pre-requisite, to achieving a person-centred attitude towards my clients, supervisees and trainees and it demands discipline. It is about self-love and self-care. I need to look after my self so that I do not tire and become distracted. I need to ensure I have the energy and resources to be present to my clients and to enjoy my work. This discipline is essential to my fitness to practise and is part of the *duty of care* I owe my clients.

I engage in what I call macro- and micro-preparation. Macro-preparation is how I care for my physical and spiritual needs: good diet (including eating out well), adequate sleep, entertainment that I find moving and inspiring such as visiting art galleries, theatre, films and exhibitions. Macro-preparation also includes my professional development, which occupies a number of concentric circles of activity, starting with training and continuing with ongoing reading, supervision, courses, workshops, case discussion with peers in a Continuing Professional Development group, and personal therapy. Micro-preparation is a finely focused exercise immediately before seeing clients, usually at the beginning of the day. I concentrate on my immediate emotional state and bodily sensations in an attempt to bracket them, or put them aside, temporarily. This helps to create a clear space in my head to concentrate on my clients.

My preparation enables me to achieve a more freely flowing inner contact with myself. This is essential as our bodies and minds are the primary vessels to convey our person-centred attitude to our clients. It helps create a greater level of congruence by helping me to become aware of what is going on in my body, mind and emotions. Tudor and Worrall (1994) argue that it is incumbent upon the therapist to 'prepare the ground for psychological contact', thereby facilitating greater congruence in the therapist. Tudor and Worrall's four requirements for congruence include:

> That we are aware of the flow of feelings and sensations within us as we work (self-awareness); that we are able to be and live these feelings and experiencing (self-awareness in action); that we are able and willing to communicate our awareness in the immediate moment of our relationship with a client (communication); and that we evolve coherent and ethical criteria for assessing when it may be appropriate to share our awareness (appropriateness). (Tudor and Worrall, 1994, p. 198)

By paying close attention to my preparation I am more able in the moment with my client to distinguish an appropriate disclosure from what Tudor and Worrall describe as 'promiscuous honesty, sloppy practice and lack of reflection in practice'.

My micro-preparation in particular helps me to create a metaphorical clearing so that I am as closely as possible in the client's world. My mind seems never to be still: I continuously find myself attempting to make sense of myself and my world. This process can get in the way of my ability to make contact, or be present, with my clients if I do not do something to alter my absence of mind. Likewise, if I'm struggling with the impact of life events I may feel inhibited from entering my client's world so as to experience it from their frame of reference. Brazier states that:

Insofar as the therapist is content and at peace, they will find it easier to avoid becoming judgemental. Insofar as they overcome self-centred concern, they will find it easier to stay with the client. Insofar as they live in the present, and are free from serious preoccupation with the past and the future, they will find it easier to flow with the client. Insofar as we are free from these contaminating influences, there will be space which is safe for us and safe for the client. *The therapist needs to create the same kind of inner space which the client is trying to find.* Therapist and client are on the same path. (Brazier, 1995, p. 30, my emphasis)

This 'inner space' is what I am trying to create. Brazier also describes it as a 'clean space' or the clearing of a mental space for his clients:

Deeper acceptance begins with the therapist creating space inside themselves: a positively receptive frame of mind . . . A cup is like the mind, when it is already full, no more will go in. If we are going to learn anything, we must first empty our minds. . . . It is our own emptiness which begins the therapeutic process. (Brazier, 1995, pp. 23–4)

Brazier goes on to say that a few minutes of meditation helps him to become in touch with the universe, 'with the common ground' between him and his clients. He stresses the importance of this in order to be fully attentive and 'oriented' to the client from the very beginning of a session:

The first few moments of encounter generally prove to be disproportionately significant . . . The client, . . . being full of need, may well say crucially significant things in the first few moments which can easily be missed if the therapist is still getting oriented. (Brazier, 1995, p. 24)

At the beginning of his demonstration sessions Rogers invites his volunteer clients to take a few minutes so that they can both mentally prepare for the session. Thorne describes a number of activities he engages in to enhance his spiritual contact with clients including taking a few minutes every day to focus on each of his clients in turn. He found that: 'The holding in mind of clients in this way can have a remarkable impact on the therapeutic relationship and its development' (Thorne, 2002, p. 42).

A simple relaxation exercise works for me. If I hold physical, emotional and psychological tension in my mind and body, it blocks much of the free-flowing energy I need to be close enough in contact for my client to experience our time together as therapeutic. I take between twenty to thirty minutes at the start of my day's work to do a thorough, focused relaxation and grounding in the reasons why I am there and why I do this work. I prepare in my counselling room, which seems to orient me in my world. This enables me to stay grounded in my world whilst moving around freely in the client's world.

Of course, there are times when preparation is more important, and therefore harder, than others. When my life seems to be going well, and I have no major concerns, I take less time. When I have a distracting family crisis then I have to spend more time preparing simply because I am so distracted that even the preparation is a challenge to my powers of concentration.

I take up to fifteen minutes for the physical relaxation stage; relaxing all my inner and outer muscles in turn. Once I have relaxed my body, I focus on where I am in relation to the rest of my world. This is a very practical orientation exercise that gets me in touch with my relative power and importance in the world, and the universe. I orientate myself by becoming aware of being held by my chair and where it is in the room, where the room is in the house, where the house is in the street, where the street is, which part of the country (north, south, east, west) and where I am located in Europe, and where in the Northern hemisphere. I remind myself of the movement of the moon around the earth, of the earth and moon around the sun and that the sun, moon, earth and stars all form the Milky Way, one of many galaxies.

This helps me to get in touch with how I fit in the evolution of my environment, of my relative importance within it. I believe that everything is connected, and that that includes me. I think about my size in the universe, the point of evolution of the universe and my environment. I think about the reality and limits of my personal power (power within) to effect change in the great scheme of things. I have always had a keen and fascinated interest in how organisms work or actualise and why, and a curiosity about what promotes or inhibits the action of atoms and their interaction with each other. I imagine myself and my client being microscopic atoms in the universe, both with infinitesimal roles to play that are nevertheless vital to the universal evolutionary process.

I believe that if I free myself up to accept and connect to the universal subtle energy it will free me and my client to actualise, without interruption, hindrance or distortion. Merry argues that:

> Not only are we connected with each other, but also more remotely to every other living thing, because every living thing is made of fundamentally the same stuff, and shares a common ancestor. (Merry, 2000, p. 34)

I think that maybe it is this connectedness that I tap in to or become aware of, which results in me feeling connected and charged with a free-flowing energy between my self and my client. I believe that environment is everything in life. This way of seeing my place and power in the universe frees me up to create a freeing environment for my clients. I cannot change my clients, either by influencing or doing anything to or for them. I can only bracket, to the best of my ability, those elements of my thinking and being that are likely to inhibit their natural growth potential, the actualising tendency. Some of those inhibiting factors can be likened to aspects of the ecological environment of plants or animals; for example weeds, acid rain, wrong kind of soil, lack of (or too much) light, conditions being too dry or wet. What I am doing is preparing the ground and grounding myself in it. This creates a fertile enough environment to facilitate growth, notwithstanding that some parts of my clients are 'not for growth' (Mearns and Thorne, 2000, pp. 114–6). My task is to provide the optimal conditions for my client's natural, integral propensity for growth, without any predetermined expectations or agendas. We cannot *make* things grow nor can we *intend* to grow our clients like some kind of hothouse plant that is brought outside in the spring after over-wintering in a heated greenhouse.

I remind myself that I have three intentions: to empathise, to be non-judgemental about my client's experiencing and to communicate congruently if I think I am not as fully in tune with him or her as I think I could be. It is not my intention to get my client to do anything, or go in any direction, or change his/her content or style of communicating. I hold in awareness that behind all my client's behaviours and beliefs is the instinct to actualise, be creative, social and constructive, and that 'Behavior is basically the goal-directed attempt of the organism to satisfy its needs as experienced, in the field as perceived' (Rogers, 1951, p. 491).

I remind myself how lonely and frightening it feels not to be understood, to believe that I am not understandable and that therefore I must be mad or bad and definitely unlovable. I remind myself that clients do not have to express feelings in order to have a therapeutic experience. Some clients of mine have made amazing changes to their lives through only relating the sequence of events in their lives between sessions. This is not to say that I have an *expectation* that clients necessarily make changes to their lives. Some clients, for example, make use of counselling as a support for stressful occupations.

Finally, I spend a moment, if necessary, reflecting on anything I've learned about myself recently in supervision. I remind myself that I am in the process of integrating that learning into my own self-structure.

This exercise reconnects me with the knowledge and experience of how it is 'the client who knows best what hurts, what directions to go, what problems are crucial, what experiences have ben deeply buried' (Rogers, 1961, p. 13). Furthermore, the client needs no active help from me in setting the pace, the agenda, or tone of the sessions. I need only to sit on the edge of my clearing, and keep it clear of obstacles to my client's process. I can listen with a free and uncluttered ear, without preconceptions and expectations. My own empathic connection can flow more lucidly, and I can more empathically communicate the sense I am making of what my client is telling me about their experience and meanings.

My philosophy, theory and practice, therefore, encompass the belief that a sense of being in my ecological niche results in me experiencing a sense of connectedness to the universe, a cosmic connection that engenders a higher quality of presence with my clients. This higher quality of presence works to enhance my love of self and my empathy, unconditional positive regard and congruence. This is probably the most important belief that I hold, for it informs everything that I do, and all of my way of being with people, most of the time. For me it is a spiritual activity that requires the spiritual enhancement of my body and psyche. From this flows all aspects of my work.

Assessment

When a client first makes contact with me I take five things into consideration when assessing whether or not I can, or will, work with them: current caseload, my physical and emotional wellbeing, client presenting issues, any ethical considerations, and any practical considerations.

I do a maximum of 24 sessions a week, including supervising other counsellors and trainees. I prefer an optimal number of 20 but will go up to 24 if some clients are due to leave. I also take into consideration how much other work I want to do such as training, writing or setting up another aspect of my business. If it is Spring, I know I'm going to want to spend much more time doing my garden before it's too late so that affects the number of hours that I work. Since my garden is a very important part of my macro-preparation, if I neglected it I would be doing a disservice not only to myself but to my clients also. It is my responsibility to avoid depleting my inner resources.

I assess my own physical and emotional wellbeing. How healthy am I? Can I cope with another client now? Should I take some time out for a while, or reduce my optimal hours? Am I competent to work with this person's issues? Are the challenges in my life the same as theirs? Can I bracket them *sufficiently* to be present 'at least to a minimal degree'? Do I even *want* to? Will I need to increase my self-care if I take on this client? Do I have the necessary financial and time resources to do that? Do I even want to increase my self-care for this client? What is going on in my immediate and extended family right now? Who is not well at the moment and may need additional support, tolerance, patience and empathy from me? Is this prospective client presenting the same issues as people in my family? Could I bracket my family business sufficiently? How is my general health and wellbeing?

The attitude I take in my initial telephone assessment of a prospective client goes something like this: 'Can I handle what this person wants to talk about?' I check with my felt sense about their presenting problem. For example, can I experience empathy, unconditional positive regard and be congruent with another client who is severely depressed? If I have two in my practice already my response would be 'no'. Is this person a counselling trainee? I like to limit the number of trainees I have so that I maintain a balance of presenting issues in my caseload so that it is not overbalanced by working with trainee clients and supervisees. Do I get a sense during our phone conversation that we can be in psychological contact? If I'm not sure about this I will invite the person to come for an initial session to ascertain the extent to which this first condition is possible; some people feel less comfortable over the phone than others. I will not necessarily charge for an initial session, especially if the person asks if I offer free tester sessions. I will also take into consideration a client's age group and how that might affect the balance of age groups in my practice. I also consider the balance of male to female clients, ethnic groups and language or accent. If a person's English is not very good then I will have to work harder to understand them and may not have sufficient energy for more than two clients like that. If the client cannot pay my full fee and my quota for low-fee clients is full and not likely to reduce for some time, I would pass the person on to someone else or refer them to free or low-fee organisations on my list. I accept a maximum of 10% of clients on reduced fees.

I also ask about the referral source — first, because I want to keep track of where people hear about me from and second, because I want to ensure I don't have a conflict of interest between members of the same family, friends or work colleagues who are already clients of mine. I would not knowingly take on people who are close to anyone I have worked with. Of course, this fact may not surface immediately in the initial assessment, and if or when it does, I would take the case on its merits after consulting with my supervisor. I would also be careful when assessing my ethical responsibilities with lesbian or gay clients as I am more likely to meet them at social events and this has implications for any therapeutic relationship.

I usually ask the prospective client where they want to be seen and what time of day within the first few minutes of our phone conversation. This can obviate any unnecessary (and tedious for the client) assessment if I cannot fit them in anyway.

All these issues I take into consideration, not necessarily consciously counting them off on my fingers as I listen to the caller, but almost automatically. I listen attentively to my feeling, and go with that. These considerations impact on my ability to experience my share of the six necessary and sufficient conditions for therapeutic change.

Contracting

I do not usually use the word 'contracting' with clients but I use it here to describe what I see as my professional obligations during an initial session with a client. I don't use the word 'contract' because I believe the word assumes I have expectations of my clients, which I don't, other than paying my fee and not arriving before time and running the risk of meeting other clients on the way out, thereby compromising both client's confidentiality. My contract emerges from what I say about what I can offer, and how I will behave in, and outside of, counselling sessions. My intention is to express my attitude about my personal integrity, which I believe is transparent to my clients — my words communicate a contractual reliability.

At the beginning I inform the client that three things normally happen in a first session. Firstly, I give information about practical issues to do with our meetings and the venue. Secondly, I let the client know that they have the opportunity to learn more about me and what the sessions might look and sound like in terms of who speaks and who listens most. They may either ask me questions or ask me to speak about my experience, qualifications and the way I work. Thirdly, of course, it is the client's first opportunity to tell me as much as they want, or feel able to, about themselves and why they are coming for counselling now. I let them know that I have no particular preference in which order it comes. I leave it to them to choose, although I do note that practical issues include information about confidentiality. I notice that most people opt for hearing about practicalities first, perhaps as an ice breaker. My contract emerges from this dialogue.

My attitude to contracting is that it primarily encompasses what I am able and willing to offer my clients. I always put confidentiality first and include my limits. I see no reason ever to breach confidentiality. If I am clear about what I can keep confidential and what I cannot keep confidential then confidentiality is never breached. I explain my legal responsibilities to disclose terrorist activities or plans I might hear about. I go into some detail about how I see my responsibilities to the public in general and to aspects of child abuse in particular. I explain the latter as *my* limit to confidentiality and that other therapists may take a different view. I explain that it is about my ability to sleep at night without worrying about what might be happening to children that renders them unsafe. I go into some detail about the process of trying to ensure the reduction of risk to children. That involves negotiating with a client who discloses what that might entail for them, whether they might prefer me to make an appropriate contact with the police, teachers or Social Services. I explain that my bottom line is that I would always seek permission from clients to disclose but, failing that, I would never disclose without their knowledge. Moreover I would always continue to support clients if that was their wish.

For me this policy is consistent with the Person-Centred Approach in that I am being very clear where I stand on the issues of public safety which leaves the client free to decide whether or not they want to go on and work with me given *my* limits to confidentiality. This policy is also about me taking responsibility for my self-care in that I need my sleep and I know I will lie awake for hours worrying about children being treated abusively. Therefore my policy is consistent with me being congruent with *me and my clients.*

I explain how I work, including my theoretical orientation if asked about it, and check out with my clients how they think my approach might be helpful for them. I let them know that I am willing to experiment with how flexible I can be about session times and duration. I let clients know that I am willing to negotiate double sessions on a fortnightly (or weekly) basis. One client woefully remarked that she thought she could do with a whole day. I offered a whole day, she took it (we separated for an hour at lunchtime) and we had a remarkable session in which she had a number of profound insights and made some resolutions that left me feeling very moved by her new experiencing of herself. What surprised me was that I half expected to feel very tired at the end of the day but I felt energised right up to 4 p.m. when we stopped.

I believe, again, that this is an idiosyncratic result of my congruent relating to myself: I felt excited at the prospect of responding freely to a client's needs as perceived in the moment. With one couple we did a triple session: I re-negotiated at the end of each 50-minute session, having mindfully looked into myself to assess my inner resources to continue *before* making the offer to re-negotiate the contract for that day. I have done this since with other couples and sometimes they take it up, sometimes they don't. Sometimes I know I can't offer it, so I don't. But the bottom line is that my clients know what is possible, given that *we all* have the resources to do it.

My attitude to money is another aspect of my idiosyncratic way of being. When contracting, I let clients know that I do not charge for missed sessions. This policy stems from three beliefs: the primacy of unconditional positive regard, synchronicity, and bad karma. Firstly I believe that charging for a missed session is inconsistent with the person-centred philosophy of trusting the client to know best. I am not responsible for anyone's integrity but my own and therefore I do not have to look after my client by making sure they do not 'take advantage of my good nature'. I think charging for missed sessions sets up the possibility of conditionality seeping into the relationship. If I am seeking to maintain and enhance my unconditional positive regard, I can't do this by insisting that clients pay for something they have not had. This policy is unconditional in its own right. I do not charge whatever the reason: illness, working late on demand from an employer, not feeling like it, transport problems.

Secondly, my experience, and therefore my trust in the synchronicity of events, is such that I make allowances for people cancelling their appointments, getting the day or time wrong, public transport being unreliable, weather, sickness. Within my maximum contact hours per week is a built-in assumption that at least two people will be unable to make their session for one reason or another. Therefore I don't need to worry about money *too much.* I emphasise this because of my third reason for not charging.

Karma is defined as 'the law of moral consequence' (Brazier, 1995, p. 158).

Therefore I believe that charging for missed sessions creates a negative energy that blocks my ability to be empathic, unconditionally positive in my regard of the client's process and congruent in my communication. I also think that all of the above might inhibit my client's ability to receive my empathy, unconditional positive regard and congruence. I believe that if my energy remains positive, enough money will come to me. My experience has always been that money for what I need always comes from somewhere if I don't block the subtle energy that allows it to flow in my direction. My experience has taught me that there is a level of worrying about, or becoming pre-occupied with money, that impacts on me to the point that I am sure my distraction with it becomes obvious and therefore unhelpful to my clients. In other words, it has proved to be bad karma for me to work with money as my primary goal.

> As long as we continue to think that acting selfishly is the best policy, we continue to create hells for ourselves and others. That is, we create bad karma. If we act virtuously in the hope of reward in the hereafter, that is better, but still not ideal. It is to create good karma. Ideally, when we act in an enlightened way, we create no personal karma at all, because our action, being selfless, is not for ourselves, but for the community. Good communities are not built by everyone serving themselves, but by serving one another. . . . Since karma is created by willful behaviour, it concerns both attitude and action. (Brazier, 1995, p. 159–60)

Endings
How or when a client might end forms part of my contracting information in that I make no demands on my clients about how they must go about, or prepare for, ending. By that I mean that I do not require clients to give me notice of when they want to end. In the practical information which I give to clients during our initial session I make it clear that the duration of our time together will, by and large, be dictated by them. For me this is, again, consistent with unconditional positive regard and the notion that the client knows best. My experience has borne this out. Whatever reason a client gives for leaving I trust that it is the right thing for them to be doing at that time. Most often the reason clients give for leaving is that they feel they don't need to come any more and I agree. I have often been aware of wondering why a particular client is still coming for therapy when during the session they will tell me that they think they can finish now: I fully accept their decision.

Other reasons for finishing have included moving away from the area or emigrating, wanting to work with a counsellor from a different background, sexuality or gender, wanting to return to a previous counsellor who had been away for a while. Some clients have been quite explicit about not wanting to look at issues that are too painful for them at the time. One client told me:

> I'm bored with only talking about myself . . . [I feel] guilty that you have to listen to me and that you don't get the chance to talk about yourself. I'm just going through a mid-life crisis and I'll just have to get on with it.

Counselling was just too much of a one-way street in her frame of reference. She preferred to talk about her life with her friends, with whom she could 'return the compliment'. Someone had suggested that she might find counselling helpful, which she did in that after four sessions she realised she had quite a good support network without it.

Some people set themselves targets for ending and stick to them, others don't. I have a client who was determined she was going to be 'sorted by Christmas' and was not and now feels amused by her ambition. There was a time she would have considered not reaching her target as evidence of her failure as a person. She is now quite content to continue until she feels:

> . . . confident enough to make mistakes without beating myself up about it or thinking people will hold it against me forever. I feel proud and open about my bi-sexuality and happy (rather than uneasy) around children.

The main reason why I would initiate an ending would be a conflict of interest. For example, a client may turn out to have a close relationship with someone else with whom I am working. I have also seriously considered ending with a client who, well into our relationship, brought an issue very similar to one that I was battling with.

In thinking about endings in general with clients I hold in mind that no matter how brief the encounter, my warmth and empathy, my way of being with them may have touched that person's life in a memorable, healing and lasting way. I do not need, nor would it be healthy, to be with them for their whole evolutionary process of healing, growing and becoming. I have been intimate without being attached, therefore I can let go without regret.

The evolving counsellor
I have explained above how my philosophy of life and people developed through my reading, training and life experience. I consider this process as ongoing in that my experience of my self (or selves) is that I am changed every day, at least to some subtle degree, by my environment. By the same token, I change my environment in some subtle or significant way. I am changed by working with my clients as they are changed as a result of working with me. If I change my immediate environment, my garden for example, I am immediately changed by its transformation when I finish working in it.

What I read, watch on TV, my training and continuing professional development, films or theatre, interaction with friends and family contribute to my knowledge and understanding of others and of me. It influences how I conceptualise myself, my configurations (Mearns and Thorne, 2000, Ch. 6). By integrating such learning into my self I continue to evolve intellectually, emotionally and spiritually as a person who counsels for her living.

I do not like to make a separation between me the person and me the counsellor. I prefer to distinguish the roles with regard to a balance between listening and speaking such that when I am with a client I am listening much more than I am speaking. Another distinction I make is that the aim of the counselling dialogue is the creation of a therapeutic environment and relationship for my client's particular goals and process; the focus of the dialogue is the client, whereas the focus in my other relationships shifts frequently from me to the other. None the less, my intention is that my fundamental attitude to the other remains the same with clients and others, and how successful I am in remaining or sustaining a manifestation of that attitude is what constantly evolves within me. For example, I currently attempt to make a distinction between on the one hand not feeling dependent on someone's good opinion for my self-acceptance and on the other hand needing some level of empathy and unconditional positive regard in order to be in an at least satisfactory relationship with them.

My level of understanding is enhanced by my reading, and my reading is guided by my curiosity and my stage of development. What you, the reader, are learning about me today will be out of date by the time you read this. I will have developed further, increased, refined, or even changed my understanding of many of the subjects I have written about here and *my* now.

One aspect of my being, however, will not change and that, paradoxically, is my belief that everything changes, or actualises. There will always be an ecological niche for me, although that might change as I change. I will always sense a universal connectedness, although how I perceive that will change as I learn and understand more about it. I will always believe in preparing for my clients, although how I do that will change as I deepen my philosophical and theoretical understanding of my self and my clients.

My intention to develop a person-centred attitude in my relationships outside my counselling practice will go on but the resolve, ability and the inner resources required to sustain such an intention will, inevitably, develop spasmodically and probably painfully. My belief in creating a moving and inspiring self-care or work/life balance strategy will remain but what I do will surely change.

I will always need to generate inner space for myself and create a 'clean space' for my clients. I like to envisage a time when I will not work on that in the way that I currently do, that I will do so more automatically, more like living in a 'clean space', in the now, achieving a contentment with living with uncertainty, unknowingness and accepting that there is no endpoint to reach, no skills to master once and for all, no perfection to achieve. There is an exciting, moving learning and becoming process to be in, synchronicity to watch out for and opportunities to recognize and grasp.

References

Brazier, D. (1995) *Zen Therapy*. London: Constable.

Cameron, R. (2002) Subtle energy awareness: Bridging psyche and soma. In *Person-Centred Practice*, 10 (2): 66–74.

Joseph, F. (1999) *Synchronicity and You: Understanding the Role of Meaningful Coincidence in Your Life*. Melbourne, Australia: Element Books.

Kirschenbaum, H. and Henderson, V. L. (1989) *The Carl Rogers Reader*. London: Constable.

Mearns, D. and Thorne, B. (1988) *Person-Centred Counselling in Action*. London: Sage.

Mearns, D. and Thorne, B. (2000) *Person-Centred Therapy Today*. London: Sage.

Merry, T. (2000) On connectedness — A humanistic, biological view. *Person-Centred Practice,* 8 (1): 28–36.

Proctor, G. (2002) *The Dynamics of Power in Counselling and Psychotherapy: Ethics, Politics and Practice.*

Redfield, J. (1997) *The Celestine Prophecy*. New York: Warner Books.

Rogers, C.R. (1951) *Client-Centred Therapy.* London: Constable.

Rogers, C.R. (1961) This is me. In H. Kirschenbaum and V. L. Henderson (1989) *The Carl Rogers Reader*. London: Constable, pp. 6–29.

Thorne, B. (2002) *The Mystical Power of Person-Centred Therapy: Hope Beyond Despair*. London: Whurr.

Tudor, K. and Worrall M. (1994) Congruence reconsidered. *British Journal of Guidance and Counselling,* 22 (2):197–206.

6

Sholto Thompson

Intention, Coherence and Spirituality in the Person-Centred Approach

Ninety-eight per cent of life is just showing up.
Woody Allen

From my birth my world has been a dangerous and unsafe place. My mother never bonded with me, had no recollection of my birth, had no memory of where I had come from and consequently did not know who I was. To this day she has no idea as to who I am. I have finally stopped trying to tell her after fifty-six years of the pain of her not being able to listen.

I have no memory of my early years: my memories start at about eight when I was sent to boarding school. I remember being asked if I wanted to go. I remember saying no, but I went anyway.

There are vague memories and sensations around those early school years, scenes that feel like snapshots, things on their own that have little or no connection with anything else. The dreams that I have now, as an adult, are filled with panic and terror because I have lost my home: I have forgotten to pay the rent and am being evicted. I am lost in some foreign city without money or tickets. I have lost my passport and nobody knows I am missing.

The boarding school regime had a profound impact on an already lost child. There were beatings that left me with bruises for months and a constant, though less tangible, threat of sexual assault and abuse. This was the system. These were the people that filled my days. At night I shivered. It was cold. My school number was 24. I desperately wanted to be loved, so I was good, but I couldn't be good for very long, so whatever I had got by being good, I would smash, by being bad. I stole cigarettes from the matron who was kind. I smoked them on the golf course in the dark before I dug holes in the green and threw the flags over the cliff. I didn't understand why I did that. I didn't understand any of it. I bullied other children into hugging me and kissing me: I am still haunted by the prolonged, premeditated cruelty I handed out to those I saw as weak, defenceless and therefore contemptible. I didn't understand that either.

I fantasised that home would save me, but the reality was different: when I did get home there was usually another new baby and I was left to look after myself. I am the eldest of eight.

Looking back at that period of my life, from about eight to twelve or thirteen, I can see that the basic currency of my relating was fear. I was afraid of the bigger, stronger ones; the smaller, weaker ones were afraid of me; the ones in the middle I either didn't notice or loved and needed so intensely that my demands could never be met. Like the smaller ones, they ran away when I approached.

It was at this time in my life that I started reading and drawing. The villains got their just desserts, the heroes were rescued in the nick of time; there was always a happy ending — I read and read. In art lessons there was 'perspective': you put a dot on the horizon line, called it the 'vanishing point' and then everything just fell into a place of its own accord, as long as you followed the rules. I got full marks in geometry. Algebra was beyond me. Why invent 'x' in the first place if you're only going to spend fruitless hours trying to find out what it was? I was told it was to help me design aircraft wings.

Aircraft wings didn't keep me warm at night.

I scraped through the eleven plus exam and was sent to a minor public school on the south coast. It was the same but bigger and more organised; not only the teachers but bigger boys called 'prefects' were allowed to beat you. There were initiation rituals, a new book of rules to be learnt and new punishments for failure or ignorance. I felt I was hanging by a thread, swinging from random sporadic outbursts of violence and vandalism to puppy-dog compliance. They couldn't make sense of me and I couldn't make sense of them. I was under constant threat of expulsion, from what or where to I did not know, but feared even more.

Amongst all this chaos, I gradually became aware of something unfamiliar. Someone had noticed me and it didn't feel dangerous: for the first time an other in my life felt safe, at least, safe enough. There was a glimmer of light on the horizon of a dark ocean. I think that glimmer saved my life.

Throughout adolescence and early adulthood, the glimmer grew stronger and I began to trust it enough to move towards it. It was a slow process and, with hindsight, I can now see it as my first contact with the healing power of acceptance. Struggling with this was my fear of acceptance and my consequent drive towards self-destruction, which, as I became older, became more sophisticated. I felt it was a race against time; I knew that the only reason I was surviving the self-punishment was because I was still young and strong. I never stayed long enough in one place to make an attachment. I was hiding the degree of my self-punishment. I was geographically and emotionally itinerant. There was a kind of map, however: writing, reading and painting helped me find a semblance of inner order. I devoured European architecture, art and literature. I painted pictures and wrote stories. I knew I had to get well before I got old.

I found myself learning to be a teacher though I hated the idea of becoming one. I used the time to try to heal myself but could make no sense of Freud or Skinner. I finished my training and escaped abroad for four years: I taught English in Morocco and Italy. It was like walking through dreamland. I still didn't understand any of it. I saw the world through a haze. I only felt connected when I read, drew or wrote something down. I still have one journal that I didn't destroy.

I had no real understanding of being in relation to an other. I was so separate, so disconnected. I could start a relationship having forgotten I was in one already. From time to time I would arrive, desperate, on my adopted father figure's doorstep and then disappear again. His acceptance and availability were unwavering. My real father was too busy to notice his children: I was all puppy-dog towards him and violence towards myself. In one year I completed a diploma in Art Therapy, got married and started work as an art therapist in a special junior day school for children with emotional and behavioural difficulties. The marriage was a disaster and lasted four years. The job was less of a disaster and lasted fifteen years.

My struggle to stay alive and somehow heal myself led me into therapy: my therapist wondered aloud why I was working with young children with emotional and behavioural difficulties. I had no idea. The beginning of my therapy took three years; that's how long I needed for this other to come into a kind of focus to become real, to become someone who was there. I was always on time, I never missed a session. After three years it was safe enough for me to speak; I spoke from within my self for the first time in my life. I can remember speaking, saying terrible things and the world not ending, the other being able to stay in the room, not running away, and my shock and amazement at that. I said all I could for six months; after that there was nothing more and I left. I had made a connection and I loved her. The me that had clung to my teddy bear in the night, dreamed of laying down my life to rescue her from burning buildings. My grown-up self wanted to tell the whole world so she could fix it for them. Looking back I realised that I felt closest when we shared a joke, when we both laughed at the same time; a full spontaneous connection. I felt most apart when I heard the smallest noise from another person in the house: her husband, her lover, her child? Some years later we met accidentally in the street; she said I had worked so hard. I said I felt I had tried her patience to the limit, but had learned that I could tell secrets.

The school I worked in was instinctively and institutionally child-centred: it was that that attracted me. The aim was to provide a safe, holding environment for these out-of-control, damaged and damaging children. We didn't have morning prayers, we had morning meetings. We didn't have punishment and humiliation, we had reconciliation supervised by a court — the judges were children elected by other children, which was a genuine alternative to retribution, somewhere to bring a grievance and find a just resolution. There were no problems with graffiti; the children felt they had a voice. Amongst a group of truants, school phobics and mainstream failures, the severest sanction was a day's exclusion.

In my public, adult life I was just about holding all this together; my private, inner, child life was in pieces. In my effort to provide for the children, I was trying to provide for myself. My self-damaging was sometimes so severe that I had to take time out to recuperate. I could only sustain and offer consistency for a limited time before crisis and collapse.

I had always suffered control and punishment at the hands of teachers and their institutions. Ironically I had found my living in being a teacher. Teaching for me was the imposition of will in order to contain chaos: and I could do it, and somehow felt compelled to do it, but I hated it. It was a huge effort of will that kept me there, that and the terror of chaos. I was trapped for nearly fifteen years: others came and went but I had no idea how to move on. What I did know, however, was that my skill lay in allowing, not teaching. And so I found my counselling training course. This was part-time over a period of two and a half years, the main feature being a week's residential every six months, linked with a monthly day-long supervision group. I applied, thinking that these courses started every year, only to discover that they started only every three years and that the closing date was in two months' time. I was accepted. The core of the reading list seemed vaguely familiar. In a dusty cardboard box that I had stored in the attic for more than twenty years I found equally dusty volumes I had collected but never read: *On Becoming a Person*, *Client-Centered Therapy*, *Carl Rogers on Encounter Groups* and *Carl Rogers on Personal Power*. Dusty books in cardboard boxes, dusty potatoes in dusty sacks.

For the first time in my life I was facing the prospect of an essentially benevolent, consistent and containing structure, though I couldn't have experienced it in that way at the time. I just knew it was right and I felt ready for it.

Held within this containing structure, I learned many things. I learned that my anger, cruelty and disparagement were not just a spontaneous expression of my own hurt, but also a device I used to try to get the acceptance and love of those I wanted to love me. The world was divided into two, the stronger ones whom you wanted to be loved by and the weaker ones whom you hated and despised. I thought that was how it worked, that to be loved by the strong ones you had to be cruel to the weak ones; I thought everyone's world was like that. I discovered that, being in a containing structure, what hurt I gave out returned to me eventually and that I didn't like or want any of it, for me, or others. This was not the vacuum that I was used to. The gradual realisation that I didn't like or want the hurt, helped me become more aware of a self that had been hiding from the beginning. There was a part of me, a part that felt like the true one, that could look at all this pain and anger and see that it was different from itself, a thing apart. Maybe I didn't have to spend the rest of my life trying unsuccessfully to hide the monster I felt myself to be. Maybe I didn't have to be hateful to be loveable.

In this holding and consistent environment I began, for the first time, to have the sense of a true me. It was a self that was separate and different from the selves I had always experienced. The profound realisation was that others could see this true self. In fact my realisation of my true self was inextricably rooted in those others speaking it to me. I had never been spoken to like this and the words were so precious that I hardly dared hold them, *could* hold them for fear of losing or breaking them, as I had been lost and broken. All I could do was receive, to let the words, the other, sink in, and to allow them some resting place: all I dared say was that I had heard what they said and thank you; to say that I too could see this true self was to put it at risk. It felt that exposure to ridicule or criticism would kill it. My acceptance of my self was a gradual, tortuous and fragile process. The world into which this self was emerging was not some utopian Garden of Eden, but what was crucially important was that it was genuinely person-centred. For me that was not about perfection, but a demonstrable intent to hold the core conditions in every aspect of the course structure. At the heart of that structure was the process of self-assessment and trust in the individual to monitor and take responsibility for learning and development. That process culminated at the end of the course in the trainee deciding whether to award him/herself the diploma, or to choose to defer. At the end of the day it was for me to decide if I was ready. I could take my diploma, if I chose, in the face of all my fellow trainees and trainers. Had it been otherwise I would probably have not completed or cheated. If the course had said to me, 'This is a person-centred course, but actually it is us, the trainers, who decide whether you pass or fail', I would have been defeated — the final abuse.

Saying one thing and meaning another is for me the insidious imposition of powerful conditions of worth and the ultimate betrayal.

The main part of the course culminated in a ceremony designed by the trainees. We dressed for the occasion and each individual trainee presented the diploma to a fellow trainee. Those deferring were not left out. Following the diploma ceremony two residential weekends were planned, the first one a year later, the second two years after that. These weekends were an important recognition of the developmental aspect of the training, giving us the opportunity to re-connect one year and then three years later. I took the chance to keep the dots joined up, to stay in relation. All that was some twelve or so years ago, and the connection continues into the present in the form of a small closed group that meets in the spring and autumn of each year. The setting is a retreat house in the Lake District, with beautiful gardens in a broad sweep of open countryside. So, twice a year, in the seasons of emergence and withdrawal, I meet with people I have known in this special way for more than fourteen years. This makes for a deep sense of natural rhythm and belonging and allows for expression of the truest congruence, the most open experiencing of the self in the accepting presence of the known other: this to me is the actualising tendency incarnate.

Another important rhythm in my life is a group that has evolved out of my supervision training: we meet for a day, every five or six weeks, throughout the year. We have also had several residential weekends.

As I look back over my training, I realise that there is a quality and a depth of relating that is dependent on just spending time together, whether it is a full week or just a long weekend. It means packing, travelling and arriving with expectation; it means sharing the day, the food and the weather; it means sharing the evening and the food, a party even, and yet more weather. Then there is the packing and leaving. First saying hello and then saying goodbye: at the heart of my every hello is the seed of my goodbye, and in between the two is my consciousness of them both. This is the space in which I work and live.

From the chaos of my not having known and my not knowing has emerged the self that does know. It knows that it is different from others but the same as others. It knows that intimacy and love are only possible when there is a true sense of both the self and the other; it knows that the depth of connection, and therefore separateness, is dependent on the depth of that sense of self in the open presence of the other.

The continuing moment deepens and broadens the sense of precious uniqueness and infinite communality. There is no self without the other. I do not exist outside relation.

In the ongoing moment of knowing, I am truly alive, separate, known and knowing, and part of an infinity of other. This, for me, is the moment of coherence and healing.

A client arrived and started: there were no preliminaries. I could have been anyone. He knew he was depressed, his girlfriend had left him for someone else. His job was shite, the transport system was shite, his flat was shite, the world was shite. He hated his body. He was ugly and no one could ever want him again, if he had ever been wanted at all. In fact he never had been wanted at all. Over the next year or so it gradually emerged that as a child it was best to be invisible: you didn't then get hit or shouted at. The only form of protest was to soil himself, the cure for that being, the doctor advised, for him to wash his underclothes in front of his family. We continued. The world was still shite, he was shite, no one had ever wanted him and no one ever could; he was ugly. Change or even hope of change was just not possible, that was how the world was. He hated himself and he despised all the others who had all the things he could not have, who could do the things he couldn't do. They took all of that for granted, as a God-given right. The complacent privileged apathetic middle class was the focus of his scorn. He had an acute sense of justice.

Mark, what do you get from coming here?
I just dump all this shite and it makes me feel better.

Another year or so further on and he said:

I think I feel a bit less depressed and a bit more angry.

Perhaps this was the end of the beginning and the start of the middle.

And so we went on as regular as clockwork with nothing changing. This whole process involved a huge effort of will on both our parts. His effort was evident in that, despite the fact that nothing could ever change, he just kept coming. He would drag himself in and fall exhausted into his chair as he always did. Life was shite; it was also exhausting. He had bought an apple because it was good for him, but it had rotted on the kitchen table. His only escape was alcohol, dope and junk food.

The degree of my effort of will surfaced into my consciousness by my asking myself before every session: how can I get in touch with him today; what on earth do I have to do? It was not a question I could ever answer but it focused my energy and somehow we always seemed to find a way. As the session progressed, I found that my world with its anxieties and preoccupations with the task in hand drifted away and my reality was able to meet his at many different levels. The nature of that meeting could be in argument, discussion, sharing, moments of excitement, despair and impotence. We were both wrestling with something other than us, some intangible, intransigent entity that could not, would not be moved or gain-said.

He believed that no one could ever really care about him. I said I did, so, I said, that wasn't true. Finally he said that he couldn't get better until his family got better. He had read that years ago. One of those psychology text books. His family never could get better so that was him then, and there we had it. Having seen the daylight it disappeared back into the darkness.

Life for him went on relentlessly, nothing working, no way out. Sometimes briefly, it seemed as if there was some kind of hope, but it was so fragile, so ephemeral that its death was in its birth; stillborn, nameless.

He took holidays, went to football. Holidays were with a friend and were all about alcohol and smoking. Amsterdam was a favourite destination. But he was getting angry with friends: they only complained and never asked about him. He began not answering the phone; he wasn't putting up with any more of their shite, they just wanted to dump it on him and walk away.

Goodbyes began to be different. It took me a while to notice it. He made eye contact and gave a sort of smile, a sort of recognition that we had come to an end for this week, we would meet again, next week, that I was me and he was him, that we could come together then separate and that there was an in-between time. Internalisation had created difference, separation, and therefore potential relationship. Despite his family there was change.

The months turned into another year and then another holiday. Amsterdam? Prague? Berlin? This time it was a farmhouse in France, in the country, in the middle of nowhere that he knew. He was going for two weeks. You had your own room and food was provided. There were things to do, like painting, yoga, things like that. Other people he didn't know would be there for the same two weeks.

It was safe enough to risk coming out of his room to meet others, to see and be seen and maybe even to join in.

He came back with a girlfriend and that was the beginning of our ending: he had found and connected with someone of his own. He still felt he was ugly and hated his body, no one would ever care about him. Everything was the same even though it was different; these facts were mutually inclusive, and that is how things still are, now, in the present. Gradually we moved to meeting every two weeks, then once a month, now once every two or three months. He and Alison are living together, able enough to make it work. They don't know how to go forward; they both hate their dead-end jobs; her flat is only a studio, hardly big enough for one, let alone two, and it's too expensive to buy. They could afford France or Belgium where the trains and buses work, but they don't know the language and so what would they do? And then there's her mother who is elderly and not too well. That's what we talk about now.

In our most recent meeting he said that he thought a few more sessions would do it. He wasn't depressed about his life anymore, though he could be depressed about things *in* his life. He knew the difference. He felt he could manage on his own now. When he said goodbye he used my Christian name for the first time in our nine years of work together.

In our next session I will tell him how much he has taught me.

There are beginnings, middles and endings: emerging, meeting and leaving. Therapy mirrors life. From chaotic darkness I instinctively look for order and light, I need them so I can understand; without understanding there is only formless unknowing. It's the edges that create meaning. The process takes me from one place, at the beginning, to another, at the end, and somewhere in the middle holds the balance between the two, the place that holds both extremes in the present moment; that is my alive, energised and knowing self that is not terrified of the unknown. But there are echoes of other earlier journeys that make it safe enough. Is this the right day, is this the right lifetime? Will they remember I'm coming? Will there be someone to meet me?

I am fearful as I set out on my journey. They said they'd be there. They said they were expecting me and looking forward to meeting me. If I miss my connection, I can always go home again.

When I arrive I wonder how it will be. I need to be safe enough to do the work I've come for. I need to ask, and ask again, to be really sure that it is safe enough to risk being fully myself, to emerge. How many times will I tell the same story, each time the same, but each time different? Will they notice that its both the same and different, or will they get bored, angry or maybe so frightened that they run away? I hope that each time I arrive I will be expected, met and find myself able to leave.

Now that I am here, in my life, I am doing the work I need to do to make the arriving worthwhile. In the act of writing or speaking I am meeting both self and other. In this meeting place the music is full of intensity and colour. It holds my intellect, my feelings, my physicality, my beginning and my end. I know that in loving the other, I love myself. I know that in harming the other, I harm myself. The fruit fly has virtually the same genetic make-up as myself and the universe is inside my head; to tread on the fruit fly is to tread on myself, to cherish myself is to acknowledge the universe and what lies beyond it. I know that my presence changes everything and nothing and that is the point of it all.

I can only be fully here if I know that I am able to meet and then able to let go. My letting go is part of my arriving and staying. Leaving acknowledges, validates my being: with no leaving there is no arriving or meeting. By letting go I know I am loved and loving, and that loving is freedom, not possession, energy, not stasis and inertia.

By an act of faith I set out on this journey expecting, hoping to be met. My act of faith has been vindicated. I have been met and have learned that I can find what I need along the way. At least I have done so, so far, and in an ongoing act of faith I have to trust that I will continue to do so. Trust in my physical, feeling, thinking and spiritual self can release me from fear and free me to move on. At this stage in my life moving on is about the manner of my leaving. Can I manage it? How can I manage it? Who will I be when I am no longer part of this present consciousness?

In the meantime, I know that intention, being the embodiment of energy, faith and will, in the presence of a welcoming other, holding similar intention, creates the context for change, coherence and healing.

Trust in my self and the other, acceptance of my self and the other, which means being safe and genuinely alive, loving and loveable, is the core issue of my continued existence.

References

Rogers, C.R. (1951) *Client-Centered Therapy: Its current practice, implications and theory.* Boston: Houghton Mifflin.

Rogers, C.R. (1961) *On Becoming a Person.* Boston: Houghton Mifflin.

Rogers, C.R. (1970) *Carl Rogers on Encounter Groups.* New York: Harper Row.

Rogers, C.R. (1977) *Carl Rogers on Personal Power.* New York: Delacorte Press.

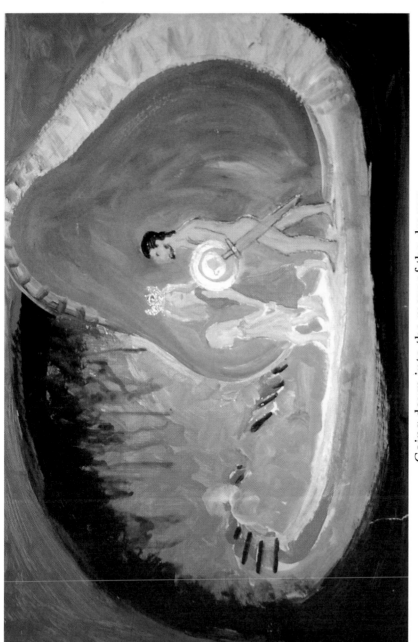

Going down into the maw of the dragon

Detail: three figures going down into the maw of the dragon

The warrior uses his shield to reflect back the dragon's rage

Detail: the warrior and the dragon

7

Dick McDonald
and
Caryl Sibbett

Companions on a Journey

The main focus of this chapter is on the interaction between three people: a counsellor, a client who is an artist, and an art as therapy group facilitator. I am the counsellor, Anna is the client and Caryl Sibbett is the art therapist who runs an art as therapy group to which Anna belongs. We have met quite frequently, both as a threesome and as twosomes, to reflect together as 'companions on a journey' on the process Anna has undertaken in therapy, and the effect this has had on us as therapists. Our approach to working together has been based on the qualitative research methodology described by McLeod (1999) and Yin (1994), and by the art therapy case study approach found in Wadeson (1996) and in the publications of the British Association of Art Therapists (2000). Thus the notebooks kept by Anna, willingly made available to us, were of great significance in a research project of this kind and earthed our work in her unique experience.

In talking through the issue of confidentiality Anna came to the conclusion that she would give herself, and those she mentions in her story, pseudonyms and leave out any specific references that might identify directly a time, a place, or a person. For much of the time our work together has centred on two rough, strong pictures produced in the group by Anna, and how these have been used both in 'talking therapy' with me, and also reflected on in the group and in discussion with Caryl.

We are glad that it has been possible to reproduce these pictures (immediately preceeding this chapter), as I have especially come to recognise that they constitute a fourth 'voice' in the shared experience of this therapy. The process of weaving together our three 'voices', and their different perspectives on the journey, has been complex. The pictures provide a way in through which others can more directly appreciate the hard graft of the ongoing struggle for truth in self-expression.

My background and approach — some basic tensions in psychotherapy and in its provision

My wife and I had returned to the UK after 15 years in East Africa where I had taught theology. My wife especially found the need both to express herself and also to contribute to the welfare of this society which was slowly becoming our own again. She was drawn to training as a counsellor with what was then the National Marriage Guidance Council. That title itself expresses the tension felt in all organisations that need to take account of the expectations of those who support them; organisations that want to guide people and promote the good of society, and yet through their practitioners seek the Rogerian 'quiet revolution', expressed here by Kirschenbaum and Henderson:

> All individuals have within themselves the ability to guide their own lives in a manner that is both personally satisfying and socially constructive. (Kirschenbaum and Henderson, 1990, p. XIV)

Kirschenbaum and Henderson go on to note:

> The half century of controversy around Carl Rogers' work simply highlights a basic philosophical and methodological question that is still plaguing the helping professions: to what extent do we rely on the individual's ability to guide his own growth and development, and to what extent do we introduce outside motivation, strategies, guidance, direction, or even coercion? That is why Rogers'

work has been so controversial, maligned, and misunderstood as well as accepted and embraced. (Kirschenbaum and Henderson, 1990, p. XV)

Yet it was largely because of my wife's pleasure, excitement and satisfaction in becoming involved in training grounded in experiential group methods that I, too, was attracted to offering myself for selection and training as a counsellor. It was mainly through the work of the Marriage Guidance Council (now 'Relate') that the influence of Rogers percolated spasmodically into Britain in the post-war years and then often in an unacknowledged form (Thorne, 1991, p. 27). It was not until the mid-1960s that he came to be studied in depth in British universities, and this meant that when Marriage Guidance recognised the need to work more directly with those experiencing dysfunction in their sexual lives and initiated a training programme based upon a behaviour change model of therapy, there was no evidence that those planning this development were aware of any incongruity involved in so doing.

Both my wife and myself became involved in the training which introduced us to the disciplines of behaviour modification, the need for careful history taking as a basis for assessment, and learning the anatomy and functioning of the sexual organs. The initial training practice for me took place under the auspices of the Department for Mental Health along with doctors and psychiatrists. We worked in pairs and quickly learned to appreciate how often the assumptions underlying our different traditions of practice are unexamined. These ranged from the basic one as to whether we sat behind a desk with two patients in front, or openly on chairs in a foursome together with two clients, to the more complex issues about whether the relationship between the two clients was strong enough to carry them through a demanding course of treatment, and whether we, in providing the programme, had a responsibility for monitoring its emotional impact on their lives together.

At the time there was no overt recognition in the inevitably brief and concentrated training programme of the tensions that were involved for counsellors accustomed to a client-centred approach in their training and supervision of being committed to a pattern of working derived from an explicitly behaviour change process. Reading again Brian Thorne's comment of some 20 years later on couple and family therapy 'that the therapist's confidence in his or her own ability to relate authentically to each member . . . is unlikely to be achieved in the absence of in-depth preliminary meetings with each person involved' (Thorne, 1991, p. 37), the contrast with our practice of simply taking a sexual history with each partner before beginning joint therapy is clear. Undoubtedly the way we worked together as a foursome over the 6 months or more which the therapy involved depended for its effectiveness on our being able sufficiently to embody those core conditions which we knew through experience to be essential in establishing a therapeutic relationship. Yet all the time our main focus was on maintaining with the couple their response to the structured programme of behaviour change for which we had contracted together, and only when difficulties arose would we have offered individual or joint therapy sessions as a way of enabling the couple to re-engage with the process.

On reflection I would see the Marriage Guidance Council's decision to provide this therapy for sexual dysfunction as an enlightened response to what was being increasingly recognised as an essential aspect of marital work. However, this pragmatic decision meant that counsellors were faced with making choices about whether they would place the emphasis upon carrying through the programme with a particular couple, or upon other needs which the couple might identify in the course of therapy. The distinction which Barry Grant makes between 'principled' and 'instrumental' nondirectiveness enables counsellors and their supervisors to identify a basis upon which choices of this kind might be made:

> In the instrumental version of nondirectiveness . . . respect for the client is not absent, but is allied to or tempered with a pragmatic concern with promoting growth. In the principled version, the therapist's actions are derived from the fundamental idea of respect for persons . . . The therapist does not attempt or intend to make anything happen — growth, insight, self-acceptance — in the client, but rather provides the therapeutic conditions in the belief that they are expressions of respect and with the hope that the client will make use of them. (Grant, 1990, p. 371)

I am aware of ambivalence in myself over this distinction about which Grant makes large claims, maintaining that these are 'not only competing interpretations of Rogers, they are competing ideas about how one ought to conduct oneself as a therapist, what is most important in therapy, what it serves, what its goal is' (Grant, 1990, p. 372).

On the one hand the emphasis given here has affirmed the sense of allowing myself to be fully present with a client, and often to hold within myself the confusion and uncertainty I may have about the meaning and implications of the disturbance that has brought this person to me, trusting that when I am able to offer a facilitative climate where genuineness, acceptance and empathy are all present, then therapeutic movement will almost invariably occur.

Yet I am also aware of uneasiness about how the discussion of what is the morally best way of doing therapy seems solely linked to an attitude of principled nondirectiveness in the counsellor rather than to the nature of the relationship that counsellor and client form together. We recognise that a human being cannot realise his capacity for creatively free activities save in society, and this is expressed in Brian Thorne's words that 'person-centred therapists start from the assumption that both they and their clients are trustworthy'. He goes on to develop this further:

> This trust resides in the belief that every organism — the human being included — has an underlying and instinctive movement towards the constructive accomplishment of its inherent potential . . . This directional, or actualising, tendency in the human being can be trusted and the therapist's task is to help create the best possible conditions for its fulfilment. (Thorne, 1991, p. 28–9)

Helping to create the best possible conditions for the client is something in which both counsellor and client co-operate and so function together as a unit through which moral discourse takes place — and language is the main tool through which this happens. That it is not the only tool is an issue that is addressed by Paul Wilkins:

> For me, it seems that there is a way of thinking that does not acknowledge that there is a powerful direction ('Talk to me') in classic client-centred therapy which is in reality no different from the 'directions' of the person-centred creative therapist. 'Dance with me' or 'Draw with me' seem to have no greater weight than

'Talk to me'. To avoid creative and expressive forms of therapy because they cannot be person-centred is not only mistaken but potentially limiting. People express themselves in many ways other than words. (Wilkins, 2003, p. 91)

I have found that one way of helping to create 'best conditions' for the client can be asking them to become aware of how they are breathing and so begin to recognise the extent to which anxiety controls how they live. Indeed, for some clients silence can be such a threat that they have to fill gaps with their own talk and they tend to put pressure on the counsellor to initiate questions that will give direction for them to continue with talk. So the invitation 'Breathe with me' allows them gradually to experience letting go of anxiety and, over time, can enable them to initiate a period of 'breathing relaxation' — perhaps at the outset of the counselling 'hour' — in which they can become aware of what it is they need to work with.

It is often possible, even at the outset of a first session, to draw a client's attention to the extent to which anxiety has altered their breathing patterns, and then to see whether they are able to experience some letting go of the tension that is there. To allow ourselves to breathe in this way is an act of trust. Perhaps for the client in the first instance it is an act of trust in the counsellor, and in the feeling of safety that has developed through sitting in the counselling room and having a sense of being accepted. I myself always accompany the client in breathing in the same way and wait for the client to become ready to continue with 'talking therapy'.

To describe working in this way is to take up a position on 'the continuum of approaches to psychotherapy characterised by a belief in the actualising tendency', which is set out and analysed by Paul Wilkins in his introductory chapter 'So Just What is Person-Centred Therapy?' (ibid., pp. 1–15). He quotes Margaret Warner's five levels of interventiveness and I would see myself as belonging to:

> **Level 3:** *The therapist brings material into the therapeutic relationship in ways that foster the client's choice as to whether and how to use such material.* The therapist may bring suggestions or interpretations, etc., to the encounter but the client is free to make use of or disregard them. I see much of person-centred approaches to creative and expressive therapies as rooted here. Many would also place experiential psychotherapy in this category. (ibid., p. 9)

I have recently undertaken to supervise a counsellor who works directly with Gendlin's 'Focusing-Oriented Psychotherapy' (Gendlin, 1996) and this has involved me both in reading and reflection, and the recognition that in some significant ways I find myself walking along the experiential path. Thus:

> Experiential therapists . . . are more likely to 'lead' their clients than are classic client-centred therapists. They may draw attention to non-verbal behaviour and interpret it, challenge, reassure, name feelings the client is (for some reason) reluctant to own and so on. Each of these is likely to be more directive than would normally be acceptable in classic client-centred practice. (ibid., p. 12)

I recognise this as describing in general terms how my practice of therapy has developed, and in particular how I have sought to integrate the insights of developmental psychology with it. For nearly 20 years I lectured to student teachers and also worked with them in applying the insights gained from the work of Jean Piaget and other developmental psychologists to understanding the way in which both children's thinking and their ability to make moral judgements develop, and how this relates to emotional maturity, their ability to understand religious concepts and the growth of conscience. For me this background remains an important resource in enabling clients to appreciate the effect their early experience of relationships in the family, and subsequently in school, may continue to have on them.

Piaget notes:

> Language always lags in its aptitude for expression. That is to say, when speaking in images we are always compelled to draw on forms of expression that we have really outgrown. For example, we say 'the sun is trying to break through the mist', which is an animistic and dynamic way of speaking, and moreover takes no account of the distance which in reality separates the sun from the mist and suggests they are actually engaged in conflict . . . It is not the child which is moulded by language; it is language which is already childish. (Piaget, 1973, p. 278)

It is out of this context that I have come to develop a kind of crude, childish, working concept of the embodied person which can provide for some clients a way in to 'owning' the tensions they experience through locating them in the body and can also enable the process of 'personal growth' as an interior dialogue or dynamic interplay of aspects of 'the self' to be consciously undertaken. For this to become a journey of discovery rather than a circular tour of the well-worn ground needs the presence of a companion who will interact from those essential core conditions. I would suggest that this approach 'resonates with the person-centred notion of the "self" as a process rather than a fixed entity' and that 'the "self" must arise from a process not merely within an individual but from interpersonal and transpersonal processes too' (Wilkins, 2003, p. 31).

It is easy to recognise that much common language usage maintains an intimate connection between feeling, emotion, and body. Phrases like 'gut-reaction', 'heart scalded', 'heart throb', 'head stuff' and many others bear witness to this physical groundedness of much living language. Taking those three basic words — head, heart and gut — what at once becomes clear is that it is through breathing that the three are connected. Breath is taken in through the 'head', flows through the throat and chest or 'heart', and reaches down to the diaphragm and so affects the 'gut'. When we go on to ask where various aspects of the person tend to be experienced we find that for numbers of people the messages about 'ought' and 'should', the judgemental critical aspects of ourselves, seem to be experienced as situated somewhere around the head. Indeed, one man who came to me described them as enclosing his head just like the motorcycle helmet he wore when he came. Others identify what they would often call the 'voice' as coming from one side of the head or the other or perhaps as located just within the head at front or back. The great waves of overpowering feeling that sweep over us in early childhood seem most often connected with the 'gut' or solar plexus and these we have to learn to control. So much so that some people learn to restrict their breathing at the throat or chest level 'on instructions', it would seem, from the voice in or around the head. This can be out of fear of the hurt and rage that might overwhelm them and everything else if it was allowed out. Another man who worked with me recognised that since childhood he had never allowed himself to breathe through his nose, which is higher up in the head, but had to allow the breath in 'secretly' through his mouth so as to trick the controlling head. Eugene Gendlin, in writing about 'a process view of the Superego', notes:

> even when the therapist is respectful of every one of the client's feelings, a very critical negative 'therapist' is at work inside most clients. Freud called it the 'superego'. It is an inner voice that criticizes and interrupts a person's every hopeful move. Even the most neutral therapist would surely intercede to defend the client's process if this negative voice were an interruption by some other person who is visibly present. (Gendlin, 1996, p. 247)

From this learning to breathe can begin a whole developmental process — a becoming adult or individual — whereby the person explores what it is like to take responsibility in the chest area or 'heart' for mediating between the controlling, often anxious, parent in the 'head' and the angry, fearful, creative, destructive child in the 'gut'. This means learning to breathe more freely and through this be in touch with the rage and fear of the child that is covering over and blocking the strength and creativity that is there. Also it means learning to talk to, and dethrone, the critical, fearful parent that is often trying vainly to control everything. This is to describe in bare outline a process that is different for every person and varies according to their particular life experience. Yet it does seem that the whole chest area becomes more and more identified with the making and taking of decisions, and that is the process through which the 'heart' grows and matures. An important way by which this is achieved is through encouraging the person to enter into an 'interior dialogue', which is yet spoken out in words, with both the 'child' in the 'gut' and the 'parent' in the 'head'. Thus for Anna aspects of her 'self' were expressed in the three images she used in her rough paintings, and they were also the 'figures' through which her 'interior dialogue' about money for the missed appointment (explained on pp. 102 and 104) were carried on both within herself, and also directly with me in 'talking therapy'.

To work like this is to make some connections with the way ancient Hebrew psychology viewed the 'heart'. For us the heart is primarily a physical organ which is sometimes understood metaphorically as the 'home' of feelings, and this is different from the Hebraic sense of the growing self as somehow belonging to the chest/heart part of the body where there is the need to mediate between the 'parent in the head' being afraid of letting breath down to fuel the frustrated rage of the child. Then having to attend to both and come to decisions about action and carry that through (often with the arms and hands giving expression along with the mouth to those decisions) and then accepting responsibility as a whole organism for the outcome of those decisions is not unlike the ancient Jewish sense of the heart as the self at its deepest centre, a level 'below' the mind, emotions and will:

> The heart . . . was the innermost spring of individual life, the ultimate source of all its physical, intellectual, emotional, and volitional energies, and consequently the part of man through which he normally achieved contact with the divine. (*The Interpreter's Dictionary of the Bible*, 1962, p. 549)

Anna had previously used the phrase 'soul journey' about the series of paintings through which she had experienced a long deep descent into the darkness and a gradual spiralling upwards towards the light. The journey that we now undertook together was one in which that spiritual dimension was explored further, though mostly without being directly named. It was as though we knew and accepted between us that the 'beyond' was also present and within.

Symbols and words — Dick, Caryl and Anna's reflections on a journey

Coming together — Dick's voice
Some five years previously Anna had worked with me over a period of two years as she explored both through words and in her painting the dynamic forces she experienced in her creativity and her sexuality as she struggled to come to terms with her relationships with two men, and to begin to find herself as 'individual'. She was then in her mid-forties. I had met and talked with her again at an exhibition of her work. Just to visit this exhibition was an emotionally searching experience: indeed, two clients who were working with me at the time described how they were both shaken by its intensity and also affirmed in pursuing their own hard journeys.

After the exhibition I met up again with Anna and broached the possibility of her painting my portrait. This was something that arose within me out of a sense of our only going this way once and not wanting at this late stage of my life to let slip away an opportunity for experiencing a reversal of our roles with someone whose courage, insight and ability I admired. I had a confusion of feelings about undertaking this 'act of self-assertion', and it was strange to sit in 'my' counselling chair and be so closely observed. I am glad of having done this — and especially of the resulting painting.

It was some six months later that Anna got in touch to say that she wanted to see me and to talk over coming into therapy with me. I had hung the portrait on the wall of the stair well as it had too strong a presence for a room. She approved of my placement and we agreed that it was not a barrier to our working together again. She identified that she wanted to work with me again because I would probe and search out things in her and not let her slip away from issues. I noticed that previously her work had centred around her father and her relations with men, whereas now her rage against her mother and her betrayals was driving her into this dangerous place. Anna was a member of the Symbolic Art Group facilitated by Caryl Sibbett. Thus the work she did in this group usually provided the focus for the process of therapy we undertook together.

When I was asked to contribute a chapter to this book I decided to approach both Caryl and Anna about whether they would be willing to explore with me the possibility of making a joint contribution. At our first meeting it felt as though we at once became committed to this.

At that meeting I decided to hand over to Anna the notes I had made of our work together during seven months in 2001. As I have the rule of destroying notes after five years, my notes of the earlier period of therapy had been shredded, but now this was the first time that anyone but myself had seen the notes I had made on my work with a client since the early days of my training. I had occasionally played out scenarios in my mind about how I would fight to avoid having to hand over notes to a client who might have the temerity to attempt to stand on their rights and breach my right to hold in confidence what I had written. In spite of changes in both law and practice I have continued to write freely 'so as to get the client out of my system' and 'not carry them around with me'. So I did have mixed feelings about deciding to break this protective shield that I had held around myself, and wondered how Anna would respond at our next meeting.

I learnt a great deal from what Anna said about reading the notes. Basically she found them to be a clear description of the process of our work together and was, perhaps, surprised that she did not discover anything new about herself . My apprehension about there being comments that would be hurtful or wide of the mark was unfounded although she did say that she could only read about two thirds of what I had written due to my scrawl and use of abbreviations. None the less this brought me to the realisation that it is in the interactive relationship in the session that response and reflection take place; that my writing up is an attempt to record this and only occasionally will involve new insights that have not been there at the time.

Anna had described the background to her coming to me through identifying a succession of emotions that flowed through her like waves moving up a beach and then running back again:

> Over the winter I have worked with two nurturing women therapists who supported me and taught me how to nurture myself.
>
> This strengthened me but now I feel rage rising that is barely in control.
>
> It's vicious and frighteningly destructive.
>
> I am afraid of letting loose this destructive power and yet I know I desperately need to let it out.
>
> I come to you because of our history, your offer to help and my recognition that you have the hard strength needed to 'survive' any 'attacks' and to 'winkle out' things I am reluctant to acknowledge.
>
> I did not want to be vulnerable. I wanted to come back on an equal level . . .
>
> I was not coming pleading to you for help. I have done a lot of work here.
>
> You are less likely to be wounded because you are not a wounded healer . . .

In his discussion of 'transference' Rogers notes the different kinds of feelings and emotions, both positive and negative, that are directed towards the therapist. So Anna brings out the tensions that are involved for her in again coming to me for therapy: 'you have the hard strength needed to "survive" any "attacks" and to "winkle out" things' have a positive feel to them. But there is also the underlying resentment involved in 'I did not want to be vulnerable. I wanted to come back on an equal level'. Rogers goes on to make the fundamental point:

> From a client-centered point of view, it is not necessary, in responding to and dealing with these feelings, to determine whether they are therapist caused or are projections. The distinction is of theoretical interest, but is not a practical problem. In the therapeutic interaction, all of these attitudes — positive or negative, 'transference' feelings, or therapist caused reactions — are best dealt with in the same way. If the therapist is sensitively understanding and genuinely acceptant and non-judgmental, therapy will move forward *through* these feelings. (Rogers, cited in Kirschenbaum and Henderson, 1990, p. 129–30)

However, for me Anna's words — 'You are not a wounded healer' — gave substance to what I had been vaguely aware of in myself. I am an eldest son who was welcomed into the world towards the end of the First World War as a kind of sign of hope for the future, especially for my mother. I am one of those who, in Erikson's words, had felt the world to be a place to be trusted by the way the first years of my life gave me that secure base. I have not had to seek counselling myself, although I have learnt to know myself at a deep level in training with my wife and David and Vera Mace, the founders of one of the most important organisations in the field of marriage enrichment. Leading workshops for groups of couples where the leader couple work openly with their own ongoing relationship — with its conflicts and enjoyments, its sexuality and power struggles — is an effective way of maintaining reality in communication with oneself and one's partner and learning how to love.

That there are both positive and negative aspects to this limitation in my exploration of myself is reflected in Anna's decision to return to me as someone who did not need protecting from the explosive rage she felt churning inside. This was despite her sense that she had in the past not felt able to trust me with the depth of despair that she previously experienced in letting go of her relationship with Callum. When Anna said to me 'you are not a wounded healer', I had to reflect on those questions with which Rogers confronted himself when he drew out the characteristics of a helping relationship. In particular, such questions as 'can I be strong enough as a person to be separate from the other? Can I be a sturdy respecter of my own feelings, my own needs, as well as hers? Am I secure enough within myself to permit her her separateness? Can I permit her to be what she is — honest or deceitful, infantile or adult, despairing or over-confident? Can I let myself enter fully into the world of her feelings and personal meanings and see these as she does? Can I step into her private world so completely that I lose all desire to evaluate it or judge it? Indeed, can I be present with her so as to affirm her as a living person capable of creative inner development?' (Rogers, 1967, p. 50–6).

Those were the kinds of issues that her expectations of me as a counsellor, expressed in that sharply focussed phrase, indirectly brought up. I was aware of my expectation to be 'just good enough' without anything to spare as the norm of working, especially when I can allow my intuitive sense of what is there for her to be given words, trusting that when it is 'off course' we can recover.

Symbolic expression — Caryl's voice
My experience of contributing to this chapter has been a similar process to that of the therapeutic quadrangular dynamic, which it recounts and explores. Both the therapy and the writing have been an interweaving of four 'voices'. I use Anna's own words transcribed both from interviews I had with her and from her own journal. I would describe myself as a researcher/therapist in this piece of work.

In June 1999 I initiated The Symbolic Art Group as a process-orientated group with experiential art as its main focus. An explicit verbal contract was made within the group, which identified that the group's purpose is art as therapy for creative and personal development. Confidentiality in the group is assured and so it hopefully offers a safe space with the potential for in-depth work. It was intended for those who already have experience of this approach and each three-hour session includes both art-making and verbal processing. The group's ethos arises out of my practice of art therapy which has a strong person-centred foundation supplemented by psychodynamic, Jungian, existential and transpersonal theories. The group provides a non-judgmental, non-directive, non-interpretative space, and is founded on the belief that the essence of art as therapy is that 'creative art practice has an integrating effect on the artist and promotes mental health' (Simon, 1992, p. xi). My person-centred approach aims to provide two conditions which Rogers (1967) suggests foster constructive creativity: 'psychological safety' through my being congruent, accepting and empathic towards the individual and their art; and 'psychological freedom' through my allowing complete freedom of 'symbolic expression'.

My approach has developed as an integration of my personal journey and my professional training. The former has involved several periods of life-threatening illness during which my own ongoing art-making process was a vital component of my expression of the experiences and of my recovery. After the first of these experiences I began my professional training, which eventually led to my becoming a BACP Registered counsellor and a State Registered Art Therapist. My way of working is underpinned by my belief that the art-making process has the potential to be therapeutic in and of itself, and particularly so when facilitated by a trained clinician.

My work with Anna illustrates some key aspects that underpin my beliefs about the therapeutic value of art as therapy. I believe that the symbolic art process can enable expression of unconscious material, thereby making it accessible to conscious awareness. It offers a dynamic multi-sensory experience where the artwork can act as a container where projections and introjections can be sifted through, the false self and projections from others disowned and the organismic self owned and actualised.

During that part of the therapeutic journey portrayed here, Anna was working in the Symbolic Art Group and other workshops I facilitated, and she shared with me that she was separating from her husband, James, due to his disclosure that he had been involved in a long-term relationship with her own mother. She felt a huge sense of betrayal by two key figures in her life, and this was compounded by her mother protesting her innocence and blaming James. Anna experienced fear and rage as she entered a long process of seeking to assert herself and the truth in a way that would not destroy her mother or herself. Anna decided she needed to recommence one-to-one work by seeing Dick again as a counsellor. She wanted to work with 'the masculine' and she also valued Dick's capacity for 'winkling things out' and his ability 'to contain'.

During that period Dick and I were not in contact but each knew that Anna was working with the other. There was a dynamic interplay between Anna's work with Dick and with myself in that sometimes something in the counselling relationship that seemed difficult for Anna to get to verbally would be brought to the Symbolic Art Group and allowed to come into consciousness there. Other times some of the art that emerged in the Group was later taken to Dick to be processed verbally in a one-to-one context. Other material emerged in the art-making that Anna felt would be inaccessible through words, and in the same way material emerged in the one-to-one counselling that had not in the Group.

Anna's voice
Dick and I had worked together in 1992–4 when I was struggling to survive the

loss of a love relationship with Callum that had allowed me to 'flower' in so many ways. I had been awakened by it in body, mind and soul and with the loss of it, I lost the 'self' I had found. He was lost and with him the keys to me.

The task of reconstruction and recovery, even simply survival, seemed almost impossible — but the choice was stark: survival and recovery, or death or endless sleep. At times death seemed easier, and I held it as the last resort if the pain was too much. That was the only secret that I consciously kept back from Dick.

I'd never worked with a counsellor before and found the discipline of it difficult. The sessions were painful, but I knew I was learning and gaining from them so I kept returning. He held up a 'mirror' to me and gradually I gained the beginnings of a sense of myself that took me past the possibility of physical death.

During this time I was working through my emotions and exploring my insights through painting. I was also challenging myself by going to classes on psychological insight — Jungian interpretation, and in time Caryl Sibbett's classes on Art as Therapy. I went to the first one thinking that I had a lot to offer art as therapy, but came away astounded at the power of what I had created within the safe space that Caryl carefully makes. This began a long-term relationship with 'spontaneous art making', and with Caryl herself.

Dick had attended the preview of an exhibition I held. When we talked, I told him that James and I had decided to separate after James had told me of his long-term relationship with my mother. Following this revelation I was in deep shock for a long time. The depth of the betrayal by the two key people in my life (apart from my children and my father who had died) was horrific. Both of them insisted on its unimportance, and I needed other people's responses to reassure me that I was not overreacting.

At this time I was receiving great support from an agency which offers counselling to those affected by alcoholism in their families (my father was an alcoholic). I also had discovered a loving woman healer who emotionally, and physically, and spiritually nourished me and taught me how to counter my mother and James shifting blame and how to empower and 'feed' myself. We went right back to the point of conception and recreated through images in pastel and clay the spark of conception, concentrating on replacing my mother's negativity and fear with love. At first this felt hopeless and using positive affirmations felt utterly daft, but gradually it began to work and in time became internalised so that I no longer beat myself up for my mistakes but accepted them and congratulated myself on the biggest and smallest positive actions. This took time to take effect, however, and the first winter after my separation was very lonely and frightening.

I had had a successful exhibition, which allowed me to relax for a while and really feel my emotions. It felt like a very 'dead' time, but looking through the journals of the months prior to working with Dick I am amazed at how much was happening and how much insight I had during a time when I felt 'stuck'.

During this time Dick had asked me to paint his portrait. It was difficult for me going back into the scene of so much pain but I was reassured by my own things — props of the job — and by Dick's careful avoidance of counselling.

Now *I* was looking at *him* with the eagle eye!

The portrait was completed in February and when he called to collect it and pay for it, we both allowed the conversation to deepen. He was insightful and succinct in his comments and I was reminded of how focussed his way of working is. That had its attractions in such a 'foggy' time, but something, perhaps pride, held me back from seeking help. However, I took on board his comment on my being in a desert — dry and barren after the jungle of emotional work.

My mother continued to press on me her innocence and to demonise James. I was struggling to assert myself with her, which meant not only going against her wishes but directly challenging her. I was terrified of killing her — if I cut away her false 'nice' persona what was there underneath? If I insisted she accept my truth, would that not destroy her? I was experiencing a lot of fear and anxiety, as well as anger, and had a number of warning 'dark man' dreams where I am being attacked and have to fight for life.

At the Symbolic Art Group I was making images of exhausted sleeping animals. Much of the time I felt zombie-like. Plummeting despair would hit me, but I realised it passed through me more quickly than before.

But when it began to swing into destructiveness, I grew afraid of the immense rage I could sense within me. I swallowed my pride and sought help from one strong enough to contain, and tough enough to survive, whatever form the rage would take — Dick.

Waiting for our first session I began an image of a man strangling a woman. It felt like my own daimon had turned against me and was actually trying to kill me.

I kept few notes of our first session, but I remember discussing Kali[1] and the necessity of destruction. I'd been pushing myself to create as this was my main way of voicing my inner state, but for the first time in years the act of creation had lost its value. Dick encouraged me to stop all painting. And I agreed with relief. He asked if I ever destroyed work. I replied, 'Very, very rarely' — and thought about what I could obliterate with relish.

In the second session we talked about expressing the rage through paint. I said there was no place that could contain the amount of paint I would want to throw about.

I came out of the session energised again and went directly to Symbolic Art. I began with a curve like that of the earth, and painted below it red and black. On the curve was grey to represent the fog I was in. Above it were flashing flickers of yellow and white — the area of energy. I am still in the grey but am now aware of the massive destructive energy beneath me and the flares of vibrant energy above me.

I felt my task was to make a connection through the layers.

From that I moved to clay and made a vicious 'beast' with open jaws and 'devil' horns. I am very against demonising animals but this felt like the only way. In talking afterwards I said something about looking forward to destroying it.

I brought these to Dick at our next session and was amazed to find he felt sorry for the beast! The quotes I made after include, 'The structure of your life is being blown apart . . . to allow the new "you" to be . . . I did not expect you to work at this depth and rate. It needs careful containing'.

After a weekend focussed on dance and movement and the elements, I had a hugely significant dream. In it I was travelling with my father and my son, eventually coming to three huge mountains that had abnormal geology — I could 'see' inside

---

[1] In Hindu mythology, Kali — 'black' — is the consort of Shiva and the goddess of death and destruction, and thus conveys a sense of God as both Creator and Destroyer.

them the magma of lava (I drew it as a tongue) under a thick layer of limestone. I wanted to explain to my father about the mountains but he did not want to know and disappeared. I was alone.

This was followed a few nights later by another sequential dream. I was to go deep inside the solid volcanoes on a quest. I *had* to go but was very afraid as no one who had entered had ever returned. When I woke it seemed it had something to do with retrieving memories — something precious.

In the next few days I felt listless and queasy — the fear of what needed to be done.

I 'forgot' my next meeting with Dick.

Then at the group meeting I 'faced' it through images. I began with the 'frozen' volcanoes . . .

Caryl's voice
I encourage people in the group to make art in relative silence and Anna reported that silence is important for her — 'something extraordinary can happen, revelatory.' She went on to say:

> Art-making brings to awareness things you weren't aware of before, so couldn't have been talked about. The words are only a reflection of what comes up in the images . . . the insights from the art can help me own things I didn't want to see. Art gives you something that the words in verbal therapy don't, in that it's often coming from somewhere you didn't recognise in yourself.

When Anna took these dreams she had to a counselling session with Dick he asked her where she was in this. Anna reported to me:

> I was unable to answer that with Dick. So I knew I could ask myself that in the Group and this led to the painting in which the three aspects of self appeared. There appeared limestone steps going down. The sedimentary rock reminded me of the grey area in the earlier magma painting. The grey got laid over with the feeding regime that my mother used. And the anger . . . it was laid down over the years, and in the dream it was cracking.

In one Art as Therapy session Anna painted an image of three figures or aspects of herself 'going down into the maw of the dragon'. Anna reported:

> In the image the three aspects of self are: a warrior figure who is resolute; a female figure who is fearful and needing the warrior to come too; and a child figure who is leading the woman down the steps.

The child wears a pink dress and leads the woman by the hand. The female has red hair and wears a red dress and a silver crescent moon headdress containing a gold circular sequin. The female is looking back to check that the warrior is following. The warrior is naked, has black hair and beard and is holding a gold shield and sword. They are going down towards steps into the open mouth of a dragon that is also a cave in the limestone-covered volcano. Anna interpreted this to be her inner child leading the afraid feminine and the strong masculine. This process seemed to me to be a form of descent into the self which might be seen as a *katabasis* or a 'going down' into the deeper self. It also parallels the myth of Persephone, which Anna reported as identifying with.

Then Anna reported that, in the last 15 minutes of the session, she created another painting to help her go deeper down into the dragon.

> I asked myself What is down there? and answered it in the art in a development of the *Going down into the maw of the dragon* picture. The big dragon was backing off. The child figure was all excited and the warrior figure was holding the mirror (shield) up to the dragon. This was the mirror of truth.

Anna described how 'the little girl claps her hands together in excitement and delight as she knows the dragon is losing power.' She journalled:

> what I see now is that the cavern is a maw and the frozen lava a huge tongue and the red glow the gullet. I can go down past the frozen word maker into the belly of the beast.

This image was a depiction of a powerful stage in Anna's self-protection from the damaging projections of her mother by, as with the medusa, reflecting them back assertively. Later Anna journalled that 'I have felt the dragon that is my mother and not given in.'

In these dragon images Anna faced and explored the 'power and the intensity of the magma' or 'source' and also the dragon or difficult dynamics with her mother. She strengthened her own sense of self by accessing her child, woman and warrior aspects. This was to enable her to access the energy and anger and move beyond the grey 'dead space' to a stronger more integrated sense of self. Part of this process involved re-creating and re-parenting herself through the artwork that helped her to enter the cave or womb. Anna reported:

> The family ethos was one of where anger was generally suppressed or occasionally erupted and there was no model of how to express it constructively. It was unsafe. The art is a safe place to express it . . .

Dick's voice

Anna described how difficult she had found it to allow herself to begin to use dialogue between the different aspects of herself she had identified through painting she had done in the group, and she brought out the two strong, rough, vivid paintings. What came out in talking with Anna was the dominant role of the child in wanting to go on down into the place of 'rage' — the open mouth of a dragon that is also a cave in the limestone-covered volcano.

What Anna now commented was 'that is the mouth that can't speak' referring to the huge grey pear shape that I now saw as an open mouth with teeth around it. 'I never trusted speech — it was never honest'.

The second picture was of the three facing the dragon — a jagged red orange yellow splurge against the black background. The child at the rear this time — though Anna described the child as both frightened and excited. The warrior in front now using his shield 'like a mirror' reflecting the 'rage' back at the dragon —

and so neutralising its power with the 'mirror of truth'. This was 'Medusa', the powerful, destructive mother. Anna described how:

> the little girl claps her hands together in excitement and delight as she knows the dragon is losing power . . . I can go down past the frozen word-maker into the belly of the beast.

Anna was not able to say much about how 'the woman' was, who seemed carried along in between the child and the warrior in a kind of unaffected way. What then came up was Anna identifying an incident when she was 11–13 years old. Anna had done something successful and her grandmother was affirming and praising her, and Anna looked at her mother and saw hatred in her eyes. She has denied this 'reality' to herself — yet it returns and she 'knows' it. When I asked about her mother's background, Anna described how she was born after a brother who became 'the precious one' for the mother as there had been a previous miscarriage— so she never got the same affection and love as her brother. This is the jealousy expressed so violently in the look when Anna, as it were, takes 'her' place in the affection of the mother.

What I then brought up with her was about her missing the previous session and not having cancelled it with me. When I asked, 'Did she owe me money for the last session?' — this led into a dialogue — the warrior saying, 'Of course you must pay' and the child saying 'We could use the money in much better ways, after all nothing happened . . . ' and the woman in the middle not being able to reach any conclusion. So I left it with her and accepted payment for the current session. I then explored with her more fully how on the Bank Holiday she had not been able to look at her filofax and being away with a friend visiting a garden, had found herself being 'lost' in the shadowy fringes of the 'no feeling' place she 'went into' as a child. I reflected with her on 'dissociation' as a place of escape yet also of nothingness.

I never did ask for payment for that missed session. Perhaps I too was drawn into 'nothingness' and was unable/unwilling to assert my needs. Anna had noted in her journal my comment, 'If I was afraid of hurting you I would be no use to you'. Here I did not live up to my own aphorism, maybe because I had a sense of Anna's dismay at not being able to find a voice for the woman.

A second meeting of the companions — Dick's voice
Most of the second meeting of the threesome was taken up with interactions between ourselves with the two paintings as a fourth presence propped up against a bookcase facing us. During the last part of our meeting Anna described herself as having been very tired over the previous week. When I asked what had been happening, to my amazement, she said that she had been away with her mother and actually sharing a room together. She maintained that this had been a good thing for her to do as she had been able to live in, and with, the separation that she had achieved from her and so begin to establish a different way of relating. She had not recognised this experience as creating enormous tension within her which she was still carrying. I suggested that here and now she explored using breathing — which she admitted she has great difficulty in applying — to see whether she could let go of the tension and anxiety. Once she attended to this she found herself freer.

Clearly this process of co-operating together as a threesome in reflecting on how therapy works is inevitably also a continuing of the journey for the main protagonist — and so too for her companions.

Another shift in the working — Dick's voice
We had arranged to meet as a threesome on a regular basis so as to develop insights from our different perspectives — but this was not to be. Caryl was not able to attend our next meeting at the last minute due to illness. This gave the space for Anna to raise directly with me her current need to work with 'separation' from James — a need which she experienced as rising out of the rage she felt within.The rage comes from:

> being controlled in subtle yet powerful ways by my mother and by James. My mother wanted me to take her point of view. I was bottle fed at precise times and not breast fed, and so was in her control.
> The mouth in the picture is the way a snake opens its mouth and the limestone is a path leading down on which they are walking . . .
> I had to go down past the frozen words into the belly of the beast . . . the limestone is cracked covering over the strength of the volcano of emotions which was bursting through . . . A mountain of layers and layers of sedimentary limestone built up over years of doing nothing . . . Creatures that die and float down . . . passive over against volcanic action which is thrusting and positive, or destructive.

I asked about her 'wilderness' time in the mountains when she had sometimes stayed there overnight for the experience of the dawn light. Anna said that this was her place and her way of both communion with, and letting go of, Callum and that intense relationship which had the power of the early child feeling for her father. She had been so constrained by her mother into her clockwork pattern of timed feeding and being wakened when she was asleep to be 'given' the bottle — and this was the mouth — the oral need — so that kissing mouth to mouth with Callum was the centre of the physical relationship. At first Callum took the initiative in the kiss, but then Anna took over the initiative and 'kissed' Callum and this was deeply satisfying. Her time in the mountains had been hard and intense — anger at being separated from Callum and despair that threatened life itself: 'the body wants to live despite so much emotional and physical pain'.

In letting go of the need for Callum she had experienced in the mists and cloud a sense of that presence which is beyond and above:

> the physicality of the mountains and the spirituality of air and cloud — within cloud you can't see much, but from a distance it is beautiful like a kiss between the element of earth and the element of air.

A further development — freedom in owning and exploring the self — Dick's voice
Anna had arranged a kind of 'ending' session with me and used it to reflect about the extraordinary recent development she had experienced in her working in a group workshop where Caryl provided that safe — indeed sacred — space:

The large image began with a horizon line (half way) which became also the line of surface. I drew little figures of myself swimming, cut them out and took pleasure in standing them on the surface, deep in the water and flying in the air. They expressed the freedom I now felt to have the choice to go deep or stay on the surface or soar above. Adding a silver moon on the left and a gold sun on the right set the scene for the life-size figures.

She described how she had lain down on the floor and had her outline drawn round on heavy paper. She then cut this out and produced three figures of herself: one from the 'positive' cut-out and two from the outline left by the cut-out, the 'negative'. I suggested 'like the positive and negative poles in an electrical current'.

These became for her the three aspects of the feminine personality — the 'crone', the 'maiden' and the 'mother'. The 'maiden' was the positive cut-out in the centre and she described this as that which is 'of herself and for herself' and not 'for' anyone or anything else. This was then clothed in filmy, watery fabrics and given her own face.

The 'crone' was the dark 'moonlit' side which was gradually explored. This was then clothed in black and the moon darkened. The 'mother' was a sensuous figure glowing with gold in the light of the sun and was then clothed in a dark red skirt — and was ready for belly dancing against a backdrop of red and gold.

Anna described the process of making the images as 'mirroring what was already there' and 'delicious — a delight to do'. When I asked whether there was any connection between the three figures and the previous figures that had appeared in the paintings — the child, the woman crowned with the moon, and the male warrior — Anna at once said 'of course, now the masculine has been taken into each figure and found its place there'.

I was struck immediately by how directly Jung's process of individuation, of the animus and the anima, was expressed here. But I took up *The Carl Rogers Reader* and read out to Anna from his description of the process of therapy the following:

> 7. His *concept of self* becomes reorganized to assimilate and include these *experiences* which have previously been *distorted in* or *denied to awareness*.
> 8. As this reorganization of the *self-structure* continues, his *concept of self* becomes increasingly *congruent* with his *experience*; the *self* now including *experiences* which previously would have been too *threatening* to be in *awareness*. (Rogers, cited in Kirshenbaum and Henderson, 1990, p. 240) (original emphasis)

She was taken by how exactly the words embodied her own experience expressed in the art-making. She had shown me photographs taken at different stages in the making process and had emphasised to me that it was the process that mattered, not what came out as an end product.

Caryl's voice
Because the artwork was tangible, Anna reported that it was insightful to reflect on it both at the time of making and over an indefinite period of time afterwards. The symbolic aspect was experienced as 'living' and holding multiple dynamic meanings.

A key aspect of this was the non-linear, spiral, timeless involvement in art as therapy as compared to the verbal process. Anna had described it as 'like dipping into a big circle' with 'smaller cycles being part of larger cycles' and 'symbols linking across time'. Thus Anna noted the difficulty she had in exhibiting her paintings, as doing this according to their chronological creation would not reflect their multiple connections and the quality of re-cycling issues again and again; whereas in the group there was 'protected space and time', 'bounded time' and so there was a structure enabling engagement in personal art which otherwise could be neglected. She reported:

> the last five minutes can be significant and you don't know you are doing something, you just do it. Then you look and say 'oh where'd that come from? It's more dynamic and more revealing. Being contained leads to symbolic vitality.

I believe the dynamic and insightful nature of symbolic art-making was a vital component in Anna's movement from 'fixity' to 'flowingness' (Rogers, 1967, p. 132). Anna commented:

> the images come before the words and then I can find the words for it. There is a lot of truth in the image . . . the art-making in the group helps me to understand the process of change I am going through. My unconscious is often ahead of where consciousness is and this enlightens consciousness.

Anna's voice
Caryl's reflection is always insightful. She has a subtle way of asking a question that will allow something to happen. The group can sometimes crystallise something that I didn't see and didn't want to see. The art-making provides a tangible record and allows meaning to unfold across time. It is many-layered in its connections. The art-making there helps me make a connection to unvoiced feelings — shock, sadness, anger, love, jealousy and many more.

Our ways divide — Dick's voice
The writing of this chapter has brought the three of us further on our journeys as we have co-operated in trust and affection with one another. We are particularly pleased that it has proved possible to reproduce the paintings that now seem to take on something of the character of a map of distance travelled. We hope they will allow 'meaning to unfold across time' for those who read and look.

As a way of drawing together our different experiences of life and the fact that it is the influence of Carl Rogers more than anyone else that has shaped our therapeutic interactions, I quote from Brian Thorne:

> Once more Carl Rogers tells me . . . what I already know. He tells me that I am trustworthy and desirable, despite my many imperfections, and that the more I can risk being fully alive the more I will be a transforming companion for my clients and for all those whose lives I touch. In short, he assures me that to be human is to be endowed with the spirit of life and to enjoy a uniqueness which paradoxically links me to my fellow human beings, my ancestors and the whole of the created order. (Thorne, 1991, p. 188)

References

The Interpreter's Dictionary of the Bible (1962). Nashville: Abingdon.

BAAT (2000) *Newsbriefing*. September. London: British Association of Art Therapists

Gendlin, E. T. (1996) *Focusing-Oriented Psychotherapy: A Manual of the Experiential Method*. New York, London: Guilford Press.

Grant, B. (1990) Principled and instrumental nondirectiveness in Person-Centered and Client-Centered Therapy. *Person-Centered Review*, 5 (1), reprinted in D. Cain. (ed.) (2001) *Classics in the Person-Centered Approach*. Ross-on-Wye: PCCS Books, pp. 371–7.

Kirschenbaum, H. and Henderson, V.L. (eds.) (1990) *The Carl Rogers Reader*. London: Constable.

McLeod, J. (1999) *Practitioner Research in Counselling*. London: Sage.

Piaget, J. (1973) *The Child's Conception of the World*. St. Albans, Herts: Paladin.

Rogers, C.R. (1967) *On Becoming a Person: A Therapist's View of Psychotherapy*. London: Constable.

Simon, R.M. (1992) *The Symbolism of Style: Art as Therapy*. London: Routledge.

Thorne, B. (1991) *Person-Centred Counselling: Therapeutic and Spiritual Dimensions*. London: Whurr.

Wadeson, H. (ed.) (1996) *A Guide to Conducting Art Therapy Research*. Mundelein, Ill: The American Art Therapy Association.

Wilkins, P. (2003) *Person-Centred Therapy in Focus*. London: Sage.

Yin, R.K (1994) *Case Study Research: Design and Methods*. Thousand Oaks, CA: Sage.

8

Tracey Walshaw

Skateboarding on Redundant Mortar

Will idiosyncrasy be the new therapy buzzword for the 21st century?

Finding a way of writing this chapter has brought into sharp focus my idiosyncratic ways of being, ranging from how I write to how I engage in relationships with clients. How I present this material is idiosyncratic. This writing is about me, not just client relationships. It feels like a 'writing authentically experiment' in that being real, how I am, how I write, has not changed for this chapter. This has challenged some of the massive introjected values I have carried from formal academic training. I had to challenge constricting thoughts such as, 'there's not enough references', 'its not academic enough', 'I should be more explicit with the theory'. What was familiar was the process I experienced that eventually shaped the structure of my sharing this with you as readers. It took several drafts for me to let go of being instructional, and trust you as readers to make what sense of this as you will.

> Assuming that the counselor adheres to the person-centered philosophy of honoring the client's perception of the world, what a counselor does in person-centered counseling is quite flexible depending upon the idiosyncrasies of the client, counselor and situation (Bozarth, 1984, cited in Bozarth, 1998, p. 127–8)

I like this quotation from Bozarth. It started a whole process of thinking about what it is like to be 'me' in a therapeutic relationship with myself, the client, my supervisor, 'the person-centred thought police' and, in moments of extreme paranoia, what seems to be everyone from the insurance company, through BACP, to BAPCA — indeed anyone who might have a definition of how I should translate my profession into a particular way of being. What is and what is not acceptable? Of course the reality of what I am asking is: what is acceptable and unacceptable about my way of working and whose locus of evaluation do I use as a yardstick? More pertinently, where did I get the yardstick? This chapter explores just what it is for me to be in relationship fully, what inhibits me and whether I can know for sure that being myself is facilitative in the counselling relationship.

When I reflect back on my development as a counsellor I can see that there is a familiar pattern that I'm sure is not unique to me. In my training I introjected conditions of worth about what a good therapist should be and even look like. I subsequently spent the majority of my personal and professional development recalibrating this 'counselling self-concept'. No one actually asked me how I thought I should be — they asked me how I thought I should be with clients. The focus of the feedback concentrated on the implications for the client and I simply got lost. Later on down the line, the implications for me and myself caught up with me like an express train. When I reflect back there seems to have been some kind of relationship detachment in my training and I know that hooked into a detachment within me. For me, training was about getting it right, passing the assessments and, in some way, being task-orientated. There was an imbalance, which, in hindsight, has been counterbalanced by the learning that has come to me from being in person-centred unstructured community groups. It is through being left to struggle with my own learning and congruence in the intimacy of these groups that a depth of self-intimacy has been facilitated. It feels disloyal saying that about my training, and loyalty, of course, is a factor that has silenced me in the past. My training was significant as a catalyst to discovering what I wanted to do: find a shape that seems to be organic, authentic and idiosyncratic within a professional framework. What started in training now seems to have progressed into a lifelong process.

Trusting the process is not a mantra for me which comes from training rules or my counselling self-concept. It is not a doing phrase. It is a being phrase. It is about being fluid in the present and being available. I wanted to include my clients in the process of writing this chapter. Here was the first hurdle. Could I? Would that be ethical? Would it damage the process? Would I get 'done'? The judgements started to arrive. I remember discussing this with a group and some folk were worried it would be unethical to ask for feedback from 'live clients' (I interpreted 'live' to mean current clients). I really could not get my thinking around this. The major objection seemed to be that it would change the relationship. My knee-jerk response was: 'Of course it would! And so?' Every time I express myself honestly in a relationship something changes. I don't see that as damaging; it is the way of life. This is how it is. Then I got tied up with, 'Am I being defensive?'; 'Is there something I do not understand?' Eventually I recognised the fundamental difference: I am a person-centred practitioner, I am not interested in thinking I know better than my client. If I ask them about the possibility of being a part of this chapter, and we have a dialogue about it and they say 'yes', I don't then have to assume, 'Ah, but they don't really know, they might not really understand'. I trust my clients.

There seems to be lots of information about what you shouldn't, couldn't, and mustn't do and not a lot about the grey areas in relationships. So I decided to tell one of my long-term clients about the book remit and asked if she would like to be involved. This felt very scary, in that it felt like asking the client for something for myself. She, without any hesitancy, said she would be interested and so this chapter is based around a dialogue we had. Who better to give me feedback about how they experienced my idiosyncratic way of being than a client? How could I not involve my clients? There have been lots of learning and challenges on many levels for me in this process.

I have been working with Molly for over two years now. She is a play therapist and we started our counselling relationship when she was in training. When we discussed the possibility of talking about our relationship, and in particular how she experiences me, she immediately agreed, sounding excited and keen. This reflects her customary willingness to engage in relationship. She suggested we set up a time which was not a counselling session and said that she would probably want to do some expressive work (working with sand, clay, figures, paint). This has been a key way of expressing and exploring her process in our relationship. I read her the remit and we taped the session.

Molly 1:   I was thinking what is different? What happens in this relationship that's different between you and anyone else I've ever seen? The way you work. There have been things (*sigh*) that either both you and I have made a note of . . . like you saying, 'I don't know if this is right, but this is what I'm feeling'. Pushing the boundaries. I suppose that's about pushing the boundaries, this is what feels right.

Tracey 1:   So is that about risk-taking? This is what I'm feeling about what you're talking about. Me not being totally reflective, including a sense of myself in those reflections. That takes me right back to our initial contracting session where you said, 'if I'm bringing things here that I need to take to supervision, I want you to tell me to take it there.' And remembering your feeling of startledness when I said well if you're bringing it here then there's a reason for that and I'm not going to tell you to do that. I feel that was a difference.

Molly 2: Some things, especially in the beginning, I was carrying as a trainee and I was struggling with my role as a play therapist, 'this is what a therapist is supposed to be'. And I've had a few other counsellors. I'd an idea about what a therapist should be.

Tracey 2: What I should be like?

Molly 3: Yeah, and because I was struggling with my own learning about how to be a therapist myself, there are things certainly in the beginning that I was doing textbook. This is what I read. What they'd told me at the course. What I think I should be. I suppose from that point your, 'if you bring it up, it's here' changed it right from the beginning. It helped from the beginning that I could bring whatever I wanted, and counselling should be like that.

Tracey 3: Sounds like you came in with some structures and I'm wondering if having those structures in place and me saying in reflection, 'well actually you don't have to do that', might have felt a bit wobbly.

Molly 4: . . . or freeing.
And there were a few things that I thought counsellors don't normally do that you've done, and how powerful they have been. How right they were. The stone, the glass stone I played with and used in sessions. In one session you said I could borrow it if I wanted, and in my training it says: 'all things in the therapist's room are the therapist's, and they stay in the room for anyone else who wants to use them.' And I remember thinking, 'this is not right'. And I borrowed it. It symbolised something.

Tracey 4: Quite a concrete thing.

Molly 5: Yeah, very visible and it was about reminding me that actually I can look after myself and I don't have to do things on my own. And one day when you said, 'it's yours, it feels right it's yours.' It was very hard for me to take it. (*Upset*) You don't come for counselling because everything's lovely dovely do you? I came because things are difficult and for you to actually hear and see that and it was like something extra, something so responsive at a time when I felt I wasn't getting the responses I needed from other people and to get someone responding in a way that felt so appropriate, it was so unexpected. And it was so unexpected and in my view to what counselling was. Like it was outside that, 'Counsellors don't give the client gifts'. It was at the time very powerful and has continued to be. And there is probably a time when I won't need that stone as much, but I still use it and that's two years ago.

Tracey 5: For me to hear that, I knew it had impact, but not that much of an impact and I feel very full hearing just what impact it had, like oh blimey that other stuff happens outside here. I knew it was important but I didn't know how or why. It sounds like the importance is not about the stone but about our relationship.

Molly 6: Yeah, absolutely. It was a symbol of that relationship and that actually I work very hard in the sessions and I work hard to try to feel better. It was something concrete of, 'I'm being listened to and my feelings are being heard and that my feelings are valid'. To say I'm hearing what you're saying, it's valid and that it brought it outside. I don't just come for counselling and come for that session. It's all the time, the work, the process stuff carries on. I took the stone to my insemination because it was like saying, 'you're doing alright and whatever you're feeling you're feeling.'

Tracey 6: You're allowed to have those feelings.

Molly 7: Very valuable and your gold boots. (*We both laugh here*) Counsellors don't lend you their own things. That's like a no-no, even if they are things that they don't need. It was like it was perfectly OK. You're a real person, you're not only a counsellor, a therapist, that actually you've got a life.

Tracey 7: I've got a life.

Molly 8: And you've got possessions in your life and on a particular occasion you had a particular possession that I could really use. I certainly wouldn't have asked, even if I'd seen you one day in your gold boots. And there you were saying, 'I don't know if I should offer this', you were hesitant. It was great. It was really nice. It was like saying you're a whole person. Links in with sometimes you've said bits of things about your personal life. Snippets and sometimes that's been about what's happening that's relevant and adds to the situation or the exploration. It added something and from my training and experience of other therapists, counsellors don't tell clients anything about themselves. It's like I do the pouring out, you reflect back, but your own stuff is clearly out of the picture. And maybe part of that is you do it in your own home, so your life is in the relationship because I'm in your house. Even if you didn't say anything at all about snippets about your life there'd still be those bits of you in the relationship because I don't come through a hallway that has absolutely no evidence of you and your family. I don't come into a hallway that's absolutely anybody's.

Tracey 8: It's personal. I manifest myself in physical things because actually it would be almost unreal if you came into this clutter and there was no sense of me in here as well.

Molly 9: I suppose it is clutter but I don't really see it as that as there's nothing that really restricts me from what I need to do. I've thought this before, that really it's quite permissive. It's all right not to have everything neat. I can play with the sand. It's all right if it goes on the carpet. I can ask, have you got paint. It's permissive. It's all right to be. Counselling I've had before had been in centres or through GPs. You had your 45 minutes and then were ushered out. Sometimes I was so upset I couldn't just go straight home, I needed just five minutes to get myself together.

Tracey 9: I absorbed in my training there should be none of me. You know I look around and think, 'oh shit', when I recognise the rocking chairs. Chairs are supposed to be still.

Molly 10: This unwritten law.

Tracey 10: Think I've shed some of this gradually. I remember contracting at the beginning and telling you about my renal disease. I know that was different because you were a trainee therapist. There could be times when we were in each other's worlds, like conferences when I might talk about my disease. I worried it could affect the relationship. You know I was telling you something massive, not just saying I've got a limp; I'm saying I've got something quite serious that could affect us. This is how it is. I've wondered if that stops folk bringing issues about death and dying.

Molly 11: I heard, and the more I think about it was you were saying, this is how it is and sometimes I might not be well and I'm letting you know. The same when I was saying when I first came to see you if we could work together because I was saying these are my issues. Have you got a problem with them? And I think its like letting me make that choice for myself, and that feels different too; it's right from the beginning showing bits of yourself rather than being this bland, faceless person.

Tracey 11: I remember a few months back when I was ill and in the middle of a session you said I looked dreadful. And I remember that really challenged me in some respect around, 'Well, why wouldn't you care about me?' That's a real challenge to me because . . .

Molly 12: You're here to look after me.

Tracey 12: She's here, it's her session and she's checking I'm OK. Its just like for an instance it was, 'oh yeah this is about being in a relationship and I do look like shite and people will notice', and something for me changed then about 'this is alright'. It's not just about you in the relationship, and me in the relationship, but about that bit about how we make the relationship between us.

Molly 13: Being honest, that thing about the thought police, the therapy counselling boundaries that says, 'this is what you should do', and 'this is what you shouldn't do'. And that sometimes that can help and sometimes it can hinder and restrict. When you're learning to be a counsellor those rules are there to help until you've got more experience.

Tracey 13: Sounds like you're grounded in yourself, like that was useful but maybe it's not anymore, like the stone.

Molly 14: Counsellors who stick to those limit themselves and the counselling. This feels right. My experience is you do, 'oh I don't know if this'll be a balls up', but trust this feels all right, a bit hesitantly.

Tracey 14: Being withholding is safer, but stops something else. I'm not that potent a therapist that if I make balls up of something you won't tell me. Something about there being a dialogue.

At this point Molly suggested we model our relationship using the expressive materials. She worked with some wooden bricks creating a structure and I worked with a sandtray and miniatures. When we were both ready, we shared what the meaning was for each of us. On the one hand this felt like very familiar turf and on the other really exciting and different in that I was sharing an expressive piece of work with Molly in this session. It felt very personal and very powerful. She asked me to go first. I went through my sandtray explaining what it meant for me; about things that affect my authenticity and things which I've had to shed to be able to be present in the relationship, especially things about rules and regulations. Here it felt like Molly was facilitating my process. Below is a transcript of a part of that process.

Tracey 15: I've taken some things on board that I've had to shed. That being in relationship helps me to identify that being a trainer, supervisor doesn't feel separate. Some things come into this room about me as a trainer, as well as a therapist. I can't deny them. There's some things about your course that I've had to keep pulling myself back from. And that was part of the process, and it was in here. You were struggling with something and I was struggling with something about your training situation, and that feels like it's changed now. You're not on the course and you found a way of dealing with it.

I explored the symbolism in the sandtray about boundaries, 'this is a bounded relationship and there are some things that I wouldn't bring in here, and some I would'. I referred to a metal anvil miniature and talked about it symbolising my weight, something solid you can bang against.

Molly 16: Before you said that, I was thinking anchoring.

Molly asked me about a skateboard I had positioned on the edge of the sandtray.

Tracey 17: Something about skating around the edges. There is a definite boundary but that doesn't mean I can't look over the edge.

I used a miniature of a woman in a boat with a baby to talk about some of the content of our sessions.

Molly 18: That's interesting, sometimes I'm out of the boat and you remind me. Its not that I've forgotten that it's the most important thing (*here she refers to her desire to have a child*), but sometimes I get swayed. It feels you reflect that bit in me that I don't lose, it just gets missed and sometimes you've said thing by reflecting, 'Oi Oi . . . What's the most important thing?' The anchoring thing. It's really powerful. Powerful that you say, 'look don't forget this thing.'

Tracey 18: Suppose it's like me being visible as opposed to saying, 'I wonder why?' Like I'm waving my arms about saying HELLO!

Molly 19: Yes. 'Hello. Wake up here!'

Molly talks about the wooden structure she created to represent our relationship.

Molly 20: Sometimes when things have been difficult I've normalised it. I've got used to it being difficult, I think it's all right. Sometimes what you say, or how you say it makes me realise I'm going up a sheer face. This is fuck hard work. It makes it real, makes me go, 'yeah I am having a crap time and I'm pretending I'm doing OK and I'm not'. That reflective thing, something extra, that moves it on. It doesn't move it on, it stops something happening, it stops the pretence.

Tracey 20: Like a bite?

Molly 21: It might sting, but then after it's OK. Sometimes it feels the kindness you've shown is very difficult, because it so needed and wanted. (*Crying*) It's good, like sometimes you've given me a hug. Sometimes it's been so difficult that really it'd be better not to, because sometimes it's like what I really want is me dad, or mum or partner to do it; or a baby, that's really hard. Maybe there were some times it would have been good if those thought police had said, 'you don't hug your client' and sometimes it might have been better if you hadn't, because I could have pretended and gone to work alright. But in the end I feel, so that particular session may be hard, but on the whole it's keeping me more in touch with my feelings. (*Crying*) I feel like I'm good at feelings. I cry a lot. I know what I felt because I can feel my feelings. I express my feelings. But sometimes I don't. I know that when I don't suppress things, at times when you have said something that just hits the mark. It was what exactly I needed? I was thinking a bit about why I've been coming for so long and I remember one time I'd been feeling OK and I was talking to someone who'd been in counselling for a couple of months and she was OK. I thought about coming to see you once a month and I came with that idea and was upset. I was absolutely sobbing and I remember saying, 'when am I going to be all right?' I remember you saying, 'perhaps you can come every other week', because I wasn't feeling all right. I remember you saying, 'you won't have to come when you can tell someone else about this stuff', and it really made me think. It was like you were saying, 'I'm (*Tracey*) no one special, you can talk about this stuff to anybody'.

Tracey 21: Precious.

Molly 22: And its like you were saying, 'whenever you can find people to talk to about this then you won't have to come'. Humble. Emm, not right word. It was very freeing you saying you're nobody special. And I want to tell you, you are.

Tracey 22: It sounds like, 'Oh I can do that'.

Molly 23: And it's like I can tell anybody anything I want to. It's only me that stops that, like the thought police. It's only me that stops me, feeling embarrassed, awkward, and guilty. What you said then has helped me talk to other people. It's good to have this type of conversation, about what things make this relationship. It feel like is a bit of a thank you. A bit of an opportunity to say this is how you've made a difference. To let you know what a massive impact you've had. I'm not saying you've done it, I know you can't do anything if I don't bring the stuff.

Tracey 23: The nature of what we're doing is unusual, but sounds like part of this talking about it is also an acknowledgement to yourself, as well as talking about our relationship. It's bigger than that.

Molly 24: Yes.

Tracey 24: The other thing that I'm aware of is I got wordy then. How difficult it is for me to accept your thank you. Don't necessarily think it's a 'being a therapist' thing. I think that, in general for me, it's stuff about receiving that's difficult. It's ridiculous I can feel myself pushing it away. I'm really touched Molly. It's hard for me to acknowledge the thank you.

There was a silence here for a while and something came into my head that Molly had not mentioned, but I wanted to hear her present response. That is the focus of the next section of transcript.

Tracey 25: There's one thing I would like to ask you about. Do you remember when you came that time and I'd forgotten your appointment and gone shopping?

Molly 25: And you weren't here.

Tracey 26: And we had a conversation on the mobile phone about me not being there.

Silence.

Molly 26: It was really horrible really. A different day and it wouldn't have had any impact, but on that day I really wanted to see you. And there are some days when I'm not looking forward to it, don't need to come. It was difficult, you were very apologetic, and I survived, it was fine. It's like I didn't think you didn't care, it was a mistake, like the time I forgot to see a child. It wasn't that I was not thoughtful, I just forgot. And I guess that empathy was there really, I know I beat myself up about it. I gave myself a hard time.

Tracey 27: I feel sad, stinging, that I made a balls up, but there's a robustness, although it's hard to hear this. I wasn't doing anything proper, I was shopping. And knowing it was upsetting, but there's robustness when it's talked about. It changes the relationship. There is something about a dialogue, things do change, and it's right it does change.

Molly 27: Don't think there's been any major surprises today. Don't know about you, but for me I've told you some of these things before. And it's like you've helped me a lot and I've helped you. Whatever, the relationship will change, don't think it'll make much of a difference.

Tracey 28: Thank you Molly. I've learnt a lot about that skateboard (*referring back to the miniature in my sandtray*). This has been a privilege. I just like being in this relationship.

Molly 28: That's good. It's good for me too.

Before I start to talk about my learning from this I want to say it is a deliberate choice on my part not to engage in a case study analysis. The dialogue speaks for itself: it is doing what it is exploring, a process within a process. I trust you as readers to be creative and bring yourselves to an understanding of what is going on in this relationship. This is exciting and also scary for me in that I do not know what is going to come back from your interpretation. In not telling you, I am surrendering control, which feels both empowering and disempowering.

I see clients at home, and I remember in training I was encouraged to have a clutter-free, client-friendly environment. On reflecting on how I present myself and the physical environment I create when working with clients it has become obvious that I am a person who is cluttered, thus my working environment is cluttered. I work in a colourful room, filled with toys, paints, objects, family photographs. I also have two rocking chairs: one for the client and one for me. There is a lot of me in this room, and there is a parallel process as is apparent from the transcript in that there is a lot of me and my process visible on lots of different levels in my relationships. Maybe I up-front things about myself via the visual scene. With Molly it has always felt all right. Only recently, when I had a new supervisee who informed me he had visual dyslexia and thus could feel distracted by lots of visual stimulation, did I feel slightly anxious about my way of being. This challenged any potential smugness I had about 'I'm cluttered and that's OK'. But none the less I didn't jump into clearing away, but rather we explored how we could both work with this.

I remember the two incidents that Molly chose to talk about: the stone (Molly 4) and the gold Doc. Martin boots (Molly 7). They were the biggest challenges to some of the introjected values I had about being a therapist. On reflection it seems ridiculous really that these could throw up such turmoil in my counselling 'self-concept'. I'm noticing more and more a feeling inside me like being on that skateboard: 'is this stepping out of the boundaries?' There is always a counterbalance of 'this is a boundaried relationship, any choices to push around the edges of these are informed choices'. They are not irresponsible whims or fancies, but choices informed and underpinned by my person-centred theoretical beliefs.

Through supervision and counselling networks I check things out professionally but always come back to that sense of rightness in the relationship. Asking my client to do this feedback session felt inclusive and working on an edge. It is the first time in client work where I have done a personal piece of expressive work. I felt very visible and exposed, but trusting of the process. It's like I know and she knows the relationship is sound and we can trust each other. There is a sense of shared responsibility.

Self-disclosure is something I use in therapy if it feels relevant. I notice my uncomfortableness with the use of the term 'use' and I feel that is because I don't go in with the intent to use self-disclosure as a tool. It just happens; there is nothing premeditated or staged about it. Clients and supervisees know things about me. Molly knows I have a degenerative kidney disease. It feels all right to tell clients because it can have an effect on the relationship. I do not have a standard contract that includes it, it is just that I recognise some clients are in my counselling world, and I'm in theirs, so I will be mindful to say. With other clients it feels less pressing, unless of course I am ill. Occasionally I've had clients who worry about my health and hold things back, but inevitably these things surface in the process of therapy, and as they do we talk about the meaning for the client. I seem to have clients who have issues around their mortality and it is strange to think they have a counsellor for whom this is a very live every-day issue.

Learning about myself from working with clients with issues around mortality is a fluid and surprising experience. One client, Bernie, whom I worked with for over four years, brought me a wealth of self-learning and revelation. One week she was ill in a session, so much so that we chose to work downstairs in my conservatory because she couldn't make the stairs. The next week she was dead. I was shocked and distressed, especially because I found out through someone ringing me because she remembered I used to be her therapist. My initial internal reaction was, 'used to be, I still am!' Her dying did not break that boundary. I really struggled with what to do. The grief felt really sticky, like I couldn't shake it off. I thought at first it was because I was a secret — very few people knew she was in therapy with me. So how could I mark her dying? The ritual of attending her funeral didn't seem like an option. Some weeks later I was in an encounter group and was hit by a thunderbolt. The reason I was so distraught was not just that I'd been in a long-term intimate counselling relationship with Bernie, but that I didn't expect to outlive my clients. In the next moment came the realisation that I didn't expect to outlive anyone. I'm sure to some of my colleagues this was not news, but to me I really got hold of something. This must have been in the relationship with Bernie but on the edge of my awareness throughout our time together. By not being in physical relationship with her any more something happened to me. This client gave me this gift. I recognised this expectation of death was something that really tied into my actualisation process: I was not born with it. What I recognise is that when all the conditions are present, they not only provide a nurturing and facilitative environment for clients, but are also a catalyst for growth for me. Hence the fundamental importance of supervision; there are always things to untangle and process. Looking at my process in relation to my clients provides a real petri dish for new discovery and growth; not to mention the identification of a few unhealthy cultures that might be festering in there too.

Humour is fundamental to me. It is an aspect of my personality that I am allowing to become more present in therapy. I have struggled with this big time in therapy and supervision. 'Counsellors are not funny' is answered in me by an indignation which shouts, 'Oh please!' Humour is as present in counselling relationships as anger, upset, depression, and joy. I am funny. I'm funny as a trainer, a person, a mum, a partner, a colleague, so why not then as a therapist? Big introjects here. I'm not talking about cracking jokes in therapy, but some things are funny, bizarrely so. Some of the imagery I use is quirky. There's nothing sophisticated about some of my images or metaphors, for example, likening someone's process to a can of corned beef, with the little key that you keep turning and, if you're just lucky enough, you get the lid off without shredding your fingers to bits.

Often if clients are describing something and an image comes to mind, or a miniature catches my eye in the room, I may reach for it. Sometimes it's not quite right and the client will reach for another one. It often feels like an added dialogue with miniatures. My miniature collection seems to be ever expanding. I sometimes think that calling myself an 'expressive therapist' has given me permission to collect lots of things that I would not otherwise house in my home. Interesting in itself that I give myself yet another label, expressive therapist, to justify why I would have art material available to clients. It almost implies that you need things to be expressive. I can honestly say I never collect something thinking, 'oh this would be good for client X's process'. It is a random collection of items. Often clients bring miniatures to add to the collection. I remember when this first happened. A client brought me a wonderful carved wooden camel from his travels, telling me how he had gone to great lengths to chose it, lining several up, inspecting the grain and colour of the wood until he found just the right one. I felt two things: extremely flattered that he had gone to such thought for me; and also worried about whether I was supposed to accept gifts from my clients. I even began to border on analytical interpretation, but managed to draw back. As is always the case in person-centred work, the process outs itself. I just needed to trust the process. It wasn't my camel at all. It was his. It soon became apparent from each session when he picked the camel up that the camel represented a relationship he was working on. So, there she stayed on my shelf and, eventually, when this client felt he could put this relationship in perspective the camel stayed and he moved on. Then, and only then, did it feel like part of my miniature collection. But how glad I was that I had accepted it and allowed the process to unfurl without pondering too much on why. The client told me why and brought his own expressive medium into the relationship.

Often my miniature collection feels like a lending library, in that clients can, if they wish, take things home with them that they have been working with. I am smiling here as very occasionally I get them back in an altered state. Once a Grim Reaper miniature returned minus his sickle. Interestingly this client did not notice the lack of appendage and it evolved into a very significant session. As I write this I recognise I have no emotional attachment to the things in my therapy room, and that the miniatures only appear valuable and special when they are at the centre of a client's process. If clients have been working in the sandtray, I may ask them if they want a photograph; sometimes they do and sometimes they do not. I feel I have nothing invested in offering this, I simply have a camera. I used to be adamant about always clearing the sandtrays, but recently I noticed I am not as meticulous. If a client wants to work in the tray we sometimes clear it out together. In paranoid moments I wonder if this disrespectful or sheer laziness? Am I cluttering up their process with other clients' work? The truth is I do not know, but I have not noticed it stopping clients building their own worlds in the sandtray.

One of the 'oughts' I have brought to my counselling relationships has been, 'Tracey Frances Bernadette Walshaw should be one hundred and ten percent reliable'. Good enough would never do. This reminds me of Molly talking about the time I missed her session. When it happened we talked about my acute sense of responsibility but I recognise now in the mere fact that I raised this issue, that there is something here that I have not let go of. I have massive introjected values about letting people down, not being responsible, not being good enough. Although I can be empathic and accepting of less than super human feats from others, I do not afford myself this understanding which can lead to me shouldering more than my share of the responsibility, which can unbalance the relationship. The feedback session with Molly was about us sharing responsibility for our relationship and me learning not to take on too much responsibility and yet recognising when I have made mistakes. Sometimes clients forget to come to sessions, there are misunderstandings about times, people get ill and circumstances dictate a late cancellation. When this happens I endeavour to ask the client what we should do about this, what feels fair so that we come to a mutual decision. My response is as standardised as the uniqueness of each relationship I am in.

Money is one of the hardest issues for me to get my head around after working for fifteen years for the NHS and then a stint in a GP's surgery. Until I went into private practice I never had to deal with the uncomfortableness around money in a session. Give me a difficult session, difficult content and process and I engage; taking money seems so awkward for me. I know all the issues about worth, being professional and so on, but somewhere inside me it feels difficult. I do it. I have a sliding scale, which really does slide. I ask clients to negotiate how much to pay me, and this feels so individual. For instance, I have had clients where it has been a course requirement for them to attend therapy. Besides all the issues this raises with some clients, I remember one client in particular whose issues clustered around intimacy. If he were to pay me what he thought was the going rate, then what he had planned out would mean we were to meet every third week. Some chance of intimacy. I challenged this and negotiated the fee down. This I rationalised as 'the relationship is important and when his circumstances change he can up the fee', which happened. For clients whose circumstances change it sometimes means dialogue or renegotiations of fees up or down. That's my commitment to them and theirs to me. I can honestly say I have never felt ripped off or cheated by a client, and I know enough about myself to feel I would challenge this. Besides which, it manifests in other ways in the relationship: process does not happen in isolation. Like illness and death the issue of money can become a big elephant in the room that, unless it is addressed, can impede true dialogue.

I have found myself recently reflecting about what Molly had said about my hallway. It struck me as important. It challenged my rigidity about routine, in particular routine of place, and I notice that recently I have offered clients the choice of working in my conservatory or my workroom upstairs. I initially rationalised this with an excuse about the weather being so nice. On reflection the excuse is the starting place for giving myself permission to challenge some of the residual rigidity from my training about clients not liking change or disruption to their routine. In fact, maybe it's not the client it's the therapist who doesn't want change. Often these rules are a means to control the client and what I am interested in exploring is how to test when this is the case; how to recognise and respond in those instances when testing the rules can prove most fruitful.

Researching this chapter has afforded me many insights into the parallels within my client, training, supervision and organisational work. My world at times seems small, with negotiating boundaries being an integral part of my working life. Counselling relationships do not happen in a sterile, vacuum-sealed flask. Each new relationship challenges all of my senses and my ability to maintain flexibility, transparency and authenticity. The process never stops, just shifts shape.

Many thanks go to Molly whose engagement in this exploration has given me great insight, and also enabled me to chip at some of the redundant mortar that has held me back. What a gift.

References

Bozarth, J.D. (1984/2001) Beyond reflection: Emergent modes of empathy. In R.F Levant and J.M. Shlien (eds.) (1984) *Client-Centered Therapy and the Person-Centered Approach.* New York: Praeger, pp. 59–75. Reprinted in S. Haugh and T. Merry (eds.) (2001) *Rogers' Therapeutic Conditions: Evolution, Theory and Practice. Vol 2. Empathy.* Ross-on-Wye: PCCS Books, pp. 131–43.

Bozarth, J. D. (1998) *Person-Centered Therapy: A Revolutionary Paradigm.* Ross-on-Wye: PCCS Books.

9

Irene Fairhurst

An Idiosyncratic Client-Centred[1] Relationship

[1] Throughout this chapter, being consistent with my usual practice, I use the term 'client-centred' when referring specifically to therapy and 'person-centred' when discussing theory and applications of the approach, which are more general.

Introduction

Whilst the major part of this chapter is a very personal account of a therapeutic relationship, I would first like to share some thoughts, attempting to link the concept of idiosyncrasy to person-centred theory. I find this practice often helps me make sense of the world.

As I wondered about the meaning of idiosyncrasy to me in my work as a therapist I began to think about how idiosyncratic personality traits might develop. I was reminded of Rogers' nineteen propositions (Rogers, 1951, pp. 483–524) regarding the personality and behaviour of the individual and particularly Proposition XI. Rogers writes about manifestations of experiences, which are 'symbolized, perceived, and organized into some relationship to the self'. These could be 'positive' personality traits or idiosyncrasies. 'Negative' traits would be manifestations of experiences which are either 'ignored because there is no perceived relationship to the self-structure' or 'denied symbolization or given a distorted symbolization because the experience is inconsistent with the structure of the self' (Rogers, 1951, p. 503). In other words 'positive' traits are in awareness and can be growth-promoting, whilst 'negative' ones are not, and can therefore suppress the actualising tendency, or growth-promoting drive of the organism.

Furthermore, Rogers suggested that the internalisation of denied or distorted symbolisation, 'negative' personality traits, resulted in conditions of worth.

> A condition of worth arises when the positive regard of a significant other is conditional, when the individual feels that in some respects he is prized and in others not. Gradually this same attitude is assimilated into his own self-regard complex, and he values an experience positively or negatively solely because of these conditions of worth which he has taken over from others, not because the experience enhances or fails to enhance his organism. (Rogers, 1959, p. 209)

So, a person can have distorted beliefs about who they are based on what they have had to do in order to feel valued by 'significant others'. Their behaviour patterns or idiosyncrasies will reflect this. As I was thinking about my own 'positive' and 'negative' personality traits, I became aware that some of my 'positive' personality traits have developed from what were behaviour patterns acted out unconsciously in response to conditions of worth. Often a behaviour pattern, which develops in response to a condition of worth in childhood, is the most appropriate way of surviving the situation the child is in. However, it can become 'negative' when it is no longer necessary in adult life and impedes psychological development. For example, through the work I have done on myself, I have realised that one of my conditions of worth was that I was valued for what I could do for others and this meant never having needs of my own, always ready to go the extra mile, or ten. In other words the message was: if I live my life at the beck and call of others, without having my own needs, I will be valued. This is a fairly common condition of worth, but powerful nevertheless. As a child perhaps I needed to behave in this way but as an adult I identified this condition of worth and the 'negative' behaviour patterns it lead me into. At that point I could have jettisoned that part of my personality which really enjoys sharing with others. Instead I feel it has become two of my idiosyncrasies: willing availability and generosity of spirit, which manifest themselves in the specific therapeutic relationship shared in this chapter. This 'negative' trait has been transformed by bringing it into awareness and is now part of my idiosyncratic way of being which I very much value.

A second type of idiosyncrasy is what I would call 'professionally developed'. These relate to me as a client-centred therapist and involve facets of my self expressed in my therapeutic relationships with clients. These expressions of my self have evolved as a result of specific training or experience in the person-centred world. Examples of this type of idiosyncrasy are: my own commitment and fidelity to the concept of the actualising tendency as the cornerstone of Client-Centred Therapy; my knowledge of the power of empathic understanding; the importance of valuing the whole person, unconditional positive regard for the 'not for growth' parts of the individual as well as the growthful (Mearns and Thorne, 2000, p. 114); and my conviction that it is the therapeutic relationship which is the healing factor in Client-Centred Therapy (Fairhurst, 2000a).

Working on this chapter has made me aware of how my idiosyncrasies are manifested in some of my therapeutic relationships and how they can sometimes be consistent with offering the three core conditions of Client-Centred Therapy. By this I mean that my empathy for a client, my understanding of their way of being with me in the therapeutic relationship, usually informs me of how much I can risk verbalised idiosyncratic empathic responses or verbalised congruent responses, whilst 'maintaining my trust in the client's self determination' (Bozarth, 1998, p. 101). Dave Mearns refers to the risk of the 'use of self' by the therapist when quoting David Tidmarsh (1993): 'There was a risk in what I had done. I had to trust that he could handle my response.' (Mearns, 1994, p. 18).

Risks were also involved in working on this chapter. It was a collaborative undertaking between myself and a client, to whom I refer here as Em. The chapter is mainly made up of extracts from Em's journal interwoven with comments from both of us. Em had from time to time mentioned her desire to write about her experiences and we had discussed the possibility of collaborating on something. I knew she had kept a journal, so working together on this chapter seemed a good opportunity to offer. The part of the editor's proposal which particularly struck us was about including 'a client's ideas and views on the therapeutic relationship, the idiosyncrasies of the therapist and the impact of this on their lives'.

Even Em's referral to me could be viewed as idiosyncratic: an example of how I respond to an unusual situation in a particular way. I had been working with a client who worked in the Social Services of a nearby Local Authority. After one of her sessions she asked me whether I would see one of her colleagues. We talked through the boundary issues and she was sure it would not affect our therapeutic relationship if I worked with this particular colleague. I explained that I would have to go through the same procedure with her colleague and she agreed. Apparently my client had realised she was running late one day at the office, and left hurriedly, saying, 'Must dash, I'm late for my counsellor'. Em had asked her the next day who her counsellor was, as she was looking for one. My client gave Em my number and she contacted me. From the start this relationship involved risk as we openly explored the possible boundary issues. She said that being a social worker she understood about boundaries. She didn't want to talk about work issues and she was sure my relationship with her colleague wouldn't be an issue. We decided to work together.

Em and I met for the first time in April 2000, and had fortnightly sessions until June 2000. We didn't see each other again until September 2000 when we had weekly sessions until January 2001. We then continued either weekly or fortnightly until January 2002, when Em began to come monthly with a view to finishing in April 2002.

The therapeutic relationship

Journal extract 1 (February 2001)

> *What can you tell about a person from their house? So much if you look hard enough.*
>
> *Take my counsellor for instance. When you stand or perch (cos the armchair's full of books) in the front sitting room you feel that you're in a personal space. You see a woman of substance, a woman who is busy, who is not slowed down by chaos, or at least has lots of balls in the air. A woman who is loved (so many birthday cards, to which I craned my neck to peek at the messages) I noticed that most were funny, unusual or beautiful and I thought that must be how they see you. You can tell she is clever and influential and people are seeking her wisdom. You can tell this by the books and the letters and the messages and the phone which rings so often before clicking into the professional, neutral message. You can tell by the tapes and the video camera and all the trappings of a woman who trains therapists and changes lives. You can tell by the mosaic of pictures, photos and paintings that she sees beauty in things and grabs it with both hands, that she holds joy to her, that she likes blue glass, which I collect. I can tell she is my kind of person, but someone who it takes courage to be. I can tell.*

Comment (mine)

For those of us who work in private practice in our own homes it is much more difficult to hide our idiosyncrasies, even if we wanted to. Em learned something of me, her therapist, from my sitting room where I occasionally make appointments after a session.

Journal extract 2

> *I'm finding it hard to sign off because I don't want to connect my name with yours. It took me days to be able to write your name, but I will sign my name with pride, just like I wrote yours with disgust and trepidation because we are linked, like all human beings are and to deny humanity is to collude with the lies that perpetuate pain. I won't do that.*
> *With Pride*
> *Em*

Comment (Em's)

That was how I ended a letter (one of my less angry ones!) to my abuser and when flicking through my journal to help me think about the questions at the heart of this book it leaped out at me. I have been questioning whether I would dare to attach my own name to this chapter and this reminded me of the importance to me of being able to be proud of myself in my relationship with the abuse, my feelings and my therapy.

Journal extract 3 (October 2000)

If I were a train . . .

I started the journey with all the other trains. There were a few hiccups, but no major delays. Until I was five years old that is. Then I derailed, froze to a halt (deadly leaves on the line). With no one around to consult, check the damage or help me repair — I carried on my journey, off the beaten track. Lost, but still moving.

I rejoined the original track at age 17, when, after coming unstuck on my lonely track I found help in a number of sources. They guided me back to join them. We discussed the original derailment and I told them of my journey so far.

Then I was off again, more determined than ever. Some said on a fast track even.

At various points I'd hear a rattle, would worry a little, but keep going.

Comment (mine)

To me Em's 'rattle' could be her actualising tendency tapping at the door of her awareness.

Journal extract 3 continued

However then came the most exciting part of the journey. I saw scenery that took my breath away. I saw mountains and streams. But I also saw red lights. I'd stop, see that there was no obvious danger ahead and carry on. I was frustrated. I did not want delays in such a beautiful part of the journey. If I could just keep going.

Eventually, after being stopped IN MY TRACKS by some flashing, blinding lights (somewhere in Norfolk) I could no longer ignore the gnawing fear at the back of my control panel. What was that rattling? Was it wear and tear or was it the engine? Perhaps it had been more damaged than I knew in the original derailment.

I tried to slow down, go a bit easier, ignore the fear, but the rattling got louder and I came to a slow but screeching halt. Luckily, because I had begun in those last few miles to anticipate the need for help I managed to stop in a good place, where at least there was help. I had heard there was a good mechanic and together we began to survey the damage.

We realised there was extensive damage in the engine, that some parts were lost or beyond repair. However, as a whole it was fixable — we could substitute some parts, oil the old parts that were still working and by making some adjustment to the control panel and to my way of driving it was possible for me to continue on my journey with a satisfactory MoT[2] pass and a renewed hope and determination.

---

[2] An MoT (Ministry of Transport) Test is a legal requirement for UK vehicles over 3 years old to test their roadworthiness.

Comment (mine)

Em's description of her understanding of her process reminds me that Rogers' theory of personality is based on the concept of the actualising tendency being about the whole organism. As Bozarth says:

> The actualizing tendency is a directional process. Although it involves assimilation and differentiation activities while maintaining wholeness, the wholeness is perpetually changing. It is a tendency towards realization, fulfilment and perfection of inherent capabilities and potentialities of the individual (Rogers 1963). It is a selective process in that it is directional and constructive. It tends to enhance and maintain the *whole* organism/person. (Bozarth, 1998 p. 29, my emphasis)

Journal extract 3 continued

I am just beginning that journey. The mechanic is coming along for the ride initially while we try out the new machinery.

Comment (mine)

I particularly like the reference to me as 'the mechanic', not the driver, and my 'coming along for the ride'. I also like the way Em refers to 'we' and the fact that the original session felt like a collaborative exploration of the damage.

Comment (Em's)

I wrote that in October 2000. That's nearly eighteen months ago. Can hardly believe that. It makes me smile, because at that time I thought that a commitment to myself and to the 'journey' meant — 'perhaps I'll keep seeing Irene 'til Christmas'. If you'd told me then I'd have carried on seeing her for so long, I'd have felt disheartened — 'Surely I'll be better before then'. I was eager to get on my way — show myself and the world that I didn't need anybody again. But we carried on — not because I wasn't 'better enough' but because I was better enough to realise that continuing to see Irene did me good, did my heart good and reminded me of my strength. And I'm thinking that's where the relationship comes in. My test drive has lasted a long time — because it was in itself a part of the journey — for its own sake and for what it's taught me and perhaps Irene.

When I wrote the 'train story' I was six months into my therapy with Irene and I thought I was over the worst (maybe I was — I can live with maybe these days). I had reached a point of self-understanding. I usually talk about self awareness, but it was deeper than that. What Irene did — beyond therapy as I'd previously experienced it — was that she walked alongside me in my mind and in the sessions while I tried on my new shoes and practised walking in them. Most importantly I found self-acceptance and explored the 'safety implications' of being who I was — who I am. She was the softest (and safest, most beautiful) cushion.

Comment (mine)

On reading this, I feel so moved and not a little embarrassed to be sharing it publicly. I hesitate to respond, feeling in danger of 'picking the petals off the rose', but I also feel it important to say that Em has sensed what I consider to be one of my professionally developed idiosyncrasies, to which I referred earlier: my conviction that the relationship is the healing factor in Client-Centred Therapy.

Journal extract 4 (December 2000 birthday reflections)

A haven is only a haven if you can leave it knowing you can always find your way back or better still if you can take it with you. If it exists within you and you know it and you trust it, you can own it, call upon it.

If you exist within it you are not free. It can be a prison — a safe one all the same, but a limiting space where you become institutionalised, creating rules that govern you.

This year has marked a change. It feels enormous and weighs heavy with endings, a mixture of sadness and release. And yet like fireworks initially and more a dawning recently, it is dotted with beginnings, openings and preview of a new and unexpected sense of freedom . . . Sometimes the sheer contentment and relief of knowing happiness like a trusted, if occasionally forgetful friend is enough to stop the searching and yet I keep finding. And when I find those moments of certainty and courage and hope and self-love and respect I want to hold them, never let them slip away. But when I do for a short or longer moment, I notice that amidst it all there is at the least a glow, an increasingly present sense of trust — in my life and of myself.

Journal extract 5

3 Jan 01

Dear Irene,

Well there's a first — never felt the urge to write to you before. I'm seeing you tomorrow. Let's see what am I going to talk about — I'm gonna brainstorm. I want you to know that I'm better. Don't laugh, you know what I mean. I'm feeling better generally all the time. Last time I saw you I felt better, back at work, coping, positive, looking forward, but not quite able to connect with the happiness I could see, so near yet so far — a bit unreachable. You helped me understand there were bits of me that didn't find the change so easy. I secretly remembered my inner child while we were talking, only briefly, then I forgot about her again. I sensed the truth and what you were saying, she was egging you on saying yes Em you want me to stop bugging you, you are getting scared of me, will I wreck things, Dan doesn't like me.

I've just realised she's been doing the talking. I'm trying to decide who's writing this — I want to be in charge — but then she shouts out — No, it's my journal too and if I want to mess up your nice little pattern I will. So ha! You can keep patting me on the head for being quiet, being there for you to ignore and reflect on at your convenience but sometimes (not too often mind, I'm not completely unreasonable despite what you think sometimes). I want or need more than a pat on the head. Yes Em that's right, I helped you, I taught you and I finally gave you back the driving seat, but you so quickly tried to forget me, strap me in the back of the car and drive as fast as you can even though I am frightened and I want you to slow down. So I shout, I call you, I throw things at you — anything to remind you that I'm there. And you notice the noise and the distraction and how it makes you feel, but you don't want to see me in the back — so you beep your horn, you drive too fast, you get frustrated in traffic and you are so busy trying to proceed or to look outside that you forget to stop and talk to me — not just about me to people in a bid to gain more insight and control over me but **to** *me.*

One of us wants to stop seeing Irene and I don't know which one or are we both unsure? Would I miss her? Would we miss her? What is it for? I need to think about what we get from her. This is a strange one. I feel that I'm getting what I need in my life. I keep noticing how happy I am — how sadness always passes, how trust and love make life so much more alive and I feel able and eager to take control back and have the drive to make the things happen that I want. I still want surprises, it's not that I want to control everything, it's just — what about the bad surprises? What if I get too controlling through fear of losing it again — or what if I can't hold things on my own? Maybe I'm scared to be left holding the baby. Maybe Irene's been a reliable baby-sitter, maybe A has too — she's been there to talk to when the baby's kept me up all night and I know she'll understand.

Irene, do you think I can do this on my own? I'm doing such a good job now. I don't want to keep paying and working at things cos that distracts me from just being and living, but maybe it reassures me, that if I forget and I get distracted by anything bad (inside and out) you will remind me and that will help me stay on track.

The best thing is that I don't need to resolve this all alone — come out with an answer now — cos we can talk about it tomorrow, but knowing me I'll find other unexpected things to talk about. I've probably just saved myself 35 pounds working out that I've got some confusion and conflicting thoughts about the counselling now. (Knew that anyway — but I guess the conflict's now more acceptable to me.) See, I can do stuff on my own — but I look forward to having you there tomorrow!

Just had a huge dilemma about how to sign off (What's the message? How do I feel about you? What do I want to convey to you?). So I guess I'm not ready to sign off just yet.

For now,

Em

Comment (mine)

In this journal extract Em writes about her 'inner child'. Dave Mearns describes different 'bits' as configurations of the Self:

> When walking around inside their existential Self, clients sometimes talk about different 'parts' of the Self . . . While clients often use the simple word 'parts' to describe dimensions of their Self, for our own understanding we use the term 'configuration' instead of 'part' because each 'part' is itself made up of a number of elements which form a coherent pattern generally reflective of a dimension of existence within the Self. (Mearns and Thorne, 2000, p. 102)

> Developing configurations within the Self is a way of becoming expert in social living and preserving sanity. (ibid, p. 116)

One of Em's configurations was a five-, or even four-year-old little girl, whom we called 'little Em'. One evening, Em's partner phoned me and said she was in a bad way, and would I talk with her. She was experiencing a flashback and I asked her if she could get to me, as I was available for the next couple of hours — she seemed astounded that I would ask such a question. At her next session she said that she had been 'little Em' and asked me how I could expect a four-year-old to drive. She had felt angry with me and not understood.

Journal extract 6

28 March 01
Irene,
Today is an Irene day — I don't feel like not seeing you is a problem (anymore than seeing you after a hard day at work is a problem) but the knowledge that I'm seeing you next week is a reassurance, something that I accept and maybe a little of what I fear.

It's not the actual session — it is at best: cathartic, validating, joyous, interesting, and at worst: dull. What scares me is even after my sessions are dull or joyous, I never know what will happen next. Where will my journey take me?

Irene, are you taking me on a journey — or am I in the driving seat? And whilst I know it's me who's taking you with me, I look to you for approval and back-up. I want to trust you to give me a gentle tug if you think I'm taking a wrong turning. You give me too much (am I too dependant?) and yet you can't give me enough.

What can I blame you for? I need to blame you. I don't know what to take from you and what to ask for and what to give you. I don't know why that suddenly matters.

I'm not sure if it's time to get closer to you or if that's a sign that I should get further away.

I wish you could tell me what this is about so I'd know if it mattered. I don't want to go fishing inside for explanations, for understanding, for reassurance (it feels too volatile, unpredictable and I may stop being so generally balanced and happy. I don't want to leave that place — cos God knows where that will take me).

I guess if I build in time for myself to go on my quests with you, or alone with my journal, I may be able to contain it, so it doesn't spill over and hurt anyone or destroy or overshadow the life with which I'm happy. I hope I can do that. I'd like to know what you think (especially if you believe in me). I want to be able to give myself what you give me and I guess I can, but at the moment I want to give myself your help.

The way things are at the moment — I am managing. If I give myself the time I need without rushing or worrying — it shouldn't need to spill over — except in good or helpful ways. If I can face things, trusting in that (and knowing that if it spills over — I'll soon realise that and adjust accordingly), then I've got the opportunity (with time and looking after myself) to keep growing and thinking and live the life I love.

Thanks Irene.
I wonder what's going on and I wonder what's going on, in the world, in

my life, but most of all within myself. It's like my memories, my hopes, my identity, my love, my fears, my dreams, my confidence, my trust is turning over, churning deep inside me, sending me flickers of wisdom, symbols of truth and pangs of pain and doubt. Overall, it feels so hard, but interesting, and I kind of trust it to progress despite the instinct to fight it and cling to what I've known.

I wanted to write a book, but don't know what about, because imagining myself out of my own story feels like something I haven't got time for. So I'll just do what comes naturally, as is my current need.

Well, firstly that feels better; big, simple and bold. I have a number of relationships that are changing and it's sending me reeling with confusion.

I want to feel settled again, on the inside at least.

Hey journal I'm scared and fucked and angry and what are you gonna do about it? Aaaaghhr Irene what am I so afraid of please help me. I don't know what to think, who I am, what I want, where I'm going.

Moved out, no gas etc. Irene lends me steamer and I wrote — 'a steamer and a counsellor' in a reasons to be cheerful list. Feeling safe (various writing about my lovely flat).

Comment (mine)

Em's courage to move out from Dan's (her partner's) flat into a place of her own had been a large part of her therapy for some time and she was so excited to find the perfect place and when she moved in she was devastated to find that there was no gas and no other possible power for cooking. After her therapy hour, on the way downstairs, I thought about lending her my electric steamer, which I rarely use, and decided it would be OK — so just said, 'how about borrowing my steamer to cook with?' She was delighted and took me up on my offer. One of my mother's sayings was 'neither borrower or lender be' but this strikes me as a very ungenerous, cold position to maintain and wielding a sort of withholding power. However, what I do try to do is put boundaries around borrowing and lending so that I don't lend things I would not be able to risk losing and so risk losing or damaging a relationship. It is also important for me to know that I do not operate from a need to rescue. I am reminded of an account of a therapeutic relationship told in *Person-Centred Therapy Today* where the therapist involved herself in all sorts of situations with a client: 'I never offered Joe more than I could sustain and I tried not to offer him less.' (Mearns and Thorne, 2000, p. 18)

Journal extract 7 (Sometime between September & November 2001)

Dear Irene
It's funny how since I've contemplated you not being there — I've felt your presence. On the end of a phone. In my journal. In my thinking. In my knowing and in my confusion.

I want (or don't want) to write 'I love you' but it seems so silly, so inappropriate. You're my counsellor and why are the tears rolling down my cheek? I don't know. You are so safe, so trustworthy, so supportive. I bet it's hard getting to be like you. And yet you make it look so easy, so natural.

I guess there are still things I want to talk to you about. I'm not perfect. I get angry. I get jealous. I get selfish. I am tired.

I need some peace. I deserve a break.

*I need to look after myself. Can I do that without knowing you are there —
soon.*

18 February 02

*Oh dear! Seems like we've reached another door. Don't like it, feel alone,
scared, toxic, guilty, frustrated, Hellooo!!!!! Can anybody hear me? Three
fucking wise monkeys everywhere I look. Angry maybe?*

19 February 02

*Everybody (except those it's directed at) wants some anger — so here goes, I'll
give it my best shot. I'm sick of feeling mad, feeling guilty, worrying, angsting,
trying to self-improve, trying to prove something, feeling like I'm not enough,
not strong enough, not assertive enough, not kind enough, not good enough
etc. etc. For fuck's sake. What do you want — blood? I don't want blood. I don't
want to think about my bad blood.*

*Irene, I need you at the moment. I should call you in the morning — cos I
want to talk about how I really feel — and I want to be held — not physically,
but contained. Don't feel quite safe enough alone or with others.*

I am enough already.

Comment (mine)

I feel that bringing my availability into my therapeutic relationship enables Em to
access me through her journal which then facilitates her to get into touch with
what she needs and gives her the courage to own it.

Journal extract 8

*Then I got to see Irene (prioritised it). She told me off for not having explained
the urgency, before going to see her. I identified that I wanted to talk to her
about (among other things) outside support — what is it right to expect?*

Comment (mine)

It is interesting to me that Em experienced this communication as my 'telling her
off'. Maybe 'little Em' was being held firmly in check and 'grown up' Em was
very convincing that it wasn't that urgent and, of course, she could wait until I
was available at a time which suited me. It was another example of my not empathising
with her over the telephone. Telephone counselling is one of my idiosyncratic
weaknesses. Turning it round, however, it feels like one of my professionally
developed idiosyncrasies is to embrace non-verbal communication as well as words
to inform my empathy for my clients. I was disappointed with myself that I had
missed all of what Em was really feeling in her telephone call and to her that was
received as a telling off.

Journal extract 9 (April 2002, after discussing book proposal)

In January 2001 I realised she was right. I often had what I thought was an inkling about what she thought — but it usually turned out to be what I thought. It was so confusing. Sometimes I'd come home to Dan and say 'Irene thinks . . .' and tell him how she was pushing me in some direction to feel anger or sadness or happy or honesty or something, something that — until I felt comfortable with it — in my head — i.e. understood, accepted and embraced it, I would think was coming from her.

I had seen other counsellors before:
2 network counsellors (Christian/voluntary)
N (Social Worker)
Relaxation therapist
Dr M (psychiatrist)
Dr U (Clinical psychologist)
Group therapy — Yuk!
Staff counsellor at X — (a few times after I was assaulted)
I don't want to undervalue how some (not all) of them helped me. I already had a strong sense of the importance of relationships and of a responsible use of 'power' within them.

Comment (mine)

During supervision, I realised that this was something I had sensed in Em which made it easier to trust her with my idiosyncrasies.

Comment (Em's)

When I came to see Irene, I was looking to do more than tell my story. I guess I wanted to master myself, my mind, regain control and hope and dissolve the growing fear within me. And as far as these objectives are possible and healthy (too much control to me is no longer an aspiration) I suppose I did.

She touched me more deeply than I had hoped possible. It also took longer than I would have initially hoped. I wanted quick solutions. What I got was the strength, understanding and support I needed to bring about more fundamental changes.

11.07.02

Hi Irene and people that are interested in Irene. I am about to look through all the stuff I've written again before sending to Irene tomorrow. But before I do, I wanted to have another brainstorm. What I've noticed is that I've come such a long way since I started seeing her. I look back in my journal and in my mind and I see that things have changed so much and thankfully not in others. I found a part of myself (that I think was always there probably) during that time that I liked. A part of me that just wanted to be prepared to ride the storms and face the demons because increasingly I believed again in life's power and to believe I had choices and that taking was OK, but that appreciating the things that brought me joy and comfort was worthwhile and helps you learn and better still that giving is even more pleasurable when you mean it, when in doing so you are being true to what makes you feel good. I don't want to lose that part of me.

When I started therapy I was wanting to do better, to cope better, to be better and most importantly to feel better. I think I got that, but it wasn't in the way I expected. 'Better' took on a different meaning and increasingly I realised I was good enough. I've also found that the more able I am to accept myself — even the bits that aren't nice (by any stretch of the imagination), the more I accept and value other people. The less I expect or demand of them the less I do of myself and I keep being pleasantly surprised by what I/we/they can do. It feels like I have my faith back. It's funny that, because my faith in the sense of my upbringing (nice churchgoing family) is one thing that I sometimes thought Irene challenged or didn't value. Mainly because she (had the audacity to) questioned the concept of forgiveness — something I suppose deep down — however much I questioned it — was still a belief in me — I'd never be 'better enough' until I forgave. And I think now that I don't have to. I just have to be true to myself and when I am my actions, words and thoughts tend to be more 'forgiving'; anyway, move well beyond my comfort zones.

Comment (mine)

On first reading, I was surprised to read this expression of Em's feelings about my 'challenging' or not valuing her faith, as I have written elsewhere about my openness and my own faith (Fairhurst, 2000b). However on re-reading this extract, I think I can see what happened. The man who abused Em over a period of years attended the same church as her family and she would become very angry with her mother who, through her Christian forgiveness, seemed to ignore what he had done to Em. He could also carry on with his Christian life, which Em perceived as hypocritical. Maybe my empathising with these feelings of anger, hurt and pain caused by Christian people, was received by Em as a rejection of her faith, rather than empathy with her own rejection of the hypocrisy of some of what happened in her 'nice, churchgoing family'.

My 'challenging' the concept of forgiveness, I thought, took the form of my acceptance of Em's inability to 'forgive' him and my empathising with 'little Em' who would have felt betrayed if the perpetrator had been forgiven, as if what had happened didn't matter and so she didn't matter. It feels significant to me that, although Em didn't experience this as empathy, she has come to accept herself with her 'lack of forgiveness' and has been able to move on despite it. The whole issue of forgiveness is important to me and I think it is a multi-faceted concept, which has different meanings for different people.

Comment (Em's)

I can hold the notion that 'I'm angry with you and I love you'; 'You let me down then, but you didn't then'. I don't know — it's hard to explain. It just sits better now. I haven't answered all my questions — I keep realising that the more you find out the less clear things are. I used to find confusion paralysing. If I didn't know what I felt (and only one definition would do) or what I thought, how was I going to fix it — to know again? I don't need certainty and control in the same way now. In fact life's surprises and my own process with its unexpected twists and turns amuse me (well after the event, at least!) and constantly remind me that whilst a little bit of planning and forethought can be wise — too much of it leads to anxiety and a desire sometimes to control too much (in myself or in others).

Comment (mine)

Another of my professionally developed idiosyncrasies is the belief in the importance of staying with the client's confusion, no matter how painful it might be for them or for me. Not to strive for clarity or meaning, but to accept the client in their confusion is, for me, a vital manifestation of unconditional positive regard.

Comment (Em's)

I remember a time when I used to say to Irene that I wanted to let go more, just be, relax, trust etc.; it seemed when I let my guard down my feelings would come up and bite me and my fear (and occasionally the reality) was that all hell would break loose — or I would (God forbid) lose control. Now when I feel good or even tired, flat, pre-menstrual, pissed off, even I'm not afraid to stick some music on, alone and see where my feelings take me — I'm less afraid if there's a need to tackle a problem. I know from experience that if I go off track a bit — I'll know and I'll find my way back — I always do. It gets easier, quicker and at times when I can step outside of my anxieties — more fun. I'm not afraid. I have my moments when things at that moment are scary or difficult, but I don't fill my moments with worrying about how to orchestrate the next. I don't need to waste my energies trying to prevent future pain — I'll need all my energy when it comes, which it inevitably will — cos that's life and I love it (mainly!).

So all in all, I guess what I'm identifying is that I feel calmer, freer, happier and more whole and real and I know myself better — and all of those things I attribute to the journey Irene and I (and Dan and a few others) have been on whilst I had therapy. In my mind also, Irene is all of those things.

I was scared about not seeing Irene any-more because I wondered if some of those things would be hard to hold onto. But they're not and I've realised that in my mind and in my heart, she hasn't gone away.

Final comment (mine)

I feel deeply privileged and strangely blessed to have shared this collaborative experience with Em. Her writings about our relationship have touched me profoundly, as she herself does.

References

Bozarth, J. D. (1998) *Person-Centred Therapy: A Revolutionary Paradigm*. Ross-on-Wye: PCCS Books.

Fairhurst, I. M. (2000a) The client-centred relationship as the agent for therapeutic change. Paper presented at the BAPCA AGM and published in *Person to Person*, BAPCA newsletter, summer.

Fairhurst, I. M. (2000b) Openness and the client-centred therapist. *Person-Centred Practice*, 8 (1): 44–9.

Mearns, D. (1994) *Developing Person-Centred Counselling*. London: Sage.

Mearns, D. and Thorne, B. (2000) *Person-Centred Therapy Today*. London: Sage.

Rogers, C. R. (1951) *Client-Centred Therapy*. London: Constable.

Rogers, C. R. (1959) A theory of personality and interpersonal relationships as developed in the client-centred framework. In S. Koch (Ed.) *Psychology: A Study of Science: Vol. 3 Formulation of the Person and the Social Context*. New York: McGraw-Hill, pp. 184–256.

Rogers, C. R. (1963) The actualising tendency in relation to 'motives' and to consciousness. In M. Jones (Ed.) *Nebraska Symposium on Motivation*. Lincoln: University of Nebraska Press.

Tidmarsh, D. (1993) In search of congruence, unpublished paper towards the Diploma in Counselling, University of Strathclyde cited in D. Mearns (1994) *Developing Person-Centred Counselling*. London: Sage.

10

Jenny Biancardi

Idiosyncrasy Through the Core Conditions and Beyond

As a psychotherapist in private practice, the Person-Centred Approach has been the mainstay of my work. I am interested in the way I am and how I interpret the philosophy and application of the Person-Centred Approach. I find examining the intricacies of how I practise and what I actually do and say in my relationship with my clients both exciting and challenging.

Authenticity has always been a crucial element for me, in both my personal and my professional life. Staying authentic, and being fully present with all of who I am, is a major aspiration. I have had many years' exposure to forms of therapy other than person-centred and have become a qualified practitioner in several of them. Because of this there is a tension in my work between using all I can bring to the therapeutic encounter and strictly keeping to the 'core' conditions as outlined by Rogers (1957). The minute I use a technique I feel I am moving beyond the core conditions, yet I feel I am still working within a person-centred framework. I experience my use of techniques as a deeply intuitive therapeutic response rather than an inability on my part to stay completely faithful to the core conditions.

In this chapter I illuminate my idiosyncratic thoughts and behaviour in my work with particular clients through a consideration of the core conditions of congruence, unconditional positive regard and empathy. I explore the need for psychological contact and how I often find my role extending as a result of my experience with the client.

Congruence

Congruence is sometimes an overlooked, or at least minimised, part of the Person-Centred Approach. It feels that in some training courses, it is expressed merely as a need to be genuine. This does not go far enough. In my own training courses, I now talk about *expressed* congruence to highlight the need to be genuine as a person and to be able to *share openly* with the client feelings I feel toward them arising from our relationship. This requires an ability to know what I feel and to be able to express this without losing the ability to empathise and value the client. This is often my greatest challenge: in the moment that I am feeling something that I believe should be shared, I am still not sure if it is my own issue and inappropriate, or something significant about the relationship we are engaged in. This means that expressing the feeling feels like an enormous risk.

Susan

To bring this to life, I begin with the example of Susan. We had been working together for two and a half years. She was a woman in her forties who had had very few intimate relationships and often experienced feeling lonely. She found her anxiety and shyness a big barrier to mixing easily. Her job was demanding, and she felt it had not been a good choice for her. Susan was also facing the possibility that due to her age and circumstances she might never have the family she had always imagined she would.

Initially the sessions were very difficult for us both. She would arrive punctually, look quite pleased to be there and then freeze. She would struggle to find anything to say, seeming more and more anxious, with only her look conveying her longing to connect. I also used to feel anxious: anxious to help her, to reach her, to make it less painful, and also not to disappoint her, as she often felt disappointed if she had not been able to share much with me. Gradually, it did get easier, and she was able to share more of her internal world. She changed her job and found ways to use her many talents, both for pleasure and profit. During our time together Susan was able to do some very deep work, much of it around her childhood and the very critical and cold parenting she had experienced.

We were working towards ending our sessions together when her mother became very ill. As she talked about this she was very distressed, saying she felt so on her own with it all. All she needed sometimes was for someone to give her a hug. As she wept she looked up and asked if I could hug her. The request was very out of character, as she never asked for anything. I should also say I have no problem with physical contact with clients if it feels appropriate, and I had hugged her in the past. However in this moment I froze. I felt no answering response in me to hold her, and yet it seemed impossibly cruel not to respond positively. She looked at me desperately and still I could not move to her across the short space between us.

I said: 'This feels so hard to say, but somehow it doesn't feel OK to hug you just now.' Susan looked shocked and very hurt and cried bitterly. I felt awful. Then suddenly, I had an image of her as a small child at her mother's knee being pushed angrily away. A scene she had described many times. I said: 'I am imagining this must have been how it felt so often as a child: needing to be held, needing comfort, and yet being rejected. The pain looks almost unbearable.'

She wrapped her arms around herself, rocking and sobbing: 'Yes, this is just how it was. I would pluck up courage to approach her only to be pushed away.' As she looked at me then, I felt a wave of warmth towards her and a desire to hold her.

I said: 'This must sound very confusing for you: I am really aware of how right it would feel to hold you now.' She said: 'Yes, it would feel right to me, I can see you now.' I held her. There were tears for us both.

A psychodynamic interpretation might include issues of transference, counter-transference, projection and boundaries. However, my focus is on how hard it is sometimes to behave congruently when I do not understand the feelings, but do trust them. This session was seminal for both of us and made the process of ending our work together a positive and rewarding time. When I froze, I did not know it was because it felt as if it was her mother she was asking for: I knew it did not feel right. When I did hold her it felt like two adults being intimate and not like a parent comforting a child. It would have been unrealistic for me to be the parent she did not have. What she did get from me was a real relationship: I was not just being a stand-in for the ideal mother. What we had was congruent. Being congruent can feel very difficult, but the courage to be congruent can bring real depth and connection.

Mary

My next example is more about the need for expressed congruence. This client, Mary, is a very successful and accomplished therapist herself. She is also someone I had known previous to our therapeutic relationship. She had done some training courses with me some time in the past and I liked her a lot.

Much of the therapy was around issues of personal development and seemed to be going well. However, after several months, I found myself becoming increasingly irritable and critical about her in my head. The irritation seemed to focus on Mary's ability to always look so well groomed, colour co-ordinated, and generally organised. Her matching shoes and bag would annoy me intensely. This petty response in myself I put down initially to my own disorganisation and an inability to do 'smart'. For several weeks I found myself having to fight this judgemental attitude to be able to be with her and to be able to hear what she was saying.

How could I be congruent? What would I say? 'I don't like your bag'? 'Your shoes are too shiny'? It felt impossible. I was clearly not a good therapist to be so distracted in this way. I worried about it, and took it to both therapy and supervision. In supervision, we decided I would have to find some way of saying something. In the last session with the client I had found myself imaging how tidy her drawers must be at home, and imaging the clean and ironed handkerchief she was bound to have in her clutter-free handbag.

At the beginning of the next session I felt really tense. I said 'Mary, this feels very difficult to say, but I have been aware for the last couple of sessions I have felt an inexplicable irritation in me. I can think of no justification for the feeling, and I wonder if it makes any sense to you?' Mary looked surprised and said: 'No. Have I done something to annoy you?' I said once again that I could not explain it, and it felt petty and ridiculous to me, and often seemed to focus on her ability to look so well groomed. Mary seemed upset and was unable to shed any light on anything happening between us.

For a while I concentrated on trying to be empathic to her feelings of disquiet, and we looked at some of the issues it brought up for her around feeling that she needed to please people. After about twenty minutes Mary said: 'Actually, I was a bit upset with you some weeks ago, I felt you minimised my distress over my cat's illness.'

I suddenly remembered the session in which I had struggled to empathise with her upset over her cat. I myself am allergic to cats and dogs, so have no close connection with them. As we explored this, Mary said: 'You know, I think I have been angry with you over that, but haven't been able to say anything.' When we tracked back to that session, I realised it had happened at the same time that I began to feel irritable. Once Mary had told me this all my irritation left me.

The session proved very fruitful, with Mary looking at how hard it is for her to express criticism to anyone she likes or admires. I felt a return of the admiration I felt for her as a person and as a therapist.

So why did my feelings settle upon her apparel? The session where I had inadequately recognised her feelings and the significance of the cat in her life, I remember thinking how different we were. I like cats from a distance, but would not have them in the centre of my life. While this was all on the edge of my awareness, what I was clearly aware of was our differences in style.

I also believe that if I am open and empathic to the other, often the feelings unexpressed by them resonate with me at a gut level. If I do not deal with those feelings at the time, I begin to own them as if they were all mine. A common next response for me is to criticise myself for having inappropriate feelings, rather than seek to see them as a possible part of our relationship, or even as something the client may be feeling towards me. My learning is that I need to try to bring to awareness between us any feelings that interfere with my ability to be empathic and accepting of the client.

Unconditional positive regard

Betty
When thinking about my attempts to provide unconditional positive regard, I am reminded of Betty, a young woman who had many difficulties due to her disruptive and neglectful childhood. During our work together her husband left her for an older woman. This was very painful for her, and evoked much of her earlier abandonment experience and feelings, leaving her unable to act. Her inability to take action over selling a joint property became serious, involving the courts and even the possibility of jail. I was getting worried for her. Even though I thought I understood how small and powerless she felt, I was very keen for her not to end up in court or jail.

During this time, I went to a person-centred conference in Belgium. In one of the workshops I acted as client for Bill Rogers, who was demonstrating the core conditions of the Person Centred Approach. In a very unsympathetic setting (large lecture room with translators), I experienced profoundly what it was really like to feel I was absolutely OK the way I was. He had no desire or need for me to be other than I was, right at that moment. The power of his acceptance was unforgettable. I still feel it as I write about it now.

I went back to Betty with new understanding and in the next session said: 'You know, I don't think I have really let myself feel just how impossible it is for you to sell this house.' Not only did I let myself be more deeply empathic, I really did let go of needing her to be in any way different. This is how she was, this was the best she could do, and it was fine. She wept and told me more of her need to stay in the property, of her rage, and of her determination not to co-operate with her ex-husband, even if that meant going to prison. I felt I really understood and was able to be with her in a different way. During the week before our next session, Betty phoned to say: 'I've done it. I've let it go!' She had sold her house.

At no time before the Belgium experience was I suggesting Betty should sell the house. However, I did want her to sell the house. How powerful the subliminal message can be.

Empathy

When thinking about empathy, I am reminded of an experience I had while running a training group. I was training some nursing staff in listening skills. They were working in threes, practising. I went into one small group because they had called me saying they were stuck. I sat down in the listener's chair facing the client. Almost immediately I felt violently sick, and actually thought I might vomit on the carpet. I managed to stand up, excuse myself and got to the toilet. I instantly felt better, took a glass of water, and returned to the room. This was the afternoon session and I had had lunch in the hospital canteen and I wondered about the food.

I wandered around the groups again, again being called to the same small group. Again I sat down opposite the client to see what was happening, only to find myself feeling violently nauseated again. I stood up, moved slightly away, and instantly felt better again. I was amazed and intrigued. I sat down again, and said to the client: 'I think I'm picking up some really difficult feelings. May I try again?' The client said: 'Please do, we're stuck.' I said: 'What I'm aware of is really physical — I feel like I want to throw up.' The client said: 'That's why I'm stuck.

I can't speak because when I think of this thing I feel so sick I dare not open my mouth.' As she said that I felt the returning sickness subside.

Although they had all been asked to talk about something that they felt might be useful to explore, I had said not to pick major issues or events, given their time restrictions and the nature of the training. With this in mind I said I was happy to hear her if she wished to say more, but pointed out the limits of the situation. She did talk about it, and I was able to hear her without the nausea returning. I was really surprised that empathy could be so physical. Since that time I am much better at noticing my physical response to clients.

Even given this, I was very shocked when many years ago after counselling a young woman dying from cancer, her face puffed up from the treatment drugs, my partner said just after she had left: 'look at your face, you look awful.' I glanced in the mirror to see my own face puffed up and moon-like. The session had been deeply moving and I was profoundly affected by her grief, rage and fear. But how could I have taken on her physical characteristics? It only lasted briefly. An hour later I looked like me. The experience gave me a different sense of how the attempt to be really alongside another person can impact upon your whole being. This client was able to come to terms with her dying, wrote the funeral service, chose the songs and poems, and died what the Catholics call 'a good death', peacefully and gently. I gained more than I can say from the experience of knowing her, and journeying with her some of her last days.

The need for psychological contact

In writing this chapter, and reviewing some of my work with clients, I realise that perhaps some of my most unorthodox work included inviting clients to live in my home, and then negotiating the role of therapist, landlady, joint-cook, friend and, in some cases, colleague. One of the major tenets of person-centred theory is that the core conditions need to be *experienced* by the other. For many people whose experience has made them suspicious and untrusting, a more intense experience of people's genuine concern and care for them may be very effective.

Pat

The first occasion was precipitated by a clash with the psychiatrist at the hospital where I worked as a psychiatric nurse tutor. I had been seeing an older woman, Pat, for individual sessions. She had been admitted after having made a serious suicide attempt. As we talked it became clear that she was very deeply distressed by some, as yet unknown, experiences in her past. As she revealed more of her unhappiness, her psychiatrist decided to give her Electro-Convulsive Therapy. I felt convinced that this form of treatment was completely unsuitable for her. In a fairly dramatic disagreement on a ward round, the psychiatrist said that either Pat had ECT or he would discharge her into my care. I made the offer and she chose my care.

I have to give credit to my husband. When I phoned to say: 'You know that spare room we have, well . . .' he replied: 'Fine.' Pat lived with us for approximately a year, and uncovered some major trauma in her life. There were times when she was dissociating, having regular nightmares, and flashbacks. We kept to our one-hour per week therapy session, and over the rest of the time I tried to provide ordinary support and friendship. My husband and son generally treated her as another household member. It was not always easy, and I needed to discipline myself to try for ordinariness most of the time, rather than getting into being a therapist twenty-four hours a day.

Initially, Pat did social things with us and shopped with us, but as she gained more confidence, and her life became fuller, she did more and more things on her own, and with her own friends. She eventually moved out into a shared flat, and the therapy continued for another year. The therapy ended when she left for college to retrain.

While I realise that this was not, and is not, the usual practice for most counsellors, I feel that in this case it worked out well. The client's own comments were that she felt that she had a safe place to live for the first time. This allowed many painful memories to surface and be dealt with. We offered her asylum in the old sense of a place of safety.

Mark

Mark was a client who had been in psychodynamic therapy for many years before coming to see me. In the course of our work together, he recognised he needed to leave his present partner: the relationship was chaotic, traumatic, and painful. The stress on Mark was such that he could not organise the leaving, or find a new home. The relationship with his partner was professional as well as personal and had many complications. In one of the sessions I found myself inviting Mark to move in with us. As he had a much-loved dog and cat (remember my allergy to cats and dogs) this was a bit reckless on my part. We lived in a small terraced house with three bedrooms at the time, so it could at times feel crowded. In the end it was agreed that the dog would come with its owner, while the cat would go and stay with friends.

This relationship — us sharing a house and also doing therapy — was made easier because of Mark's psychological sophistication and experience as a client. Once again my family was supportive, and, when we moved to a larger home, Mark moved with us. This therapy continued for a couple of years, stopping after another move. This first move to a larger house gave us extra space, which meant for a while yet another client, Lucy, who I believed to be at great risk also lived with us. During this time Mark was involved in offering support and on one occasion played a life-saving role by taking Lucy to hospital after a suicide attempt. Lucy stayed with us until the major crisis in her life had past. She has gone on to have a very successful career and has stayed in contact despite living abroad. Lucy has said that the time spent with us saved her life. I believe that it did.

The main key for me in managing these mixed roles was being congruent about the day-to-day issues, like who leaves their cups in the bathroom or does not stack the dishwasher correctly or has not done their share of household chores. At the same time in the therapy session I tried to offer unconditional respect and support. I was helped in this process by my years working and training at the Cassel Hospital in London, where the model of psychosocial nursing meant working side-by-side with clients with the day-to-day living tasks. The bonus for these clients, whose life experience means that they have difficulty in believing that they are acceptable, is that they find it much harder to stay with this belief when they are accepted on a day-to-day basis.

If we really do believe in the actualising tendency, then it is inevitable that our roles in people's lives will change. Usually this may just be that the client no longer needs to see us and leaves our lives, but in Mark's case he became a much-trusted friend. In over 25 years as a therapist, there have only been four clients who I felt needed to live with more support, and where I felt I could sustain a therapeutic relationship in that situation.

There have been clients whom I have met for coffee, who after therapy stayed in touch, and who I occasionally meet to catch up. There have been many students who have attended ongoing training with me, who have later become close friends and often colleagues as well. Each relationship is unique which makes rigid rules about boundaries almost impossible. It is crucial not to set up an expectation in the client of a relationship that cannot then be sustained.

After living through the awful stress of a complaints procedure, where many of my idiosyncratic acts of support were interpreted negatively, I am now more cautious. I was cleared, but it was a very stressful, time-consuming, and career-threatening experience. I now find myself less willing to be spontaneous, and generally do not move out of the safety of the boundaries of the consulting room. I feel oppressed when I cannot just trust my own internal process and judgements, but have to also be thinking: 'How would an external regulatory body view my response?' However, times change, and we live in a much more litigious society. Does this mean I am being less idiosyncratic? Probably, yes.

I would not now offer sanctuary to a client in my home, nor would I advise anyone else to, as it would not fit into current professional codes of practice. I am now more conventional. Having a unique relationship with a unique human being needs unique responses, but this is hard to justify within a society that wants rules, regulations and restrictions to be in place and observed. In many ways I can be sympathetic to this need to control and regulate, as this is very responsible work that we do. However, often the most creative and exciting moments of connection and healing come out of a spontaneous and intuitive response, that in turn comes from a feeling of openness and freedom, which feels opposite to adhering to the rules.

To be a reliable and professional therapist, I believe I have to be constantly willing to monitor myself and to look at my own motivation, needs and prejudices to ensure that, as much as possible, I am responding to the needs of my client and being as genuine as I can be in my therapy relationships.

Extending my role
Person-centred therapists generally do not give advice — they are non-directive. Most of the time, I do not; but, with some clients, when they ask, I do.

Maria
Maria is a client I have worked with for approximately ten years, on and off. After a period of initial therapy, which was very much conducted in a client-centred model, she took a break. Some time later she phoned asking for a couple of sessions to get my advice. I should say that Maria is a very articulate bright woman who has run her own very successful business. In the session she wanted advice about a family issue and was clear: 'I want to know what you think.' I told her. She said that it was helpful.

Maria is very clear in asking for what she finds helpful, and will also book sessions not seeking advice, but to explore something and be heard. For me it feels respectful of Maria's ability to allow her to pick from me what she finds useful. I am interested in how this can feel all right with some clients, while with others I feel most uncomfortable and very reluctant to give my view. In those cases, I do not.

Julie

I have also worked with a client, Julie, whose early experiences were so terrible, so cruel and abusive, that I occasionally gave medical advice based on my past experience as a nurse. In one session it became obvious to me from the symptoms she was describing that she may well be quite physically ill. Although I had suggested in previous sessions that she might want to see a doctor, she had not done so. Her history made any medical examination extremely stressful. Also, she was so used to pain, she did not react to it but just lived with it. Not showing hurt had been a survival mechanism for her in the past.

In the end I persuaded her to promise to go to the GP the next day, and I sat and helped her write out all her symptoms so her GP had a proper picture (Julie minimised all of her own feelings). I phoned the next day to see how she had got on. She was admitted to hospital and scheduled for major surgery. At her request I wrote to the doctors at the hospital to give some explanation of what had happened to her and why she would find some things very stressful. In this case I felt I needed to be a supportive ally and a practical advocate. My sense with this client was that her damaging early experiences had so affected her ability to take care of herself (or even to believe that she was worth taking care of) that this meant she was at times in serious danger when she need not be. With negotiation, I could help her.

Alice

Sometimes I will move into action in a session with a client. As a qualified psychodramatist it occasionally seems to me the client is showing what psychodramatists would call 'act hunger'. This is the need to do it or say it directly, not just talk about it. Recently, a client, Alice, while talking about some unexpressed anger towards her brother, said: 'I just wish I could tell him to his face.' I said: 'Well, we can get close to that.' I got up and got an empty chair and said: 'OK, here he is, where shall I put him?' She pointed to a space. I stood beside her looking at the empty chair and said: 'What is it you need him to hear?'

She began to express her anger, looking surprised at what she was saying. Years of unspoken hurts and disappointments were expressed. After the action she said: 'It feels so good to have cleared all that. I may never say it to him, but I'm not carrying it around any more.'

This moving into action I find very releasing for the client when they have already indicated that is what they need to do. What would not feel right would be for me to prescribe or decide before the session what action work the client needed to do. I believe that if it comes up from the client in the session as a need, then it is very legitimate for me to find a way for the need to be met. It feels very empathic.

This same client also had a couple of phobias that were causing her difficulties and restricting her life. It felt completely reasonable to use the fast phobia cure[1]

[1.] The fast phobia cure was popularised by Joe Griffin (Griffin and Tyrrell, 2001) and others and was originally developed by Richard Bandler, one of the co-founders of Neuro Linguistic Programming.

with her, which worked after one session to remove both phobias, one of which she had had for a long time.

I am aware that some person-centred therapists might balk at using a technique. I feel that as a therapist, if there are ways of relieving distress, and the client wishes this, then I feel it is responsible to do so if I have the skill. My main concern is to be an effective therapist, and if that means moving outside of the purist's definition of the Person-Centred Approach, then I will do so. It is really difficult, because one either believes that the core conditions are sufficient or one does not. I believe that most of the time, when I can really provide them in a way they can be experienced, then this is a very healing, positive and enabling process for the client. However, if I am to use all of myself, I have to trust the occasions when I intuitively feel something else is called for.

Given the recent research and knowledge about how the brain stores trauma and debates on what is the most effective way of working with post-traumatic stress (Griffin and Tyrrell, 2001) I believe we have to take on board the concerns that just re-experiencing trauma can in fact be damaging, reinforcing the trauma instead of relieving it. Person-Centred Therapy has been criticised by some of the recent research (identified in Griffin and Tyrrell, 2000) as an inappropriate way of working with trauma and depression. My experience is that I have certainly had many successful outcomes from person-centred work with both depressed and traumatised clients, but it is not usually short-term work.

What I have come to appreciate is that some techniques, like EMDR[2], do speed up the healing process for some clients. Many years ago I was at a conference where a well-known person-centred therapist was asked whether, if she knew there was a technique which would reduce the therapy needed by half, she would use it. She said no. I talked with her for some time, and certainly respected her belief and commitment to the Person-Centred Approach. I feel that now my position is that I would do anything that was life-enhancing and freeing for the client that I was qualified to do, that was ethical, and that they wished to try. For example, freeing the client of a phobia that stops them from travelling can often be done in a single session.

Conclusion
As my own practice is steeped in person-centred theory, I feel like a member of the person-centred family. There is no other family I feel I could belong to. My hope is that this family continues to welcome any members who cherish and practise the Person-Centred Approach in their own unique way. It saddens me when supervising therapists to hear them denying their intuitive response to a client through a fear of not being person-centred. I was present at a conference, during a vigorous discussion about people doing different things and describing them as person-centred. Some people were getting very indignant, while Carl Rogers' response was to say how interesting it sounded and to ask more about it. I was very impressed at the time because it was his life's work we were talking about, and he seemed to

---

[2.] EMDR, Eye Movement Desensitization and Reprocessing, is a method which uses repeated stimulus of sight, sound and touch to speed up the processing of traumatic events. This technique is used in the treatment for post-war trauma for soldiers, for victims of torture, but also for more general post-traumatic stress and anxiety states.

have no fear or need to be defensive or protective.

Being a person-centred therapist is complex. I feel passionate about people's right to work at their own pace, to have power in the relationship, and for therapy to be a collaborative effort. I also believe that it is the relationship that matters, and for that to be most effective, I have to be authentic and fully myself. Part of who I am is someone with enthusiasm and an interest in new ideas and theories. These I try to make available in the work I do with my clients. This is not an 'anything goes' approach, but as a trainer and therapist I have learnt that people learn and change in different ways, and having a range of ways of responding to the client's needs is essential.

To restate my therapeutic position: if I feel I can meet the needs of the client then I will do so, rather than leave it entirely up to the client to find their own way. Only they know where they want to go — I may have ways to help them get there.

References

Griffin, J. and Tyrrell, I. (2000). *Breaking the Cycle of Depression: A Revolution in Psychology*. East Sussex: H. G. Publishing.

Griffin, J. and Tyrrell, I. (2001). *The Shackled Brain: How to Release Locked-in Patterns of Trauma*. East Sussex: H. G. Publishing.

Rogers, C. R. (1957). The necessary and sufficient conditions of therapeutic personality change. *Journal of Consulting Psychology*, 21, (2): 95–103.

11

Rose Battye

Beads on a String

Alice

Alice was telling me about a business meeting that had gone horribly wrong. On the journey home she had felt more and more wretched as she realised that an important contract was not going to be honoured. She felt angry and hurt and deeply betrayed. I listened to and reflected her feelings back to her. She felt furious and powerless.

'I wish I was a steamroller squashing a gingerbread man and then I'd be the right shape and could hang on the wall and wouldn't have all the awkward bits.'

This was powerful, if confusing, imagery. In previous sessions we had looked in depth at her struggle to believe that it really was all right for her, after an extremely conditional and non-valuing upbringing and education, to feel and think the way she did rather than how other people expected her to. It was very unusual for her to produce such a metaphor. A highly intelligent woman, she tended to talk and think very fast. At times I had found it hard to help her be in touch with her feelings and to stay with them.

'A steamroller squashing a gingerbread man! What a powerful image, Alice. It's given me a thought; you know this course I have been doing that I told you about?'

'Yes?'

'I've learnt a way of working with images which might be interesting to try here; would you like to hear about it?'

Alice looked intrigued, so I continued.

'The idea is to 'be' the image, so I'd ask you to get up and I'd be beside you and ask you to imagine being the steamroller and the gingerbread man and we'll see what that is like for you. I think the idea is that these images could all be expressions of how you feel. What do you think?'

'It sounds a bit odd, but, well, why not, let's give it a go.'

Alice looked a bit puzzled but attentive and definitely game, so we both stood up.

'OK, if at any point you want to stop just say so.'

I checked again and she was looking fine.

'Now just imagine you are the steamroller; you can shut your eyes if you like.'

Alice stood rather awkwardly, shutting her eyes and then she laughed.

'It feels really good, I'm going to smooth everything out completely flat.'

'You're going to smooth everything out completely flat?'

'Yes.'

'OK, now when you're ready, can you come out of being the steamroller?'

Alice opened her eyes and looked at me.

'That was really odd!'

'Are you happy to carry on and be the gingerbread man now?'

'Yes.'

'OK, move to a different place if you like and shut your eyes again and imagine you are the gingerbread man.'

Alice was silent for a few moments.

'Oh this is quite different.'

She sounded very surprised.

'What's it like?'

'The steamroller is huge and it is going to flatten me and I shall die.'

'Mmm.'

'I want to say, let me be a bumpy bit of road; I don't want to be like everyone else.'

I noticed how the image had changed. As in dreams, images often do not remain consistent or logical. I waited a few seconds.

'Is there anything else you want to say from there?' ('There' because I wasn't sure if she was gingerbread man or bumpy road at this point.)

'No.'

'OK, come out of there now.'

She opened her eyes and looked at me with astonishment.

'I had no idea it was like that for the gingerbread man, I could only see the point of view of the steamroller.'

'Shall we just try and see what it is like for the steamroller now?'

'OK.'

She moved her position and shut her eyes again.

'I don't want to roll him out any more. I'm just going to stop here.'

She opened her eyes again and looked at me again with real surprise.

'Shall we end there? Is there anything else you would like to say or do?'

She shook her head and we sat down and talked about it.

She said that it had helped her see very clearly the two parts of herself that had become familiar to us: the part that wants her to conform to the expectations of others and the part that wants her to be herself. She was very struck by the point of view of the gingerbread man and the bumpy road and also by the change of heart in the steamroller once it had heard their point of view. In future sessions we were able to proceed with a greater sense of a dialogue between these conflicting aspects of herself. It also enabled us to consider other parts of herself which it was hard to give attention to because they didn't fit in with the kind of person she wanted to be.

The great embrace

This is my idiosyncrasy: my belief that person-centred theory identifies such fundamental truths about human nature and relationships that ideas from other orientations can be included in its great embrace. I think that as a therapeutic approach Person-Centred Therapy is grossly underestimated and dismissed and this shocks and saddens me. But I do not, on that account, want to succumb to sectarianism and in turn be afraid of learning from other approaches. I celebrate what is extraordinary about the Person-Centred Approach at the same time as being open to other ideas. I find it exciting to read what other people have thought about the development of the self, the personality, the role of the therapist and the therapeutic relationship. When I hear new ideas, I am always thinking, how does this fit in with person-centred thinking? Usually it seems to me that alternative theories can be seen as a development of the key issues that Carl Rogers identified.

In the eighteen years since beginning my person-centred counselling and psychotherapy training, I have attended many workshops and, in the last eight years, two other trainings: a cognitive therapy course (arranged by colleagues who work in the National Health Service) and psychotherapy training with the Centre for Transpersonal Psychology, London. I have learnt ideas that I include in my work. They are all ones that have increased my understanding of myself and feel true to me. They have become part of me. Not to offer them, if they are relevant and the moment feels appropriate, would be to withhold something of myself from my client. I would feel incongruent. With some clients it would also feel rather patronising. I believe the client knows best and is able to show, in various ways, when something is not wanted or useful. It is essential that I am ready, through empathy, to see if that is the reaction.

In the episode with Alice we worked in a Gestalt[1] (McKewn, 1997) way with her image. Because of the way I offered and facilitated it, I would describe the whole process as person-centred. I responded empathically to her image; I had the idea that exploring the images in the way I had recently learnt might be helpful because it could give access to her feelings in a more direct way; I considered it and decided to offer it to her. I was being congruent. I was monitoring her reactions all the time. I was being empathic. I was working with our relationship, firstly by assessing whether it felt mutual enough to offer the idea, and then continually checking by listening and watching her, to see whether what I was suggesting was acceptable, and not disempowering for her. Given that I knew Alice often found herself pleasing people I knew I had to be particularly careful. It all happened in a moment. There would hardly have been a pause in the conversation.

I believe passionately in the key tenets and concepts of Person-Centred Therapy and would describe myself as a person-centred counsellor and therapist. My person-centred training changed my whole way of thinking and being. I discovered the phenomenological view that we each have a unique experience of the world and attach a unique meaning to it. By careful and accurate empathic listening, by being genuinely present and by creating an unconditionally accepting relationship so that a person may feel fully able to safely reveal themselves, the fundamental life force, the actualising tendency, can be encouraged to actualise.

Whenever I look at a different theoretical approach my respect and affection for person-centred philosophy and practice increase. I do not see my inclusion of other ideas as a way of being person-centred *and* something else. It is as though I have eaten the other ideas and digested them, keeping only those which feel true and make sense to me. The ideas are now part of my psychological understanding and are present in me as I work, just as my other experiences are there to be drawn on.

By introducing and offering other ideas, I understand I may appear to be breaking a fundamental person-centred principle of letting the client decide the direction of therapy. I hope I shall show in this chapter, that my idiosyncratic understanding of unconditional positive regard, empathy, congruence and the therapeutic relationship makes sense of my belief that the way I work deeply respects the centrality of the subjective experience of the client. I shall look at the ideas that have enriched my work and show that there have been themes which have been consistent over the years.

To further illustrate my practice, I will give two more examples of working with people where I offer ideas I have discovered in a way I consider to be person-

---

[1.] The references to different therapeutic ideas I give throughout are the ones I prefer and by no means the only ones or the most well known.

centred. They show how my congruence is tempered by empathy and knowledge of the person, so that the way that I am with each person is different according to what they require from me. Both cases show how our relationship is collaborative: we are working together.

Louise

I saw Louise for 3 years. She was the director of a successful business. She used her time with me to reflect upon herself and her difficulties in relationships. She made it clear what she required of me: my undivided attention and my honest input to what she had to say. She was interested in and knowledgeable about psychology and psychotherapy. I told her about psychological ideas which were relevant to her story and together we tried to make sense of her experiences.

I shared with her Rogers' view of personality development: the locus of evaluation, the conditions of worth and the development of the self-concept. It helped her understand why she lacked belief in herself. I offered her what I had learnt about reciprocal roles (Ryle, 1995) and it made sense for her of the relationships she found herself in.

Reciprocal role procedure describes how we fall into patterns of interpersonal and intrapersonal relating based on our early experiences. Thus according to Wilde McCormick:

> ... if our early experience is of a rejecting other, we will carry the wound of the rejected inner child and perhaps feel unworthy and useless. We will also carry the image and experience of a rejecting other. In relationships the rejected aspect will anticipate and expect the rejecting other because of the unhealed wound. This may be played out either in the rejection of oneself or of unconsciously anticipating and seeking others who are rejecting and so confirm the core wound. (Wilde McCormick, 2000, pp. 31–2)

Louise saw how she was repeatedly attracted to people who needed her but who ended up rejecting her, when she herself became needy. This 'thinking' approach was accompanied by immensely deep and painful experiencing of feeling. There were many sessions in which she wept and little was said at all. Patterns in her relationships, which had been entrenched, began to change. She became trusting and accepting of herself and realised that it really was all right for her to consider what her needs were in partnership.

She knew nothing and clearly wanted to know nothing about me at all. In another sense we knew each other extremely well. At every moment in the session we were intimately in relationship. I followed her every word and movement and she responded to me. She experienced a very wide range of emotions with and towards me, including suicidal despair, extreme anger, frustration, disappointment, irritation, boredom, delight, joy and fear. Sometimes I gave her feedback on how I experienced her and together we used this to find out what was going on in her. She did not want any more of me than this and I was careful not to show more of myself at all.

Jeff

With Jeff I could not have been more different. I had seen him a couple of years previously for another problem. He was a very friendly, impulsive, young man and we had got on well. He made a new appointment to see me because he was depressed.

The night before I saw him I had watched a television programme about obsessions. One obsession was hoarding. I watched fascinated as we were shown around two homes filled with twenty years of clutter. Each room was packed up to the ceiling. In one home, the owner had to bend to get through the doors because the floor level throughout was raised due to several inches of trodden-down layers. As I watched, I recognised something of myself and the process I had been going through for the last two years, throwing away things I had collected over nearly two decades.

The next morning Jeff walked in for our first session. We greeted each other warmly. He sat down and the first thing he said was, 'I'm a hoarder.'

Spontaneously and immediately I said, 'Did you see the programme?'

He laughed. 'Only the end of it.'

I thought, why was this the very first thing he said?

'Is this your problem?'

'Yes, I think it is.'

And he told me about his house and garage full of things and how it was getting him down, how impossible it was for him to throw things away. He was describing the same extreme symptoms and attitudes as the people on the programme. I realised that indeed he did have a problem and that, possibly, I could share what I had learnt. I was aware that he had come about his depression but I thought it was very likely they could be related. A connection appeared as he told me about problems with his new partner who was tidy and hated the chaos. He also loathed his mess and felt it was 'doing his head in'.

He asked, 'Was it a good programme?'

'Would you like me to tell you about it?'

'Please.'

And so I did. He got more and more interested. He felt he couldn't sort out anything until he had cleared things up. I passed on the tips I'd gleaned. For example, it is important to admit there is a problem, to do a little bit at a time, to push through the anxiety barrier of actually throwing something away and believing one can live without it.

He said, 'I only managed a drawer yesterday.'

I replied in a heartfelt way, 'No, not "only", that was marvellous; a whole drawer is incredible.'

This was not an empathic response. It came entirely out of my struggle; there are still times when to do a whole drawer feels insurmountable. There was something in his face. Something like shame. I realised that as he didn't know about my side of things, my response could have sounded condescending. I decided not to respond to the shame as that might make it much worse, and chose to tell him about me. I told him about my dusty heaps, the filing cabinet full of newspaper cuttings, catalogues, programmes and calendars, the drawers full of tights which I haven't worn for years, the carrier bags full of cards from at least five Christmases, the bin bags of other people's cast off clothes and the kitchen cupboard full of ancient spices and beans.

He looked immensely relieved and laughed.

I asked, 'Did you feel uncomfortable talking about it with me?'

'Yes a bit. I haven't been able to talk about with anyone. I felt ashamed.'

Out of a mixture of empathy and congruence I told him about myself rather than draw attention to his shame. He so immediately and totally relaxed I was reassured it was the right time for a rare moment of self-disclosure. He began to talk again about his feelings of depression. We talked about it a little but then we had to consider what to do. I was about to go away for a fortnight so we wouldn't be meeting for at least four weeks. We made a plan for him to begin tidying and throwing away and we agreed to look at the depression when we met up again.

The following month he returned quite exhilarated. He had reached the point of throwing out boxes and bags that had been unopened for twenty years. He was feeling a lot better.

He said, 'If I have managed without the things for this long, I can manage without them forever.'

He said that when I told him about my battle it had made all the difference to him.

In following sessions we looked at the meaning his possessions held for him. They represented more than his history and his identity; it was as though they actually were him and his past. Throwing things away felt impossibly dangerous. He was learning that he and his past could exist and survive without them.

I was being a very different aspect of myself with Jeff. I was tuning into his impulsiveness, friendliness and spontaneity. I think I was working very rapidly with empathy, congruence and unconditional positive regard and I knew, using empathy, that Jeff could handle it. In fact it suited him. I was equally myself with Louise.

Each client required a different use of myself. In each case my empathy determined my congruence. We all have our own understanding of the core conditions, (Rogers, 1967, pp. 60–3), and, in that sense, we are all idiosyncratic. In order to look at my idiosyncratic understanding I have divided the following exploration into five sections: meeting, unconditional positive regard, empathy, congruence and the relationship.

Meeting

I enjoy my work. I am totally absorbed, involved and deeply interested in the experiences of my clients and the therapeutic encounter. As soon as we meet, the process begins and my attention is attuned to them, to myself and to what is happening between us. Being with my client, attempting to understand their world, attending to what it is to be me and what it is for us to be together, is an activity that continually fascinates me.

Before anything else I allow myself to simply be in the presence of the client. This is a difficult thing to describe. I am listening with all of me. I have to use words like openness, sensing, shape, flow, beauty and awesome mystery, to catch something of the phenomenon of being in the presence of another in the protected space and time that therapy allows us. Somewhere I am also noticing, thinking, remembering and connecting; ideas are coming into my mind, but that is all behind the immediate experiencing of my clients which is where my moment-to-moment attention is. It is very important to me that this immediate attention always, always comes first.

Unconditional positive regard

Unconditional positive regard is the foundation upon which all therapy rests. My own belief system and faith lead me to see each of us as a phenomenon of being of great value, whatever our personalities and behaviours may be like. At this profound level I feel totally accepting of the whole self of the person I am with. I feel that I am in the presence of the whole person: everything they have been, who they are at that moment and all that they are capable of being.

As we meet and engage I have all sorts of other feelings as our personalities, attitudes and behaviours interact. These may become useful material for the therapy, but I do not ever want to lose sight of the sense of the fundamental, sacred preciousness of their being.

With each client I say to myself, 'Namaste'[2] (which means, 'I bow to the divine in you'). This is the bedrock of my practice.

Empathy

Empathy feels to me to be the key that can unlock the discovery of the self. It requires attention in every moment. The process of knowing the self can be eased or totally blocked by the tiniest deviation. It is an extraordinarily powerful attitude. I never cease to be struck by the impact of being properly understood or misunderstood, and every day I see the consequences of getting it right, and getting it wrong. Every day I know I shall learn something more about it. My client's experience of their world can be understood from the very first moments of encounter: how we meet and greet each other, how they are looking, how they are moving, how they come into the room and sit down, how they look at me, how they begin the session.

I am waiting, watching, listening, engaging and responding. The person before me is entirely unique: the experiences, the history, the feelings and thoughts, the beliefs and the meanings, the hopes and fears, the humour and imagination are all entirely unique and sitting there before me. What am I going to be shown of the person? What of them will I not be directly shown? What will happen when our two beings meet? As they begin to speak I listen not only to their words, their imagery, feelings and thoughts, but I am also aware of their body, any movements, facial expressions and the look in their eyes. There is so much more to listen to than the words. Everything is information. I want to find out what their meaning is and try to make no assumptions at all. Often different kinds of information are coming across. They may be describing a situation and how they feel when, in fact, everything suggests another feeling may be operating. For example, a teacher I saw recently who failed to get the promotion to headship he had expected and hoped for, described his feelings of weary frustration and despair. But his face seemed very tight, he could not look at me and his body was all hunched up. It

---

[2] 'Namaste' is in origin a Sanskrit word. It is used as a greeting across the Indian subcontinent and beyond.

looked and felt like anger and so it turned out to be. He admitted to absolute rage.

There are different aspects of the person to be aware of, hear and understand and this is what I am particularly interested in. I am prepared to extend empathy to the whole of the person I am with and I think this is where I am probably most idiosyncratic.

> The skill of the person-centred therapist is to help the client to unravel the uniqueness of his own structures and dynamics of self. And so the person-centred therapist listens as openly as possible to all the different parts, meanings and conflicts gradually unveiled by the client. (Mearns and Thorne, 2000, p. 127)

My understanding of empathy goes further than this. It is very elastic. I extend it in the widest possible sense. It stretches not only to all the parts that are 'gradually being unveiled', but to all aspects of self, veiled or unveiled, that the person is capable of being. It extends to their whole potential. I believe this potential being of themselves exists and, if it wants to, it will recognise itself and may respond to me.

I feel as though I am reaching out to the actualising tendency of the person by offering this broadest form of empathy. This wider understanding and use of empathy has been enhanced through what I have learnt from other approaches. They have increased my ability to hear what may or may not be said. It is empathy which safeguards how I offer the things that I have learnt, by listening and watching very carefully to the reaction my offer may have.

Congruence

What does it mean for myself as a person to be present with the client? My responses to my client come out of a mixture of my attunement to them and their world and from what is going on in me. I am not just a reflection of what they are saying to me. It is my self that is listening. I have a personality and I do not think it changes very much when I am working, although how I am varies with each client according to the relationship we have. My whole self includes everything that I am: my own history, my interests, and everything I have learnt along the way, including my psychological learning. All of this I understand may contribute at any moment to my 'self-experience'.

> Congruence is the accurate symbolisation and integration of self-experience into awareness and the accurate expression of this integrated experience into behaviour. (Lambers, 2000, p. 204)

My understanding of congruence may be considered idiosyncratic because I do use myself very fully in relationship with my clients, both in how I am and in the way I offer my learning and ideas with them. It is the number one lesson for me, that, despite my enjoyment in my work, my clients are not there for my interest: I am there for them: to help them to know and understand and accept themselves better. This is the sole purpose of our meeting. In order to do this I need to understand what is going on in me so that it will not interrupt the process of listening to them and so that I may use myself for their benefit. Becoming aware of the ideas from different approaches has helped me better understand what is happening to me whilst I am with the client.

I used to think I was very open. I see now that although I intended to be and was probably as open as I was capable of being, in a way I was not completely present because I did not know myself or the dynamics of relationships very well. The way I offered the core conditions meant that I was a bit hidden; a lot of me was not properly involved. There were quite a lot of things I was avoiding knowing about myself. For example, I have learnt that when I have strong reactions to a person, it is almost certainly an indication that something within myself is reacting; something that I am not familiar with, that I do not know or do not want to know; a hidden aspect, which Jung described as the shadow (Jung, 1964, pp. 171ff). It could be a positive aspect or a negative one.

A few years ago I was struggling with one or two clients that I felt were being unusually demanding and needy with me. Through looking at this reaction in therapy, I realised that there was a side of myself that found it very difficult to express my own needs. I was feeling impatient with people who were better at demonstrating their neediness than I was. I see these kinds of reactions in myself and in my clients every day and understand them to be clues which can lead us to important knowledge about the parts of ourselves we prefer to avoid. Our congruence changes all the time as our self-knowledge increases. Mine has changed a lot as a result of what I have learnt about the shadow aspect.

The relationship

Hundreds of thousands of words have been written about the therapeutic relationship. Nearly everyone acknowledges its importance, though few, I think, sufficiently acknowledge Rogers as identifying precisely the factors which make it so important. Even therapists who claim not to 'use' the relationship would not get very far if their clients did not experience them as being genuinely and warmly interested and attempting to understand them.

The client and I share time and space together. We are not doing anything else. We affect each other and react to each other. If the client is having a reaction to me or vice versa, then I can use myself as a source of learning for them. Being willing to use myself in the relationship as a source of information for the client is something that I am continually finding out about. Our relationship is a place where the whole of the client's situation may appear; it is a unique opportunity for them to find out what may be giving rise to their problems.

I see now that I was less than fully present to my clients because of a lack of knowledge about the dynamics of relationships. An understanding of Jung's shadow has helped me to see how my reactions to a person may be due to something I do not know about myself. Whereas the theories of transference (Kahn, 1997, p. 27ff), counter transference (ibid., p. 125 ff), projective identification (ibid. pp. 136–8) and attachment (Bacal and Newman, 1990, p. 209) have shown me that the reactions I am having to someone, or that they are having to me, may be due to previous experiences we have both had. For example, there are occasions when I notice I may be feeling protective and motherly towards a client. To recognise this does not feel as though it interferes with the way we relate. It is helpful because we can use it in all sorts of ways. For example, are they reminding me of one of my children or is there something about them that brings out this feeling in people?

Our relationship is also the meeting of two subjective realities. This is the approach taken by the intersubjectivists (Stolorow, Brandchaft and Atwood, 1987). What happens between us can be a source of information about how the client is in relation to others and to themselves. It is also a source of information about me, but as that is not the purpose of our meeting it is my responsibility to deal with it in my time, such as supervision or therapy. My reactions are appropriate to use in the session when they are of benefit to the client.

There is a tension between seeing the relationship as the meeting of two unique subjective realities and the idea that there are familiar dynamics that may be operating between people. For me, they are both true and knowing about them has enriched my understanding about being myself in relation to another person.

I see different ideas as helpful to bear in mind but it is essential that they do not lead me. I hold them at the back of my mind so that they do not get between myself and my client in the immediate experience of our being together. I respect Rogers' caution with regard to theory, as Thorne remarks:

> He discovered in his early work that a reliance on theory could lead to a situation where the therapist attempted to fit or mould a client into a preconceived cognitive structure rather than engaging with the client's world as he or she experienced it. (Thorne, 1992, p. 24)

I do believe that ultimately the client knows best. I always respect the centrality of their subjective experience but I am aware that the self is a complicated process with many aspects which may have different points of view about what is best for its wellbeing. My empathy, therefore, is offered to the whole person, veiled and unveiled, sometimes going beyond what is immediately being presented. My congruence includes being fully present and involved in the relationship, sharing myself and ideas, monitored and tempered by my empathic understanding of how the client is, what they may be calling on in me and how they are responding to what I am offering. Our whole encounter is underpinned by my understanding of unconditional positive regard.

The treasure chest
I have mentioned some of the ideas that have influenced me and in the following section I shall expand on this and show how they have become an integrated part of me rather than a collection of random fancies. As well as workshops, conferences, training programmes, textbooks and journals, ideas that affect the way I work come from all over the place. They come from conversations with colleagues, friends and relations, experiences in supervision and therapy, programmes on the radio and television, newspaper and magazine articles, books of all sorts, poetry, painting and sculpture, music, opera, and theatre. In this respect, life feels like a treasure chest of things to be discovered. I feel endlessly curious.

Learning about other approaches and ideas has been my way to educate myself in subjects that have always interested me and continue to interest me. There are always new ideas to consider, such as the extraordinary mapping of our consciousness by neuroscientists (Schore, 1994). Some of the things I have learnt make me feel more comfortable knowing what people are talking about. I used to feel awkward not understanding terms like 'attachment theory', 'ego strength', 'schizoid' and 'object relations'. I was also intrigued. There might be something there for me. Almost always there was.

But it has not just been curiosity that has attracted me. My approach to therapy is not merely an eclectic mish-mash of novelties. From the beginning I have investigated approaches which deliberately invite both our imaginative and thinking faculties into the therapeutic process. In the second year of my counselling training, I went on two transpersonal workshops, which invited imagination through visualisations, and an introductory weekend to Cognitive Analytic Therapy (Ryle, 1995). Throughout my eighteen years working as a counsellor and therapist I have been fascinated by the multifaceted nature of the self and have learnt how to gain awareness and understanding of it through these cognitive and imaginative aspects. At the same time my attention has been consistently drawn to the universality of human experience. My attempts to understand the transcendence of self has led me to consider the interface between psychology and spirituality which helps find a place that takes us beyond our personality.

The multifaceted nature of the self
There are a multitude of ways to discover, understand and contact the complex process that is the self. The idea that the self has many aspects is an old one. Jung identified opposing forces in the psyche which he described in terms of the persona, the shadow and the archetypes (Casement, 2001). Transactional Analysis introduced us to our adult and inner child (Berne, 1975) and most of us have met our sub-personalities (Rowan, 1993). Configurations of self have now entered person-centred theory (Mearns and Thorne, 2000) and listening to our different aspects has become a normal part of working practice. Years of working with dissociative clients (Mollon, 1996), has taught me that while I am apparently in the presence of one, I am in the presence of many.

I am also interested in the aspects of the self that are presented less immediately. Narrative therapy, as developed by Michael White and David Epston (Payne, 2000), has a social constructionist approach to therapy which has shown me that we may become trapped by the stories we make of our lives. We may selectively remember experiences which reinforce the stories, often destructively. It can be helpful to look for the 'untold stories'. This phrase still gives me a thrill. Narrative therapy listens or asks for exceptions or 'unique outcomes' (Goffman, 1961), times when the familiar story was not repeated.

I worked with a man who repeatedly told me about his terribly unhappy childhood with two alcoholic foster parents. I asked him if he could remember any times at all which felt less awful. He quickly said he couldn't. I pressed him. Then he remembered the dens. He was leader of a little gang and they used to make dens. We found some happy memories which opened up the possibility of looking at those qualities of play and leadership that he had lost sight of. It could be protested that I wasn't letting my client lead or choose the direction of therapy in his case. However, I think that this is a case of my elastic empathy. The whole man was there. His qualities of play and leadership were there. He had completely lost sight of them. By inviting him to search for an exception I gave him a chance to reconnect with that part of himself and bring it back into his consciousness. If he had continued to be unable to find a memory I would have dropped it. I persevered because he answered so quickly the first time that I felt he wasn't really believing there could be anything else but the familiar horrors.

At one of those early transpersonal workshops I was shown how to listen to my self: to separate out the intuitive and spiritual part, the thinking mind, the feelings and the body. I have found this extremely helpful, both for myself and for clients, in all sorts of situations but particularly when there is an inner conflict or a difficult decision to make and no clear way forward. A very common example would be when someone is driving themselves into the ground with overwork. It has helped me to ask: 'You sound very tired. What would your body say about it if it could?' in response to a weary sigh. Sometimes I tell a person about the idea and see if they want to try it out in its entirety. I do not feel that I am imposing the idea on them.

I remember a client saying, 'I know this is this the right thing for me to do in terms of my career, but there is just something that doesn't feel right about it.' I empathised with this statement and added, 'Would it be helpful to hear what different aspects of yourself have to say about it?' I introduced the idea to her. It helped her identify strikingly different points of view which showed her exactly why there was something that didn't feel quite right about it.

I have learnt how to listen to the body in a gestalt way, treating it as though it can talk and asking questions of it directly, such as, 'Foot is tapping rather fast isn't it? What does foot say?' Shortly after I learnt this approach, I had a client whose legs were always on the move, swinging about. I had always been a bit nonplussed and used to carry on talking above them but it was like ignoring an energetic child gambolling about between us. I decided to try it out and, feeling rather idiotic, I said, 'I notice there is a lot of energy in legs. What do legs say?' My client was amused but then attended to his legs and found that they wanted to dance and leap about. It led to him recognising that the dissatisfaction he had been expressing about his job was in fact a frustration far greater than he had realised.

I have noticed that when people are considering a new way of thinking or are identifying an important feeling they often squirm or grimace or look uncomfortable. Noticing this feeling can help them realise that something is changing. Focusing (Gendlin, 1978) would identify this as the 'felt sense'. Attending to the felt sense is an extremely sensitive and powerful way of finding out what is going on in us by becoming aware of the wordless sense of ourselves held within our body:

> This 'inner referent' or felt sense holds a highly differentiated set of implicit meanings. For these meanings to be made explicit, the person must express the felt sense in a symbol, such as a word, phrase, statement, image or even bodily movement. The act of symbolizing an area of meaning in the felt sense allows other areas to come to attention. Accurate symbolisation therefore brings about a 'shift' in the inner felt sense of a situation or problem. (McLeod, 1998, p. 105)

'Accurate symbolisation' leads me to consider the different ways we can work with images and symbols.

The imaginative and cognitive aspects of the self
The creative and imaginative part of our selves can be accessed by listening to the imagery we use. Our speech is full of imagery and one way that listening to images can be helpful is to monitor inner feelings. Clients have described their inner states to me in various ways: a river, a portcullis, a Viking ship which can move in many ways using wind and oars, a window that is open or closed to a varying degree. They have told me that when they want to know what they are really feeling they

check to see what is happening to their image. The image can also be played with in the imagination and this may open up different ways of thinking, feeling and behaving.

In my transpersonal training I learnt to 'walk the dream' (Somers and Wilde McCormick, 2000, p. 164). This is a way of working with images in dreams in the same way as with images that appear in conversation, as happened with Alice. Sheena brought me a dream in which she was standing holding two saws above her head. In each saw she could see people moving. We 'walked' the dream. When she got to holding up the saws, she said she felt completely exhausted. I asked her what she wanted to do. She wanted to put them down but it felt too frightening: what would happen to the people inside them? We waited a little and then she thought she would see if she could. When she did she felt the most enormous relief. The people were still carrying on their business. She realised that she had been holding them up for years out of fear of the consequences of putting them down. Later, she said it all felt part of letting go of the protective front she had put up to the world and her overdeveloped sense of responsibility. The dream helped her realise what a huge amount of energy it has taken to 'keep it up'.

> We are working, equally with the client, on material which is either already in his awareness or in the process of coming into awareness. An important discipline of the Person-Centred Approach is to work at the level of the client's current level of symbolisation so that the client is at the centre of the endeavour. (Mearns and Thorne, 2000, p. 103)

In these cases where images appear in dreams or conversations, they are at the level of the client's current level of symbolisation. I want to go beyond this and invite a person to find an image where none currently exists. It is like calling on the imaginative faculty of the actualising tendency. All creative thought comes from this kind of imaginative leaping. Any painting or creative writing has actually to be *created*. It is apparently coming out of nothing but it must in fact come from the creative self of the person. It may not fall within the 'current level of symbolisation' referred to above, but I take great care that 'the client is at the centre of the endeavour'. This idea of imaginative leaping has crossed paths with what I have discovered in cognitive therapy.

Cognitive therapy works in the area of the imagination. One way of using it is to invite a person to look beyond an immediate situation and imagine themselves doing things differently or to imagine anything at all that would be embodying the qualities that they are wanting and, from this, to identify what it is that needs to change. I think it is empathising with the part of a person that can be reached by the imagination and that may not be in awareness.

James had to give up work in the prison service due to overwhelming stress over many years. He felt frustrated and stuck with the hideous memories of work. We had been here for many sessions and I felt stuck too. I said so and asked if we could try something different. I asked him to take a great imaginative leap and pretend it had all never happened; to imagine doing something and feeling free and good about it and what would that be like. It was very hard. Eventually he looked up and said, 'It would be something with no responsibility at all.' It was a completely new way of looking things and was something he had never allowed himself to consider.

Another client, desperate with family pressures, at my invitation to 'leap' found herself imagining the spaces between the seeds she had been planting in her vegetable garden. She realised she was metaphorically choking and it showed her what she needed to do.

Cognitive therapy has helped me think more clearly. Some people seem to think clearly more easily than others. I have had to learn how to think and cognitive therapy has helped me introduce some order into what sometimes felt like a rather too chaotic internal world.

In recent years, as I have been involved in both the writing and marking of essays I have found that it is not enough to say that something is interesting or difficult; we have to say why it is so. I think this can be a useful way to approach life. I like the way cognitive therapy asks questions like: what was it about the holiday that made you feel good? What did you do differently this time? Most of all, cognitive therapy has shown me that we can develop troublesome habits of thinking, feeling and behaviour based on beliefs and assumptions formed from our experiences. By challenging these thinking patterns, different ways of being can have room to appear.

I am acutely aware that paying such particular attention to the thinking part of ourselves could feel intrusive and alien, crushing to the imagination and be the last thing that a person might want to do. As with all these ideas that I may offer, I am extremely careful about whether to offer it and when, and to be sensitive to the reaction it receives. My empathic antennae are on full alert.

The universality of human experience
The outstanding feature for me of Person-Centred Therapy is the importance it places on and the respect it holds for the centrality of subjective experience: the phenomenological viewpoint. There cannot be any argument about this. We all have a unique experience with our genes, our histories and every experience from the moment of our conception (and some would say before), shaping us into who we are. Discovering this singularity of experience was a liberation for me and attending to it continues to be my guiding principle at all times. The question is always: what is the meaning for this person? At the same time, I have always been interested by what we share in common, by the universality of our experience as human beings.

In the second year of my counselling training I worked with some family therapists who introduced me to the idea of systemic thinking (Draper and Dallos, 2000). To see ourselves as part of some system and not merely as individuals was a complete contrast to the phenomenological view I was learning about. It fitted in with my lifelong interest in ethology and the extraordinary way animals operate in groups, as in migration, or the organisation of insect populations such as bees, ants and termites where the individual exists for the whole population, sharing complex patterns of behaviour and means of communication.

These commonalities are reflected in human terms. We have been sharing experiences for hundreds of thousands of years. Unless a life is cut off short or there are exceptional circumstances, we all share the experience of being born, having a gender, being a child, maturing into an adult, having some sort of relationships, growing older and dying. As Campbell has so thoroughly discussed these are archetypal experiences that we share with each other and they appear in myths and fairy stories and folk lore which show repeating themes from different cultures and times (Campbell, 1985).

There have been many attempts to describe the phenomenon of the human personality in a systematic way. In their book *Character and Personality Types* Totton and Jacobs (2001) look very thoroughly at this history from ancient descriptions such as the enneagram, based on early Sufi mysticism, and ayurvedic chakra types to the situation today where typologies abound. Our western secular therapeutic world is dominated by the psychological categories listed in *The Diagnostic and Statistical Manual of Mental Disorders* (American Psychiatric Association, 1994). Because of my deep respect for the value of the subjective experience, I used to have a horror of categorisation. Now I feel that knowing about what we have in common is important and cannot be ignored. However, I believe there are many ways of looking at it, including different cultural viewpoints, and that they are descriptions that must be handled with enormous care.

> The argument about the merits or dangers of character and personality types is, then, perhaps about the appropriate balance between the wisdom of experience and the wisdom of 'beginner's mind'. And this balance — like all living balances — has to be a dynamic one, which sways between its two extreme positions in each session, and over a week, a year, a lifetime. (Totton and Jacobs, 2001, p. 3)

I have often noticed how therapists from all sorts of different backgrounds, and people in general, gravitate towards the Rogers' core conditions as a comfortable way of being in relationship. This I consider to be Rogers' great achievement: at the same time as celebrating our uniqueness he identified the common qualities of human relating at its best. Going further than this, I would say that he identified qualities of relating that bring us closer to our spiritual nature. This leads me to the belief I share with many people that what we have most in common is that ultimately we are all part of one reality: the Everything and the Nothing as described by Meher Baba (1963).

The transcendence of self

In the second year of my original training I had an experience which completely changed my spiritual understanding of our existence. It led me to believe that ultimately there is only one reality of which we are all part. The individuality of the self is an illusion. Buddhism describes our Buddha nature as 'One's own true nature, True Self. Buddha nature should not be misunderstood as a separate soul' (Jiyu-Kennett, 1999, p. 304).

Over the years I found I was increasingly faced with a dilemma. Psychologically we give all our attention to understanding and strengthening the self, whereas spiritually, the goal seems to be to transcend the self. I began to seriously question what I was doing in my work. In devoting my time, enthusiasm and interest to the phenomenon of self, was I in fact going spiritually in the completely wrong direction and taking my clients with me? Was I encouraging the illusion?

As I continued to work, I saw, as Rogers predicted and described, people becoming more accepting and fully understanding of themselves, including most importantly their shadow sides, as they internalised the core conditions I attempted to offer them. It was hard to see that this could be harmful in any way.

Many writers have examined the area where psychological and spiritual practice meet. (Wilber, 1998; Wellwood, 1983; Kornfield, 1993; Epstein, 1999). Nigel Wellings (2000) has summarised writings on the interface with Buddhist beliefs. It became increasingly clear to me that the two practices are very different disciplines, but there are areas which they share in common. One area felt particularly relevant to my concerns:

> Wellwood identifies the quality of *maitri* or unconditional friendliness. In transpersonal psychology we link this to the compassionate observer. In practice this is the essential ability not to judge one's ideas, feelings and actions, particularly when they first become conscious, but rather let them be with a kindly acceptance which does not make us wrong for having them . . . Maitri then, is the unconditional friendliness that we extend to ourselves during the explorations of therapy and also as we sit in meditational practice. (Wellings, 2000, p. 183)

This feels similar to the Buddhist attitude of mindfulness: 'Mindfulness or bare attention requires a careful noting of everything that happens in the mind-body spectrum as it unfolds' (Epstein, 1998, p. 67). For me, something of this is present when cognitive therapy is used sensitively, and gently attending to the felt sense as encouraged in focusing offers the same approach. We can become less attached to the hubbub of our personalities. The strength of the Person-Centred Approach for me is that it offers the most facilitative conditions for the development of the compassionate observer.

This view provides a challenging alternative to some current attitudes to psychological disturbance. Our fears, desires and even our suffering, become states to 'be with' rather than to avoid.

> Rather than see the self as an expanding and contracting, coalescing and dissolving, separating and merging organism, Western psychology views the self as something that has to be developed or improved throughout its one-way journey to separateness . . . if we continue to see development in linear terms, as proceeding from a merged state of oneness to differentiation and autonomy we will continue to miss the essential role of letting go in our lives. (ibid., p. 85).

The Person-Centred Approach is unusual, and is sometimes criticised, for its lack of intention in therapy, its 'non-directiveness'. For me, it respects and values the changing process as described above and for the moment, these areas that psychological and spiritual practice share in common have settled my dilemma.

I realise that these are my understandings. I deeply respect that this area of belief is extremely personal. I work comfortably with people who have no belief in anything other than the world they directly experience and who have reactions ranging from indifference to outrage at the idea that there could be anything else. I work entirely with and within our relationship and what arises for the client. For me the core conditions offer the best analysis of a spiritually attentive and caring relationship and, spiritually speaking, for me, nothing more is required.

Two clients' experiences of therapy

I asked two clients if they would be willing to give me some feedback on what had been useful or not useful about our work together. When we met after a summer break, Sheena and Alice brought me something they had written. I felt very nervous. What would their side of it be? This is what they wrote.

Firstly Sheena, who had the dream about the saws and who experiences dissociation:

> *One of the most helpful things, at least in the long term, was the unconditional positive regard (UPR) shown to all my aspects, that was constant no matter what the content shared. At times this was most painful to receive depending on whomever internally was listening. Suddenly I was exposed, and it took a while to get used to the light. Or again, UPR to me is the experience of suddenly being on centre stage, in the limelight when I thought I was backstage. For the child aspect this was what was deeply desired, to be noticed and loved and yet the experience was unfamiliar and until used to, very painful. It brought to feeling, what had felt lost and never to be.*
>
> *This OK to be your self, as shown by Rose's way of relating to me and the world generally, has allowed me to be more brave in allowing others to see other aspects of myself and feel less self-conscious about my differences, rather than conforming to what I would think each person would think acceptable behaviour, according to my perception of the time.*
>
> *One particular way of 'walking the dream' proves to be invaluable for checking my internal state. Without the total acceptance of who I am and have been, I would never have been able to open myself to work in this way. I would add that the dreams used in this way have been ones with a different quality about them to the normal run of the mill dreams. They have all felt significant, and until 'walking the dream' I would have missed their real value.*

And Alice:

> *I came to Rose at first because I wasn't sleeping. I was pretty unhappy really, although I didn't allow myself to admit that because it would have made me feel guilty. I had absolutely no reason in the world to be even the tiniest bit unhappy, so I kept trying to do everything right, the way I had been taught to but found everyone else constantly breaking the rules and getting away with it. I think I was pretty angry about it. Anger again was something that might have been hard, but not as hard, to admit.*
>
> *I probably wanted an answer, over about three visits, and then I would get on with my life. I didn't get an answer and still don't have one now, not really. And I'm so glad that that's how it has turned out (over far longer than three visits) because the world is more complicated and fascinating and bewildering than I was brought up to believe or that answer could explain. I've discovered instead that I am unique, a product of a difficult upbringing involving amongst other things a new school every year or two from four until eleven, a regimented boarding school, divorcing parents . . . parents with their own set of problems and understanding of the world. Taken from the point of view that I am unique, with unique experience it dawned on me (slowly) that my particular view of*

the world is just that; mine. And all the more precious for it.

Feelings hadn't been encouraged/valued/important in my past. It came as a surprise to gradually trust feeling above whatever my head told me I should feel. There had been a war going on; what I felt, covered by what I should feel. The should generally won and left me feeling confused and angry.

It was often very difficult to admit what I was feeling and the non-judgemental atmosphere in which to talk and which I have rarely, if ever, experienced before, was so important.

Once we literally acted out a particular image that had been going through my head and I came to realise what I was trying to do to myself. I was being more critical of myself than I could believe; trying to destroy whatever didn't fit it in. Another time we drew the people in my life and my different feelings in different coloured pens. The exercise made me see the complexity of the relationships and my own position and contribution to them, for better and worse. Both of these exercises have stayed with me as a powerful image of how it is possible to get to a deeper meaning behind what we are experiencing.

It was useful to see a spiritual dimension to what we were talking about, like the relaxation exercises we sometimes practised as a form of meditation when my mind was racing, as with the Buddhist idea of monkey mind. It helped me put what I was discovering in a context that makes sense to me. And I will always be searching for a deeper more profound answer just because that is me.

Talking about dreams, the emphasis on feelings and more than anything, going over and over and over again. It has been a slow gentle process of letting go of the habits of a lifetime and learning a new way to experience the world. For someone used to getting things done in a hurry, to understanding quickly, it has been a lesson in patience. But it couldn't have been rushed. I had spent thirty-nine years learning what I now tried to unlearn.

Rose has focused on me as a unique person, not a term or a label. And she has taken time to help me discover this for myself. If this approach is idiosyncratic then I would understand that to mean from my experience, varied, adaptable, informed, patient, kind. I felt understood. For me it has been a very valuable experience.

Beads on a string

Some people might describe my approach as integrative (O'Brien and Houston, 2000). I do not mind if they do. I am concerned not to contribute to adversarial attitudes. But I would describe myself first and foremost as person-centred. The spiritual teacher, Meher Baba, said:

I have not come to teach but to awaken . . . I am not come to establish . . . a new religion. The religion that I shall teach gives the knowledge of the One behind the many. The book that I shall make people read is the book of the heart that holds the key to the mystery of life. I shall bring about a happy blending of the head and the heart. I shall revitalise all religions . . . and bring them together like beads in one string. (Cohen, 1977, p. 80).

Rogers identified fundamental truths about the formation of the self, the therapeutic process and the therapeutic relationship. I feel the core conditions he identified are the string on which all other beads of therapy hang.

References

American Psychiatric Association. (1994) *Diagnostic and Statistical Manual of Mental Disorders* Fourth Edition. Washington D.C.: American Psychiatric Association.

Bacal, H.A. and Newman, K.N. (1990) *Theories of Object Relations: Bridges to Self Psychology.* New York: Columbia University Press.

Berne, E. (1975) *What Do You Say After You've Said Hello? The Psychology of Human Destiny.* London: Corgi.

Campbell, J. (1985) *Myths to Live By.* London: Paladin.

Casement, A. (2001) *Carl Gustav Jung.* London: Sage.

Cohen, A.Y. (1977) *The Mastery of Consciousness.* Twickenham: Eel Pie Publishing.

Draper, R. and Dallos, R. (2000) *Introduction to Family Therapy.* Buckingham: Oxford University Press.

Epstein, M. (1999) *Going To Pieces Without Falling Apart.* London: Thorsons.

Gendlin, E. T. (1978) *Focusing.* New York: Bantam Books.

Goffman, E. (1961) *Asylums.* London: Penguin.

Jiyu-Kennett, P. (1999) *Zen is Eternal Life.* California: Shasta Abbey Press.

Jung, C.G. (1964*) Man and his Symbols.* London: Picador.

Kahn, M. (1997) *Between Therapist and Client.* New York: W.H. Freeman and Company.

Kornfield, J. (1993) *A Path With Heart.* London: Rider Books.

Lambers, E. (2000) Supervision in Person-Centred Therapy: Facilitating congruence. In *Person-Centred Therapy Today.* (Eds) D. Mearns and B. Thorne. (2000) London. London: Sage, pp. 196–211.

McLeod, J. (1998) *An Introduction to Counselling.* Buckingham: Open University Press.

McKewn, J. (1997) *Developing Gestalt Counselling.* London: Sage.

Mearns, D. and Thorne, B. (2000) *Person-Centred Therapy Today.* London: Sage.

Meher Baba. (1963) *The Everything and The Nothing.* Berkeley: The Beguine Library.

Mollon, P. (1996) *Multiple Selves, Multiple Voices.* London: Wiley.

O'Brien, M. and Houston, G. (2000) *Integrative Therapy.* London: Sage.

Payne, M. (2000) *Narrative Therapy.* London: Sage.

Rogers, C.R. (1967) *On Becoming a Person.* London: Constable.

Rowan, J. (1993) *Discovering Your Subpersonalities.* London: Routledge.

Ryle, A. (1995) *Cognitive Analytic Therapy.* London: Wiley.

Schore, A. (1994) *Affect Regulation and The Origin of Self.* Hove: Lawrence Erlbaum.

Somers. B. and Wilde McCormick. E. (2000) Dreaming in depth. In N. Wellings and E. Wilde McCormick. (Eds) *Transpersonal Psychology.* London: Continuum, pp. 157–76.

Stolorow, R. Brandchaft, B. and Atwood, G.E. (1987) *Psychoanalytic Treatment: An Intersubjective Approach.* Hillsdale, NJ: Analytic Press.

Thorne, B. (1992) *Carl Rogers.* London: Sage.

Totton, N. and Jacobs, M. (2001) *Character and Personality Types.* Buckingham: Open University Press.

Trower, P., Casey, A. and Dryden, W. (1996) *Cognitive Behavioural Counselling in Action.* London: Sage.

Wellings, N. (2000) Naked presence. In N. Wellings and E. Wilde McCormick (Eds.) *Transpersonal Psychotherapy.* London: Continuum, pp. 183.

Wellings, N. and Wilde McCormick, E. (Eds.) (2000) *Transpersonal Psychotherapy.* London: Continuum, pp. 177–205.

Wellwood, J. (Ed.) (1983) *Awakening The Heart.* Boston: Shambhala.

Wilber, K. (1998) *The Essential Ken Wilber.* Boston: Shambhala.

Wilde McCormick, E. (2000) The Therapeutic Relationship. In N. Wellings and E. Wilde McCormick. (Eds.) *Transpersonal Psychotherapy.* London: Continuum, pp. 20–51.

Tony Merry

Epilogue

Person-centred theory gives us a sense of direction in what we do as counsellors, but no theory is ever adequate to explain the complexity of human relationships. In a counselling context, theory should be held lightly. It is always inadequate in that it reduces complexity to a series of simple statements. We can say, 'empathic understanding is, theoretically, a necessary condition of effective therapy', but this does not convey (nor is it intended to convey) the feeling that accompanies the experience of being deeply understood and accepted for who we are. To capture some of this feeling, we need to enter into the counselling relationship not as curious and objective observers, but as involved and active participants.

The various authors of this book were set a most difficult task. They were asked to describe what 'being person-centred' meant to them, not only in theoretical terms but also as involved and compassionate people. I know, from experience, how hazardous a task this can be. Writing chapters for this book was, I believe, a risky undertaking since every time we write, or say anything, we run the risk of being misunderstood, or judged. Writing something down can convey the message that here is a finished work, the final product, the last word, but to read these chapters as if they represented a 'final product' would, I believe, be a mistake. In the Person-Centred Approach, we talk a lot about 'process', of 'becoming', of 'change' and of 'growth'. There is a dynamism in those words, a feeling of flow, of movement, of transition from one state to another. As each counsellor represented here grows and changes, so will his or her work, but each will retain their own uniqueness and identity — their own idiosyncratic way of being.

Each of the counsellors contributing to this book describe themselves as 'person-centred' in their theoretical and philosophical orientation, but this tells us little of who they are as persons and as practitioners. It tells us that they base their work on the hypothesis that growth and change are natural and common experiences; that change results from the urge to become all we are capable of becoming; that to 'actualise' is a property of life itself. It also tells us that each of these practitioners derive their inspiration, in some measure, from the pioneering and revolutionary work of Carl Rogers, and that it is relationships that count, not technique, and not theory.

The counselling literature is replete with arguments about the relative merits of adopting a 'single theory approach' or a more 'integrative' one in which the concepts and strategies developed in a number of approaches to counselling are combined together to create something new. In the person-centred world there are debates and arguments between those who adopt the 'classical' or 'orthodox' position, and those who reach beyond 'mainstream' person-centred theory and are influenced by other ideas and perspectives. However, the most important task for any counsellor, of any school of thought, is to develop her own approach. In effect, this implies an assimilation into the counsellor's self-structure those ideas, theories and philosophies that most closely match her own personal values and experience. This is certainly true in person-centred counselling, where theory is useful only to the extent that it represents a congruent expression of the counsellor as a person. This means that each person-centred counsellor expresses, in her work and perhaps in her life, the theory and philosophy of the Person-Centred Approach as it comes alive within her.

Part of the problem with the word 'theory' is that it is associated with scientific method. Theories are designed to explain events and observations, and to predict and control the future. Person-centred theory is a good example of theory presented as testable hypotheses and propositions: '*if* these conditions are present, *then* these changes will follow.' To this extent, Rogers was a good scientist. Trained in scientific methods, Rogers presented his ideas to the world in the form of hypotheses and propositions, challenged the scientific community to disprove them, and set about accumulating evidence to test them for himself. Interestingly, however, Rogers never returned to his 1957 and 1959 theory statements in order to refine them, or discard them, or adapt them in the light of new information. To some, this is evidence of stagnation: 'How can a statement of theory written during the 1950s still be relevant in the twenty-first century?' To others, it is a testament to the thoroughness with which Rogers approached his task.

Rogers suggested that counsellors are better equipped to facilitate change if they can be empathic, experience unconditional positive regard, and remain congruent in their relationships with clients. To the dismay of some, he didn't tell us *how* we were to be empathic, *how* we should be 'congruent' or *how* we should communicate our positive regard. He showed us how *he* did it, but he didn't expect others to do things the way he did. He described the characteristics of empathic understanding, he offered a portrait of the hypothetical fully-functioning, congruent person, and he discussed the non-judgemental nature of unconditional positive regard, and he admitted how difficult it is to be all of these things. Rogers wasn't interested in telling us how we should 'do counselling', but he did invite us to try and *be* a certain way, and to see what happens.

The problem is even more complex, however. If there is a 'certain way' to 'be', then we could all practise being that way, and everything would be fine. But Rogers said, to paraphrase him, 'This is my way of being. I do it like this because this is who I am. Woe betide you if you try to be like me. Be like yourself.' To try to be like Rogers would be to portray the therapeutic conditions as if a portrayal were sufficient. We know it is not. In fact, we know that a portrayal is the worst kind of deception; and we know that to deceive is the worst kind of betrayal.

Many clients seek help because, in some way or another, they have been deceived and betrayed. Those who should have cared for them did not, and those who should have been genuine with them deceived them. Their 'genuineness' was a sham. As counsellors, we work with the deceived and the betrayed every day, and the last thing we should do is to deceive them again by portraying a 'genuineness' that we know to be a sham, particularly if it is done in the name of 'theory'.

All person-centred counselling is idiosyncratic in the sense that all of it is an expression of an individual, and all of us are different. This is not, however, an excuse for an 'anything goes as long as I'm being congruent' approach. In itself, this reveals a misunderstanding of the meaning of congruence. This book contains the accounts of a group of counsellors struggling to 'be themselves' in their relationships with their clients. In particular they present their work with an honest determination that, however difficult it proves to be, what they value most of all is their genuineness or, as Rogers sometimes put it, their 'authenticity'. This authenticity manifests itself in a variety of ways throughout the book. Sometimes it is represented by a counsellor's internal dialogue as he or she contemplates what 'being person-centred' means. At other times we are privileged to witness the moment by moment encounter between a counsellor and a client as, together, they try and understand chaotic, confusing or frightening thoughts and feelings.

There is dynamism, flow and movement in each of the chapters contained within this book. The practitioners describing their work and themselves each communicate a depth of engagement with their clients that involves them as whole persons. An unusual and welcome dimension is that this 'engagement' is brought to life through the voices of clients who tell us what *they* think and feel. Indeed, some chapters invite us to think about the process from the client's vantage point, as 'spoken' directly by the client. The book is unusual also because it shows person-centred counselling 'in the raw'— uncut and as it happens. It is very immediate and honest. While there is theory here, and science, there is also art and artistry. All of the chapters deal with 'the relationship' in one way or another, some directly, others indirectly. Some describe their preparation for entering into relationship with clients, some describe their own journey towards becoming 'person-centred'. Others take a particular relationship and explore it, or allow it to speak for itself.

Perhaps for me the most exciting thing about this book is that none of the counsellors included is 'Rogerian' (there was only ever one of those), yet all are person-centred. This is not so simple a thing as a matter of 'style' or 'emphasis'. All are person-centred in that they proceed from a trust in the client's ability to take what they need from the relationship, yet each behaves very differently. There is something broader, altogether more profound being communicated than 'accurate empathy', though that is present too. It is the personality of each of the counsellors that insists on being expressed — their sense of humour, what concerns them, touches them, moves them.

I have learned a number of things from reading this book. Firstly, I have learned (again) how crucial it is for a counsellor to trust her 'inner experiencing', and not to be afraid of it. At the same time, I have been reminded of how important it is to think about this experience, to live with it and to use it wisely and responsibly.

Secondly, the term 'idiosyncratic empathy' has taken on a deeper meaning for me. Life experience, intuition and sensitivity all combine uniquely to enable each of us to 'hear' subtlety and nuance differently, and to respond to it in ways that go far beyond the formulaic and mechanical way that 'reflection of feelings' is sometimes misrepresented.

Thirdly, this book demonstrates that it is clients' self-healing resources that become available to them through relationships with counsellors who are prepared to accompany them rather than guide or direct them. This process of 'companionship' is not always easy, and it isn't a passive one of silent observation or non-involvement. The counsellors in this book are inventive, creative and committed. They actively reach out to their clients so that between them they can achieve something that may have been impossible alone.

Finally, I am reminded that Rogers' theory was, in essence, a 'working hypothesis' that could be tested again and again with each new client. Every counsellor in this book tests that hypothesis in different, unique and idiosyncratic ways and each arrives at their own internal formulation of a personal theory. Rogers has provided the framework, but each practitioner personalises it and makes it 'come alive'.

At the very heart of the book lies a deep honesty. There is no deception here. If mistakes are made, they are honest ones. The authors simply say, 'This is me. This is how I take Rogers' theory and shape it so that the way I am with my clients reveals something of who I am as a person.'

Contributors

The Editor

Suzanne Keys works as a person-centred counsellor in Newham Sixth Form College in London and as a therapist and supervisor in private practice. She is a participant in a local Independent Practitioners' Network (IPN) group. She comes from Northern Ireland and has lived and worked in France, Italy and the Ivory Coast, West Africa.

The Contributors

Annette Ansell has been in private practice for eight years and works from north-east London and her counselling rooms in central London. She has had a wide variety of jobs including dairy farming, being a nanny, selling underwear, mending cars, setting up a housing association for homeless women with babies, and fundraising for an HIV/AIDS organisation. Her career in the charity sector, before moving into private practice as a counsellor, culminated in becoming a supported housing manager for a pan-London project helping single homeless people. It was this work which finally motivated Annette to become a full-time counsellor when she recognised a gap in provision for homeless people. She now has a large, holistic practice in central London providing rooms for other counsellors and psychotherapists, including alternative and complementary therapists, and a placement scheme for person-centred counsellors.

Rose Battye writes: I live with my husband Ian in the country. I love it when Tom and Nell, our son and daughter come to stay. Recently I have given up my counselling work in a GP surgery so that I have more time for such things as walking with our dog, Wigram, gardening, watching birds and seeing friends and family. Sometimes I do absolutely nothing at all. I completed my person-centred diploma (FDI Britain) in 1988 and work as a person-centred counsellor/therapist, supervisor and trainer.

Jenny Biancardi is a BACP accredited counsellor, UKCP registered psychotherapist, qualified psychodramatist, Senior Trainer for the BPA and has a Certificate in Counselling Supervision. She writes: I have varied management experience in the health service and regularly run staff development and management training courses for both the public and private sectors. Person-centred theory and principles inform my practice both as a therapist and as a trainer.

Terry Daly works as a person-centred therapist, supervisor and trainer in Glasgow. Working in these areas creates the ideal situation for Terry to meet those of his passions that can be shared in public. The first one being a deep belief in the quality of relationship and that offering the core conditions can have a profound and powerful effect on individual lives. Secondly, as a trainer, Terry has a strong commitment to the principles of equal opportunities along with the idea of self-learning and, through a person-centred way of working, he has found a medium in which the two can be brought together. Being a supervisor working with many experienced counsellors has given him an ideal place to see how the approach is making a fundamental difference in the fabric of Scottish culture. As a gay man, who is severely dyslexic, his experience of not fitting in to society and the education system has sharpened his desire to create space where people can find their own individuality and self-acceptance. Terry believes it is ironic that in the process of having to challenge labels and barriers you first of all have to adopt them, so that you can define yourself, rewrite these labels and then become free from them.

Irene Fairhurst is a BACP Senior Registered Practitioner and a consultant to various educational and training organisations. She was a member of the BAC Individual accrediting panel for a number of years and co-founder and President of the British Association for the Person-Centred Approach for its initial seven years. She has completed an MA in Counselling at the University of Hertfordshire. Her home is in Essex, which as well as housing her private practice, also, at present, is the base for the Institute of Person-Centred Learning. Irene edited *Women Writing in the Person-Centred Approach* for PCCS Books in 1999, and, in what little spare time she has, enjoys playing tennis, gardening and reading. Aims for the future include cutting down on work and spending more time with her grandson!

Jan Hawkins is a person-centred therapist, supervisor, trainer and group facilitator. She is married and has three children, two of whom are now adults. Jan is committed to offering experiential learning opportunities from a person-centred perspective on the legacy of childhood abuse, learning and/or physical disabilities and loss and bereavement. These learning environments allow deepening of empathy and self-awareness around particular issues.

Dick McDonald is a priest in Anglican orders, formerly a tutor in theology and 'trainer' of clergy in East Africa and a lecturer in religious studies and a 'trainer' of teachers in the UK He is now in private practice as a counsellor and supervisor and is a Senior Registered Practitioner and Fellow of the British Association for Counselling and Psychotherapy.

Omar Sattaur trained as a counsellor after a successful career as a journalist and broadcaster in Britain and Asia. He received his diploma in person-centred counselling in February 2003 and now spends part of his week counselling at a GP practice. He spends the remainder as a freelance editor and writer, mostly for development and environment agencies.

Caryl Sibbett, BA, Dip.Couns, SRATh, M.Ed. (Guidance & Counselling), writes: I am a Lecturer at the Graduate School of Education, Queen's University Belfast, where I teach on courses including the MSc Art Therapy. I am a BACP Registered Counsellor, a UKRC Registered Independent Counsellor and a State Registered Art Therapist. I am Vice-Chairperson of the Northern Ireland Group for Art as Therapy (NIGAT). I have published papers in journals such as the British Medical Journal and presented nationally and internationally.

Sholto Thompson, B.Ed. (hons), Dip. Art Therapy, Dip. Ed. Psych., Dip. P.C.T., Cert. Supervision, was born in Toronto, Canada, on 12th April 1947. He was brought up and educated in the south of England and has lived in Morocco and Italy. He spent 15 years working in special education with children with emotional and behavioural difficulties and their families. He now has a private therapy and supervision practice.

Tracey Walshaw writes: I am 43 years old, have a huge collection of Doc Martin boots and live in Oldham with Martyn, my husband, and two children, Jenny and Peter. My life is varied and full of people and all that comes with being in relationships. I work as a counsellor and supervisor in private practice. I am a director of, and trainer with, PCCS Training Partnership in Manchester.

Index

Also in this series

Idiosyncratic REBT
Edited by Windy Dryden
ISBN 1 898059 52 7

PCCS Books
•
publishers of

the largest list of English language
Person-Centred Approach books in the world
•
Critical Psychology Division
•
the best selling *Steps in Counselling* series
•
Journals
♦ Person-Centred Practice
♦ Person-Centered and Experiential Psychotherapies
♦ Journal of Critical Psychology, Counselling and Psychotherapy

www.pccs-books.co.uk